SCOTLAND

FREE OR A DESART

THE
RADICAL INSURRECTION
OF 1820

T J Dowds

Published by T J Dowds
Publishing partner: Paragon Publishing, Rothersthorpe

Text and notes © T J Dowds 2020.

www.cla.co.uk

ISBN 978-1-78222-749-6

Book design, layout and production management by Into Print
www.intoprint.net, +44 (0)1604 832140

CONTENTS

PREFACE

2020 marks the bicentenary of the Radical Rising in Scotland: an event about which most people have no knowledge. Yet what the men who took part were seeking is today taken for granted: namely the right to form trade unions, the right to vote, and the creation of a Scottish Parliament. On Monday 3 April a one-day general strike closed down most industry in west-central Scotland, and two days later a small band of Radicals engaged troops at Bonnymuir, while next day, the anniversary of the signing of the Declaration of Arbroath, another band marched from Strathaven to Glasgow, before disbanding. Three of the leaders were later hanged and beheaded for their part in the 'Radical War' and eighteen others transported to Australia.

Where attention has, with justice, been given to the Tolpuddle Martyrs who came after them and the victims of the Peterloo Massacre who preceded them by a few months, the sacrifice of the Scots radicals in the spring of 1820 has been largely ignored. It is not part of the history curriculum in Scottish schools, and most history books tend, at best, to gloss over it or more often, bypass it completely. Earlier publications on the subject, such as those of Ellis and Mac a'Ghobhainn, and the late James Halliday, attract a small readership and commemorative events to preserve the memory of those who were killed or transported, enthusiastically attended by huge crowds in the 1840s, now attract but a handful of spectators. The 1820 Society is a small, and sadly reducing, group that has endeavoured to preserve the memory, not just of those executed and transported, but of the civilians and police officers killed and wounded in Greenock by troops sent to the town to maintain order.

This year the Society, along with a number of local history groups, has planned a series of events to mark the anniversary at sites as sociated with the Radicals. The Society's main focus will be in September, to coincide with the executions of John Baird, Andrew Hardie and James Wilson, while at the same time avoiding a clash with the seven hundredth anniversary of the Declaration of Arbroath which coincides with the date of the Radical War. There are plans for a visit by a number of the descendants of the transported radicals who never returned home, and the commemoration at Sighthill in September will be one of the highlights.

This book is an attempt to give an updated account of the important events of 1820 and to expand on what was previously known by incorporating new information recently discovered. It also gives a brief account of work done in Australia that explores what became of the Radicals sent as convicts to New South Wales.

Tom Dowds
Hon. Vice President
1820 Society

P.S. As this goes to the publisher, the country is in the grip of the Coronavirus pandemic, which has led to the cancellation of some of the early commemorative events. But, these are only postponed, and like the Radicals of 1820 we will persevere and ensure they are not forgotten.

ACKNOWLEDGEMENTS

Like most historians, I am greatly indebted to many people without whose help this book would not have been possible. In first place, thanks must go to those who have gone before in researching the Radical War, in particular the efforts of Peter Berresford Ellis, together with the late Seamus mac a'Ghobhainn, and the late James Halliday, whose work has opened a door onto events that had been forgotten or hitherto neglected and shone a light on what would otherwise have remained in the shadows. This book is in many ways an extension of the research they began, and hopefully will be a spur to others to take the work further.

For their help with the present undertaking I am indebted to the professionalism of the staff of a number of libraries and institution, who gave of their time and expertise to assist with the research by tracking down the documents that have proved invaluable in preparing this work: in particular the staff of the National Records of Scotland, the National Library of Scotland, Glasgow Police Museum, the Scottish Police Trust, and the Andersonian Library University of Strathclyde. Local libraries have provided much relevant material, some of which had not previously been utilised on this subject. Thanks must also go to the staff of Airdrie Library at Wellwynd, Condorrat Library, Dumbarton District Library and Heritage Centre, Falkirk Archive Calendar House, the Mitchell Library Glasgow, and the William Patrick Library Kirkintilloch, who sought out and made available papers that uncovered documents that have provided valuable information that has expanded our understanding of the events of that fateful year.

A number of research centres that could not easily be visited were prepared to provide much needed information by telephone and copies of documents. The prompt and helpful assistance of these are gratefully recognised: Devon Record Office in Essex, the Public Record Office at Kew, and, with special thanks, the State Library of New South Wales, and the State Library of Queensland.

This work was greatly assisted by members of the 1820 Society, who shared their research with the author; particularly Ian Bayne, Gordon Bryce, Mary McCabe and Marion McMillan, together with Tom Crainey whose work on the Radical War and Kilsyth was most helpful. In addition, Allison Symon, a descendant of the Condorrat Radical John Barr, and Nea MacCulloch of the Scottish Australian Heritage Council, who is descended from the Radical Thomas MacCulloch, provided valuable material about the transported Radicals.

Finally, but by no means least, I am grateful to Professor Sir Tom Devine for his agreeing to provide a foreword to this work, and to Ruth Dunachie, who read through the draft and made several helpful suggestions.

To all, thanks!

Foreword

On April Fool's Day 1820 the *Address to the Inhabitants of Great Britain and Ireland,* compiled by the 'Committee of Organisation for forming a Provisional Government', was circulated widely throughout the manufacturing districts of the west of Scotland. Thus was triggered the beginnings of the so-called 'Radical War', a revolutionary attempt to change the course of Scottish history and bring about the political emancipation of the working classes.

The Proclamation was unambiguously subversive, an overt challenge to the prevailing undemocratic order of the day. It even called upon the forces of the crown to cease the support of despotism and instead join the ranks of the workers in their struggle for freedom.

2020 is the centenary of this remarkable episode and it is therefore fitting that Tom Dowds has produced a new study of the dramatic events in commemoration of those who took part in that tumultuous period. As he points out, the history of Scottish radicalism of that time has much lower profile, even today, than contemporaneous events in England, such as the Massacre of Peterloo, which has been recently immortalized on film. It is books like his which will help to rescue the Radical War from the neglect of posterity.

Tom Dowds explores the background and origins of the insurrection and, with new material based on his own researches, provides a detailed reconstruction of its evolution from then until the final judicial trials and gory executions of some of the key activists.

I warmly recommend his book as a lucid, readable and evocative account of a group of courageous Scottish working men who gave their lives for the democratic freedoms which we all now take for granted.

Tom Devine
Professor Emeritus Sir Thomas M Devine
The University of Edinburgh

1. INTRODUCTION

By the beginning of the nineteenth century Britain had been in a state of war with Revolutionary and Napoleonic France for almost 25 years, and when this finally ended at Waterloo in 1815 the economic consequences were enormous. Large numbers of ex-service personnel were released into a labour market that was already shrinking, due both to the technological changes of the industrial revolution, and to the disappearance of continental markets as a result of the French embargo on British goods. The result was high unemployment and reduced wages for those able to find work, at the same time as the government introduced the Corn Laws to prevent the import of cheap foreign grain, thereby increasing the price of bread.

Without pensions or any type of state security, the condition of thousands was desperate and, aggravated by immigration, put severe strain on the old Poor Law that it was unable to meet due to the increased demand placed on it. Trade unions which represented workers had been declared illegal, as were public meetings to discuss grievances, leaving the bulk of the population without a voice. Only parliament had the power to take measures to improve the situation, but there was no possibility of this as the franchise was restricted to the propertied classes, It was members this class that were the beneficiaries of the Corn Laws, and who saw in any demand for change echoes of the revolutionary confusion that had gripped France at the end of the previous century: a situation that the establishment was prepared to do anything to avoid.

In Scotland a number of working people decided on armed insurrection against the British state to win the right to vote, the right to form trade unions, and for the creation of Scottish Parliament. They were motivated by the republican ideas of the American and French revolutions, by the writings of Thomas Paine, and by the egalitarian poetry of Robert Burns. James Wilson, one of the oldest of the 1820 radicals, probably knew Thomas

Muir, the Glasgow-born advocate who had attempted to get military assistance from Revolutionary France in 1795 to establish a Scottish Republic, and who had been tried and transported to New South Wales for sedition.

In early 1820, central Scotland was the scene of a widespread general strike, that was followed by an armed rising of workers who demanded political reform. The immediate military object of the rising was Carron Ironworks near Falkirk, where they hoped to gather arms for an attack on Glasgow. However, the radicals were intercepted by cavalry at Bonnymuir, and, after a short conflict, taken to Stirling Castle to await trial.

Troops were sent to several towns in the area, with Glasgow becoming an armed camp, and suspected radicals were rounded up to face trial on charges of high treason. Public resentment at the heavy-handed action of the authorities and the searches by police and military grew, leading to confrontation, and in Greenock, troops fired into a demonstration protesting at the presence of political prisoners in the town jail. The action of the Volunteers resulted in the killing of eleven men, women and children, and the serious injuring of dozens of others. The crowd then stormed the jail, and released only the Paisley prisoners. In the aftermath further searches led to the arrest of several people accused of being part in the affray, but no court martial or public inquiry was ever held into the killings by the troops, who were commended for their action.

When the trials of the suspected radicals who had been arrested throughout central Scotland were held, the government decided that the cases should be heard under a Special Commission of Oyer and Terminer, i.e. the court was to use English Law, rather than the law of the country where the offenses took place. After a series of trials in Stirling, Glasgow, Dumbarton, Paisley and Ayr, at which eighty men faced sentences of death by hanging, beheading and quartering, two of the leaders of the Bonnymuir force, John Baird of Condorrat and Andrew Hardie from Glasgow, were hanged and beheaded, together with James Wilson who had led the Strathaven men part of the way to Glasgow, and nineteen others were transported to Australia for terms ranging from five years to life.

The aims of the strikers were the right to form trade unions to protect the rights of workers and the extension of the franchise to allow all the vote: although, in the early nineteenth century, the demand for 'universal' suffrage was unlikely to include the right of women to vote. These demands were also being aired by workers in England and Wales, and were regarded by Westminster as, at best an attempt to reduce the power of the establishment, and at worst the overthrow of the constitution by the lower orders of society. In the aftermath of the French Revolution, neither alternative was likely to appeal to Parliament, and their suppression of this 'dissent' was ruthless. Repression was even more rigorous in Scotland where the reformers had added a third demand, the creation of a separate Scottish Parliament.

Against a background of scandal that brought the monarchy into disrepute, any change to the constitution was something that could not be countenanced by Lord Liverpool and his government. The administration was already deeply hated for its repressive measures in tackling dissent over the Corn Laws and for not only condoning the actions of the magistrates and troops during the Peterloo Massacre, but for sending to trial the organisers of the peaceful meeting in St Peter's Field. It was seen as significant in official quarters that the trial of those arrested for this meeting were in progress at the time of the Radical War, which led to the belief that the events in the north were a display of sympathy for the defendants, and evidence of cross-border collusion between dissident elements.

Unlike political agitation in England, where the Peterloo Massacre and the later transportation of the Tolpuddle Martyrs became part of the history curriculum in schools and universities, and, more recently the subject of film and TV coverage, the Radical War in Scotland remains virtually unknown. Indeed, many history books do not even mention the events in Scotland, although a few local history writers, to their credit, have done so.

In the immediate aftermath of the insurrection, this neglect was understandable. Faced with condemnation by the kirk, opposition from the middle classes, and repressive action by government, it is not surprising that the radicals of 1820 were not given publicity by their contemporaries, as praise for their motives would have been interpreted as criticism of the government, royal authority and of the constitution, as well as being contrary to accepted religious opinion. But in the following decades, the aims of the men who died and were transported, i.e. the right to vote and to form trade unions, and the setting up of a Scottish Parliament have all been realised.

The political objectives of the men of 1820 were carried over into Chartism, and that movement's physical force section encouraged working class agitation for the vote, and the early radicals were held up as precursors of the new reform movement. Similarly, the demand for recognition of trade unions did not disappear but continued until recognition was granted in 1824. With the passing of the Great Reform Act in 1832, limited through it was, the franchise was opened to a wider range of the population, and in the following years more people were granted the right to vote.

Throughout the nineteenth century, particularly in the heady days of Empire, the idea of establishing a Scottish Parliament did not figure in the minds of most people. With wars and the threat of war dominating most the first half of the twentieth century, tending to bring the United Kingdom together to face a common enemy, the concept of a shared British identity predominated, and nationalism was shunned as having been at the root of the war in 1939. Towards the end of the century, however, there was a change as the established British political parties were perceived as being out of touch with the conditions and needs of the mass of the population. This feeling was particularly keen in the north of the United Kingdom, and the idea of a distinct Scottish identity grew, and by the last quarter of the century the Scottish National Party had become an accepted part of the political life of the country. In response the UK Parliament agreed to the creation of a Scottish Parliament, which opened on 1 July 1999, thus fulfilling the third demand of the men of 1820.

Rightly, the struggle of the Chartists, the political reformers and trade union activists, and more recently the valiant women who fought for the vote, have been given their place in the history of the country, but little has been said about the sacrifice of the 1820 radicals. Now, as the bicentenary of the Rising takes place, and with all three of the rights they set out to achieve having been won, the time is surely right to give these martyrs for those causes, their rightful place in the history of both the United Kingdom and Scotland.

2. BACKGROUND

Political

In spite of great changes in Britain during the 18th and 19th centuries resulting from revolutions in agriculture and industry, together with the dawning of the Enlightenment, the system of government remained as it had been in previous centuries. The accepted belief was that only those with a stake in the land had a right to govern the country, and thus only those who owned property could be trusted with the vote. This meant that in Scotland, as in England, not only were the small landowners excluded from managing the country, but also the wealthy merchant and industrial classes that had emerged with the industrial revolution. In effect, the franchise was restricted to the propertied class in the counties, and the members of the old-established merchant guilds in burghs, and the new trades and powerful industrial classes were not recognised as sufficiently important to have the right to the vote. Elections were held every seven years, which meant that once elected the government was virtually unchangeable for a prolonged period.

The situation in Scotland was devised in 1707 and remained unchanged, despite the growth of towns as a result of industrial change and immigration, mostly from Ireland, with the result that by 1800 only about 0.2% of the population had the vote. Where in England each county and borough had two MPs, Scotland's 66 royal burghs, with around 2,600 voters, and 33 counties, with a total of 1500 voters, had to share 45 members, one less than the county of Cornwall. This resulted in the 27 largest counties having one MP each, while the other, smaller counties and burghs were grouped together to share one member, with some of these seats taking turns to elect an MP to represent them at Westminster.

Scotland's cities were virtually unrepresented and the largest, Glasgow, had no member as it was part of the Glasgow Burghs constituency, whereas

Liverpool had two MPs. The 88 electors in Dumbarton, Glasgow, Renfrew and Rutherglen ('The Clyde Burghs') sent one member to the House of Commons: each burgh taking turns to be the 'returning Burgh.' In the burghs the system produced a small clique of councillors, who frequently re-elected themselves, that had the power to choose the fifteen members to represent the Scottish interest at Westminster. During the eighteenth century some of the burghs had even proposed, unsuccessfully, making the right to select the MP hereditary within the then current group.

Even in counties where tenants held property that entitled them to the franchise, they had to declare their vote in public, making it impossible to vote against their superior's choice without risking the loss of their tenancy. In the Scottish counties this led to the creation of political empires such as those of the Argyll, Buccleugh, Bute and Sutherland families, who manipulated elections to extend their power and strengthen control over their estates, and often beyond. In the burghs, only a handful of merchants and tradesmen had the vote; there were only 33 voters in Edinburgh.

In most of the burgh constituencies, like Anstruther Burghs and Wigtown Burghs, each of the individual burghs had one vote and this was easily manipulated by the local landowner to ensure the election of his candidate. Scotland's senior legal figures, including the Lord Advocate and most of the Justiciary were appointed as Members of Parliament, and not always for Scottish seats, which gave them a vested interest in preserving the electoral status quo. Lord Advocate Sir William Rae who prosecuted the 1820 radicals had held seats in England and Ireland as well as several in Scotland.

By being able to control the system of elections, power was retained by a small clique, and in 1790 only nine county and burgh elections were actually contested. Henry Dundas built up a network of clients dependent upon him, and by 1790 he controlled 34 of the 41 Scottish constituencies, and Prime Minister William Pitt the Younger relied on him delivering the northern vote to secure his power. But the Dundas influence was wider than Scotland, as his family had control of 'rotten boroughs', like Gratton (lying between London and Brighton), which helped deliver another batch of supportive members. With around one-sixth the population of England, Scots held a quarter of official pensions and one-third of state sinecures, and such was the demand for preferment that Dundas was able to choose candidates on the basis of talent and ability. As Tom Devine has put it,

> This gravy train was vital to the careers and family prospects of many in the Scottish landed and professional classes, and few were likely to risk preferment by rocking the boat too much.

The Paisley poet Alexander Wilson, writing in 1793, was equally scathing in his appraisal of the local politicians,

> O happy that man and blist
> Who in the Council gets him:
> Soon may he cram his greedy kist
> And dare a soul to touch him.

An example of how the system worked comes from Glasgow. On 11 February 1820, as elections were pending, Kirkman Finlay, MP for Malmesbury (Wiltshire) and formerly for the Clyde Burghs, wrote to Lord Provost Henry Monteith indicating that he intended to support Archibald Campbell, son of the judge Lord Succoth, as the Tory candidate for Glasgow Burghs, and expressing the hope that the Lord Provost would support him also. A week later Campbell wrote thanking Monteith for his support, and was later elected, and served until 1831.

A major problem for the authorities was that Scotland was at the time one of the most literate countries in Europe with the working class being educated, and the ideas of the Enlightenment and current events were debated throughout the country, which was experiencing growing dissent arising from the disruption of the Church and a growing spirit of egalitarianism. Radical agitation reached its peak in Ireland in the rising of the United Irishmen in 1798, where the 'Scotch-Irish' especially in Antrim and Down were noted as being particularly prominent.

In Scotland the Church was of greater local importance to the general population than Westminster, and formed a 'parish state' that looked after the welfare of the congregation. Poor relief was administered at parish level and the local kirk punished minor offences, educated the children and buried the dead. At national level, law was at the centre of government and the judges and senior law officers in Scotland were independent and not easily influenced by business or class interest, and as a result, they dealt fairly with wages and allowed combinations of workers.

By the 1780s where there was a demand in England for extensive reform of the franchise, and Thomas McGrugor (alias ZENO) wrote criticising the system because it excluded the intelligent and the propertied middle classes, but was opposed to giving the votes to the lower classes as he believed 'the dregs of the populace are disqualified by ignorance.' Even Dundas was inclined to be sympathetic to modest change, as Scots did not pose a threat to the regime and there was a lack of interest in meaningful reform.

Many Scots expressed support for the revolutions in America and France, setting up Societies of the Friends of the People and forming the Society of United Scotsman to advocate greater democracy at home. The government feared militant action could happen here similar to that which had happened abroad, and declared strikes and gatherings not authorised by the authorities to be illegal, stifling opposition but alienating middle as well as working class critics.

Anxious to stamp out agitation for reform the authorities decided on action against the Friends of the People, stressing its links with the revolution in France and the Society of United Irishmen. Reports were received from the meetings that indicated the members wanted political reform, and that members of the Society of United Irishmen were present, and the government decided to act. Leading members of the Society were arrested in 1793, and faced trial towards the end of the year on charges of sedition. The lawyers, Thomas Muir of Huntershill and Joseph Gerrald, together with William Skirving, Maurice Margarot, and the Unitarian minister Thomas Fysche Palmer, were found guilty of sedition and sent to the penal colony in New South Wales.

There was popular condemnation of the harsh treatment of the 'Scottish Martyrs' but government had made an example of reformers from the educated middle class, and hoped this would send a message that no one was exempt from arrest and punishment for seeking to change the constitution. Of those sentenced, only Maurice Margarot returned home; Gerrald and Skirving died of dysentery while in captivity, and Palmer and Muir, having escaped, died in exile. The fact that most of those who had been transported were never to return home, must have had the effect of making the public regard transportation as a virtual death sentence.

The excesses in France, however, alienated many in Britain and turned public opinion against revolution. The middle classes promptly distanced themselves from reform groups, leaving them in the hands of the educated working class. When the Society of Friends of the People was formed in Strathaven by a group of Whigs, the Duke of Hamilton objected to its aims and most of the middle class members withdrew, leaving the working class, who previously had only been allowed to attend with listening powers, in charge of the organisation. A local long-time radical, James Wilson, became more active in leading and organising the local society, and came to be regarded as the main proponent of reform in the area.

Economic

Industrialisation of the textile industry enabled employers to hire less skilled workers at wages lower than those previously paid to skilled employees, and this latter group found that job opportunities were reduced and incomes declined. The influx of Irish and Highland workers, particularly in the last half of the eighteenth century, flooded the labour market and further depressed wages. At the same time, the price of food increased as a result of demand by the expanding population, adding further to the distress of the poor. An economic downturn in early 1787, compounded the situation, leading to the wages of handloom weavers, the best paid workers in the country, falling by up to 50%.

To remedy their plight Scottish handloom weavers united to ask for an increase in their rate of pay. When employers rejected their call, the weavers stopped work and held mass meetings to highlight their plight. On 3 September 1787, around 7,000 striking Calton weavers and their families gathered in Glasgow to draw attention to their case for higher wages. The city magistrates, fearing a riot and with the support of the manufacturers, called in troops from the 39th (East Middlesex) Regiment to suppress the disturbances. Colonel Kellett ordered his men to fire volleys into the crowds at Drygate, and they killed three weavers and wounded others, inluding three who later died of their injuries. One strike leader, John Grainger, was put on trial accused of 'forming illegal combinations' and found guilty and sentenced at Edinburgh to be publicly flogged and banished from Scotland for seven years. After a few days, the Glasgow weavers were obliged to return to work on the employers' terms, and by October the city's first major strike was over, but there was a lingering distrust of the manufacturers and authorities, who had been prepared to use military force to suppress protests by workers.

Further industrial unrest erupted in 1810-11, when Glasgow cotton spinners were involved in a protracted dispute, the 'Reign of Oppression.' Forced to end the dispute on the employers' terms, the incident led to the creation of the first union of cotton spinners. In response, employers formed associations with the aim of strengthening their position against workers' actions and to enable them to hire and fire as the market dictated.

Previously, the old Scots Poor Law had been effective in dealing with periodic episodes of illness, unemployment and trade depression. But by the early nineteenth century it was struggling to cope. Based on each parish raising the funds to look after the needs of the local population, it was not equipped to manage the strains imposed by the growth of towns, where parishes were fewer and had large numbers of immigrants requiring aid. As the century progressed and experienced economic downturns, the numbers requiring relief grew to a point where local resources were inadequate, and appeals to government fell on deaf ears. The new strains on the Poor Law throughout the United Kingdom led many to suggest the need for change to adapt to the new conditions.

As early as 1803, Thomas Malthus, in his *Essay on Population* had argued that 'generous' poor relief was encouraging 'imprudent marriages' which led to a high birth rate and an increased labour force which in turn reduced wages and further exacerbated the numbers in poverty. With the Enlightenment well under way, many found Adam Smith's view of a free market that responded to supply and demand, attractive and in accord with Malthus's theory. In Glasgow, Dr Thomas Chalmers of St John's parish argued that poor relief should be based on charitable contributions rather than taxation, which broke 'the charitable bond between donor and recipient.' Many believed that this added ecclesiastical weight to what Malthus had claimed and came to regard the Poor Law as the cause of poverty. Many towns happily accepted this and applied more rigorous standards for relief in 1810-11, to ease the burden on those paying the poor rate, just as a recession was throwing yet more people out of work.

In 1812 the government abolished income tax, which had been introduced in 1799 as a temporary wartime measure and which fell on the wealthy. To find the money needed for governing the country taxes on essential goods that were used by the mass of the population were increased, making the price of tea, sugar, salt, soap, shoes and candles soar. With incomes falling as a result of export markets having been lost during the war, and employers reducing both wages and work forces, Lanarkshire weavers petitioned for a minimum wage 'with fair hours and proper application, to enable them to feed, clothe and accommodate himself and his family.'

In an effort to avoid confrontation and aware of the reaction that that might provoke, they used the long-established custom of asking the magistrates and justices to examine their case and decide on a fair rate of pay. The justices heard their argument and proposed a modest increase which the workers were prepared to accept. The employers refused to implement this, arguing that wage rates should be determined by the law of supply and demand not that of the justices. When the workers took their case to the Sheriff and Lanarkshire Justices, they accepted the earlier ruling, but manufacturers again refused to implement the new wage. On appeal, the Court of Session, initially agreed to the previous legal decision, but when employers still refused to comply with the ruling, the Justiciary declined to force the employers to implement the increase, and the weavers went on strike.

With 30,000 looms idle, the Lanarkshire and Renfrewshire sheriffs became alarmed at the sheer scale of the stoppage and had the organisers arrested, sending them to prison charged with 'forming a combination' – the first such large-scale case in Scots Law. The cotton merchants and manufacturers argued that 'antiquated laws' were hampering economic progress, and quoted Adam Smith to back their case. The 'enlightened' legal elite agreed and repealed the 1661 statute that had allowed JPs to regulate wages, thus freeing employers to implement whatever rates of pay they chose, and to enforce them through their associations. As a result, the only course open to workers was to attempt to change the way the state was governed by having their voice heard in parliament and they turned to political radicalism.

Despite the economic distress, in 1815 the government, following the new policy of mercantilism, introduced the Corn Laws which imposed duties on imported grain in order to keep grain prices high to favour domestic producers, i.e. the British landowners. Designed to make it too expensive to import grain from abroad, the policy effectively increased the cost of food. With wheat selling at 65 shillings and seven pence a quarter, the price of a loaf of bread rose by around 11%, to 11d. At the same time, as a result of a duty of £30 a ton on salt, the price of this essential commodity rose to four pence a pound, thus increasing the cost of living, and further eroding the living standards of the poor.

William Playfair in 1821 studied the relationship between the price of grain and the income of 'a good mechanic', i.e. a highly paid craftsman, between 1575 and 1821. This showed that while the worker's wage rose by 50% between 1775 and 1820, the price of a quarter of grain had risen by over 100%, and that to buy one loaf a day would cost 30% of his weekly income by that date. Even when food supplies were short, the government refused to relax the Corn Laws, insisting they were in the best interests of the country as a whole: indeed, it was not until the disastrous potato famine in the 1840s, particularly in Ireland, that mercantilists gave any attention to these laws.

Early Radicalism

That there was a radical element in Scotland before the French Revolution has been ignored by many writers, who have concentrated on the growth of radical movements in England from the 1770s. But Paisley weavers had been sent to prison for forming 'combinations', and the press reported troop mutinies in 1778 and 1779, indicating that disaffection was quite widely based. General Adolphus Oughton was concerned about the situation in Scotland and wrote to Lord Weymouth at the Foreign Office (then the Southern Department) in 1779, suggesting that Scots troops could not be relied upon.

> I should think it highly advisable to withdraw all the Fencible regiments from this country, replacing them with an equal number of English; as I discover too many seeds of discontent, especially among the lower people. Great numbers of dissenting Ministers, and several of the Established Clergy are avowedly Republicans and Americans.

As the war went on, the economy suffered and social problems increased accordingly, causing further discontent.

Faced with rising prices and stagnant wage rates, there was dissatisfaction that spread widely during the 1790s. The period after the French Revolution saw a huge increase in the number of newspapers advocating political reform. Where there had been eight newspapers in Scotland in 1782, the number had expanded to 27 by 1790, and all the new publications championed some measure of political reform. Radical publications like *Wooler's Gazette, The Spirit of Union, The Black Dwarf* and *The Scottish Patriot*, were eagerly read. As education was widespread in Scotland most people were able to seek information from the press. Even government attempts to restrict circulation of these 'inflammatory' publications, by increasing the tax on newspapers, failed, as many towns organised Reading Clubs where subscribers had access to the newspapers. Rev Robert Anderson described how that at Kilsyth operated.

About 1820 newspaper clubs began, each member reading in the order agreed to, and getting an hour to do it. There were second-hand readers at a cheap rate, and it was a poor rag of a newspaper before all was done.

A result of the greater interest in politics can be gauged from the creation of Political Clubs and Reform Societies in almost every town and village in Scotland. Frequently these met in secret to avoid the wrath of the landowners and magistrates. By 1810, some felt strong enough to organise public meetings, such as that held in a field at North Barrwood in Kilsyth that attracted a crowd, estimated at 15,000, from the surrounding countryside, who marched through the town with banners and a band. It is said that the factor at Colzium House expressed regret at not having a cannon to use against them. Having made their views heard and asked for government to listen, the crowd dispersed without trouble.

Government became concerned that such meetings, and strikes by groups of workers were a sign that seditious elements in the country were planning an armed insurrection, and promptly labelled all who sought change, no matter how modest, as 'Radicals.' Alarm was caused by the spread of radical publications like *Cobbett's Register*, the *Black Dwarf*, and the *Manchester Observer*, which gave publicity to the grievances of the working class and sought political change, arguing that the increased cost of food and reduced wages were example of the exploitation of workers. *Government* suspicions seemed confirmed when there were reports of secret drilling, the presence of caches of arms, and printing presses turning out posters urging workers to take up arms.

With declining wages and worsening living standards between 1812 and 1813 causing hardship many weaving towns throughout Scotland witnessed strikes, but faced with employers' resistance and the threat of arrest for forming combinations, the strikers were forced to abandon their action after a few weeks. The leaders of these strikes were often obliged to flee the country to avoid arrest and imprisonment.

One of the strike leaders was Alexander Richmond, who fled abroad to avoid prison, but returned to Glasgow penniless in 1816, and sought help from Kirkman Finlay MP and Lord Provost Henry Montieth, who, in Richmond's words, 'were at the head of manufacture in Glasgow.' Finlay recruited Richmond to 'a respectable permanent situation' where he could spy on workers and report 'every second or third evening' to Finlay at his home in Queen Street, and later, 'to avoid suspicion', at the home of James Reddie, the Town Clerk. As Finlay was in almost daily correspondence with Lord Sidmouth, it is most likely that the Home Secretary had a very clear picture of what was happening in Glasgow.

As the war drew to a close and troops were released the labour force increased rapidly, and wages fell as employers could employ desperate workers at very low rates of pay. According to one account, it is estimated that weavers who before the French Wars had earned 40 shillings (£2) a week were, by 1819, reduced to 5 shillings (25p), and with the high cost of essentials many had to claim poor relief. As the poor rate was collected from landowners, this gave rise to concern among the wealthy that they were subsidising 'laziness and idleness', and they looked to parliament to ease the burden on them.

Low wages also impacted on the manufacturing sector, as the general population had little enough to spend on the necessities, let alone any surplus to purchase manufactured goods. As a result, in the first three months of 1816 the inability of workers to buy goods led to many bankruptcies, estimated at close to £2 million in Glasgow alone, as merchants and manufacturers had no domestic market for their produce.

In Glasgow, a committee was formed that sought to address the issues affecting workers, and in late 1816 permission was sought to hold a meeting either in the Trades' Hall or on the Green to discuss a petition to parliament, but this was refused by the magistrates. Even Alexander Richmond, a former leader of the 1812 weavers' strike, and now an informer for Kirkman Finlay, was moved to observe that,

> Official robes are not always found to cover the highest attainments... The influence of the wearers frequently

depend more upon the power they have of concealing them from the gaze of vulgar eyes than on intellectual superiority.

One of the committee leaders, James Turner, offered his estate as a venue for the meeting and on 19 October a crowd, estimated at 40,000 people met at Thrushgrove in Glasgow, where they passed resolutions seeking redress of their grievances and repeal of the Corn Law. This so alarmed the city's magistrates that they placed the 42nd Highlanders, based at the barracks in Gallowgate, on alert, and the Duke of York sent the 7th and 10th Hussars under the command of the leading cavalry officer, Sir Richard Hussey Vivian, to reinforce the garrison there. The troops were not needed as the people dispersed having made their peaceful protest and there were no further assemblies.

In the months following the Thrushgrove meeting, Richmond and one of his associates, Macdowal Peat (or Pate), set up a branch of the Reform Society at a meeting of around a dozen people in the home of William Legatt, a spirit-dealer in Tradeston. At this meeting they urged members to take an oath to support reform: this came to be known as the 'Treasonable Oath' and was one of the charges faced by the radicals during the trials in 1820. Similar to the oath of the United Irishmen, a factor not missed by the authorities, it bound members to secrecy and the use of whatever means was necessary to achieve their aims.

In the awful presence of God, I ,(name), do solemnly swear, that I will persevere in my endeavouring to form a broth-erhood of affection amongst Britons of every description, who are considered worthy of confidence; and that I will persevere in my endeavours to obtain for all the people of Great Britain and Ireland, not disqualified by crimes or insanity, the elective franchise at the age of twenty-one, with free and Annual Parliaments; and that I will support the same, to the utmost of my power, either by moral or physical strength, as the case may require. And do further swear, that neither hopes, fears, rewards, nor punishments, shall induce me to inform on, or give evidence against any member or members collectively or individually, for any act or expression done or made in or out, in this or similar Societies, under the punishment of death, to be inflicted on me by any member or members of such Societies. So help me God, and keep me steadfast.

This oath was administered at further meetings at Ingram Street on 11, and at Gallowgate on 18 January and 15 February.

As early as 1816, the Solicitor General, Alexander Maconochie MP, was able to inform the Commons that there were secret meetings in Glasgow demanding 'the elective franchise at the age of 21, with free and equal representation and annual parliaments.' Armed with this information the Home Secretary, Lord Sidmouth, succeeded in getting bills passed by parliament in February 1817, aimed at preventing radical activities. Political meetings of over 50 people without permission were declared illegal, and any such meetings that were held were deemed treasonable. The suspension of the Habeas Corpus Act was the most significant measure, as it gave the authorities power to hold suspected radicals without trial for an indefinite period of time. A further response to government concern about popular agitation for the vote was the employment of spies to report on such meetings.

The authorities, anxious to stamp out any demand for reform or criticism of the king and government, ordered the arrest of the known leaders in Glasgow. On 22 February, eighteen members of the Glasgow committee, who had arranged the Thrushgrove meeting, met at 8pm in Hunter's in the Old Wynd Glasgow, and immediately after Richmond's associate George Biggar left the meeting, the police, led by the County Procurator Fiscal and the Sheriff, raided the premises and arrested them. When Biggar was seized by an officer, he told them he had informed the authorities about the meeting and he was released. Those arrested were taken to Glasgow Jail and held in separate cells, awaiting trial for sedition. Richmond later pointed out that the police who took part in the raid were from Edinburgh, as the local police were well known in the area, and would have been recognised before the raid.

Along with the radical leaders Andrew McKinlay, John Campbell, John Keith and William Edgar, the elderly Rev Neil Douglas, who had preached in Anderston Church about the licentiousness of the Regent, Prince George, was also taken into custody. On 23 February *The Scotsman* asked if there was any evidence of plots against the people, while the *Glasgow Chronicle* on 27th expressed surprise that there were any 'extreme reformers' in the city. Kirkman Finlay informed the Commons that he was 'deeply convinced of the necessity and propriety of the measures proposed by ministers' to prevent disturbances.

When Maconochie brought the prisoners to trial he used the 1812 Act that made administering an oath binding a person to treason guilty of a capital offence. When John Keith, a mill owner, and Mr Edgar, a school-master, were put to the bar on 18 July, John Campbell was called as a witness for the prosecution, but told the court he had been promised a reward by the Advocate Depute and the Sheriff of Edinburgh to give evidence against McKinlay and the other accused. Despite the evidence of other witnesses, the jury returned a verdict of Not Proven, and the men were released. Kirkman Finlay accused Maconochie of 'imbecility' for his conduct of the trial.

Many members of the public were convinced that the government had set out deliberately to entrap the reformers, and Earl Grey, in Parliament, condemned the Glasgow authorities for the use of 'hired spies and informers' to ensnare the accused. His criticism was echoed by the press, led by *The Scotsman* on 24 July, and the *Glasgow Chronicle* went further on 14 and 19 August, and named Richmond. Years later, Alexander Richmond sued the press for damages in an English court, claiming his character had been defamed by the accusation that he was a government spy, but lost his case in 1834.

It is difficult to be certain about the strength of revolutionary activity in Britain, as members of reform groups tended to keep a low profile, and government agents had much to gain from exaggerating their 'findings.' It is true, however, that there was growing discontent as is evidenced by the Cato Street conspiracy of February 1820, when English radicals plotted a rising against the new, and unpopular king, George IV. As the depression continued, meetings were held complaining about the Corn Laws which kept the price of bread high to appease the landowners, whose interests dominated Parliament, and which affected most severely the lives of the poor.

Against this background that saw the weekly wages of weavers fall from one pound to eleven or twelve shillings, radical groups held meetings throughout Britain to demand political reform, and delegates from Scotland attended the meetings in England to coordinate action. The government panicked, fearing a French-style revolution, and resorted to the use of military force. At a peaceful rally in St Peter's Field, Manchester, on 16 August 1819, troops opened fire on the crowd that included women and children, killing fifteen people and wounding hundreds, many seriously. In response some radicals decided to take up arms to defend themselves, while the government decided to prosecute the organisers for holding an 'unlawful meeting.'

3. MILITANT RADICALISM

Between 1810 and 1820, the term 'Radical' came to be more widely used to distinguish the working class who sought political reform from the middle class 'Reformers.' This last group were Whigs who also wanted an extension of the franchise, but were not keen on the vote being given to workers, and who agreed with the Tory philosophy that only those with a landed or financial interest in the country had a right to determine how it was run. In addition, the Reformers were more interested in using moral force, and constitutional methods to persuade the aristocracy to introduce reform, and shunned the very idea of using physical force.

There was a further and to the government, more alarming change around this period. For most of the eighteenth century there had been little in the way of cooperation between reformers on opposite sides of the border, partly as a result of lingering doubts about Jacobitism, and partly from a fear that the 'backward North Britons' would be a drain on national resources. This attitude was summed up by that great advocate of the English lower classes, John Wilkes, who used *The North Briton* in 1763 to paint his picture of the Scots.

> … the River Tweed was the line of demarcation between all that is noble and all that is base – south of the river was all honour, virtue and patriotism – north of it nothing but lying, malice, meanness, and slavery. Scotland is a treeless, flowerless land formed out of the refuse of the universe, and inhabited by the very bastards of creation.

By the turn of the century, this rivalry was diminishing. Scots troops had been active in the wars in America, supported the government during the 1798 Rising in Ireland, and played a major role during the war against revolutionary France. During the wars, workers in both countries were experiencing similar economic hardship, and social discontent and unrest grew north and south of the border. At the same time, the revolutions in America and France had shown that the power of the elite was capable of being challenged, and that cross-border cooperation was required if the redress of grievances was to be achieved.

Reformers set up societies and groups to discuss their grievances and to seek a means of improving their lot, and as these spread widely Scottish groups were in regular communication with those in the south, particularly with groups in the industrial towns of northern England. The formation of unions to negotiate wages and conditions at work figured prominently, but faced with the resolute opposition of employers and government belief that such groups were a cover for those intent on the destruction of the constitution, such meetings were made illegal. The only means of redress left was to seek reform of parliament itself to allow workers to elect MPs to represent their interests.

In Scotland a number of radical societies had been formed and meetings were regularly held in Airdrie, Ayr, Dumfries, Glasgow, Kilsyth, Neilston, Paisley, and Rutherglen. When these groups received reports of the 'Peterloo Massacre', all meetings vehemently condemned the government for its brutal and heavy-handed approach, with collections being taken up to support the victims. When the news reached Paisley, a crowd of 5,000 rioted after a memorial rally in the town on 11 September, and it took the cavalry a week to restore order. In Airdrie a crowd of 15,000 gathered to protest at Albert Place, at the head of Broomhill, on 16 October, and on 1 November anothter large march took place at Broomknoll. These protests caused the alarmed authorities to raise a troop of Yeomanry and two companies of Volunteers, with 150 men in each, to protect the town from 'trouble-makers.'

But not all workers had joined the protest, as some were prevented 'by the petty tyranny of certain little-minded employers in and about Glasgow', and one master had warned them the protest amounted to blasphemy and an affront to religion, although the same man had, according to the *Spirit of the Union*, forced his employees to work on a religious fast day. Despite the apparent quiet after these events, the military remained on alert and their presence, it was hoped, would avert more serious trouble.

The *Glasgow Courier* reported on 2 November 1819 that 'Great meetings of the Radicals were held on 1st November at east end of Gallowgate, Paisley and Kilsyth', and, on 9 December, that two men had been arrested after the Airdrie meetings,

> At Airdrie on Friday, a man by the name of Roger, a carpenter, and Miller a weaver, chairman and secretary of the Union Society were committed for further examination and lodged in Hamilton Jail on a warrant of the Sheriff of Lanarkshire.

'Roger' is clearly William Rodger who was the chairman of the local Union Society, and who had taken in Alexander Richmond as a lodger for a time earlier that year. Miller was given a sentence of six weeks in Glasgow Jail, and was later re-arrested in 1820 and spent three months in Hamilton Jail, where he was held during the rising that year. In his history of Airdrie, James Knox states that when Miller was sent to Hamilton a large crowd had gathered outside the prison, and Major Smith of the Rifle Brigade asked Miller to tell them to disperse, which he did, but only after he was allowed to get them to give 'three cheers for the good old cause.'

Volunteer units had previously been raised for service in Ireland, and when the threat of violence broke out in 1819 many English local authorities formed units in centres like Huddersfield, Leeds, Newcastle and Cheshire, where their main task was to be an armed force to assist the police in the event of disturbances. Scotland followed suit, and Airdrie was not alone in raising Volunteer units, as most towns raised at least one such unit during the disturbances of 1819/20. In Glasgow, the editor of the *Glasgow Herald*, Samuel Hunter, who had served with the Volunteers in Ireland during the 1798 Rising, raised a force, the Glasgow Sharpshooters, that was of regimental size. Unlike the Yeomanry and Militia, they were to be disbanded when radical activity subsided after the failure of the insurrection in

Scotland. In Airdrie, the badge of the Volunteers, which had been awarded as a shooting trophy, was attached to the Provost's chain of office when the unit was disbanded in 1828.

As the demand for redress increased, so did violence. In October a meeting in Stirling was attended by 2,000 people, while a demonstration in Airdrie was led by a band playing *Scots Wha Hae*, for which the band was arrested and fined. The following month there were workers' demonstrations in Renfrewshire, Ayrshire, Fife, Stonehaven and Dundee, all raising in the mind of the government the spectre of a French-style uprising.

Kirkman Finlay, the MP from Glasgow, together with Provost Henry Monteith, had concerns about the growth of radicalism in the city and gave assistance to the infiltration of radical organisations by agents provocateur. Finlay later admitted to the *Glasgow Evening Post* in 1833 that he had paid three agents to 'stir up' the revolt of 1820. Alexander Richmond, a weaver recruited by Finlay as an informer and spy, who infiltrated a number of radical meetings and reported back to James Reddie, the Town Clerk, was known to be active in the Glasgow area at this time. James Anderson in his *Reminiscences of Sixty Years Ago* noted that in 1819 there was an,

> undercurrent of disaffection prompted by spies sent by the Government. One Richmond was sent to Airdrie and lodged with William Rodgers, a wood merchant, who lived at the foot of Hallcraig ... (who) wrote to my father.

Rodgers was one of those arrested and imprisoned for organising the meetings in Airdrie to protest at the Peterloo Massacre.

The same year, the head of Edinburgh police, Captain James Brown, was sent to Glasgow, 'disguised as a reformer' according to the Lord Advocate's report to Sidmouth, but found that the fears were exaggerated as most members wanted peaceful change and the few men involve who had more radical views could, he believed, easily be dealt with by the local magistrates. This was corroborated by Richmond's reports, which confirmed that the main activities of the reformers' meetings were the distribution and discussion of radical literature.

But by the turn of the year the reports became more alarming. Richmond had provided the names of some of the leading radicals and their meeting places, but no details about their plans. Of more use to the authorities was George Biggar, who had been employed by Sheriff Robert Hamilton of Lanarkshire as an informer, and had gained access to the inner circle of radical leaders by early 1817, and was sending regular reports on groups in Paisley, Kilsyth, Campsie and Airdrie. He supplied details of names, meeting places, and even passwords used at meetings, warning that there was talk of gathering arms in preparation for a rising.

Militant Action

By 1819 economic problems caused heightened tension in central Scotland, and in Glasgow in particular, as a combination of increased immigration lowered wages at the same time as due to the Corn Laws food prices were high. The situation prompted some Scottish radicals to take action.

Early on Monday 13 December, three hundred armed men arrived in Kilsyth from Falkirk, on their way to join a rising planned for that day in Glasgow, but they were sent a message that the insurrection was postponed and returned home. The authorities, however, were aware of the plot and Sir Thomas Bradford, Commander-in-Chief of His Majesty's Army in Scotland, and his staff had been sent to Glasgow the previous day to organise the military response, but found the city quiet. So successful were the government spies that Lord Hope, Lord President of the Court of Session, was able to write to Lord Meville telling him that the rising had been cancelled, the day before the radical army arrived in Kilsyth.

The demand for reform of the franchise was not limited to the working class, but had wide support from manufacturers and some of the landed gentry who did not have the vote. One such was George Kinloch of Kinloch, near Blairgowrie, who had spent time in France during the Revolution and returned home a convinced radical. Between 1817 and 1819, he attended meetings demanding parliamentary reform and was arrested in 1819, but escaped to France before his trial.

By the turn of the year, there were meal riots in some towns, and strikes by colliers and shoemakers, causing James Mitchell, Glasgow's Chief of Police, to report to the Home Secretary that there was an increase in the number of 'Thieves, Rogues, Vagabonds and Defendators of every description in the city.' He warned that there was increasing demand for parliamentary reform; a change that he and his political masters viewed as revolutionary. On 10 January Lord Provost Monteith was informed that military precautions were being implemented to prevent trouble, and Sir Richard Hussey Vivian had been appointed as commander of the troops in the city, presumably to impose a more strict military regime there.

Gilbert Macleod, the editor of *Spirit of the Union*, was arrested that month for publishing demands for Annual Parliaments, Universal (male) Suffrage, and Voting by Ballot. In his address to the jury the Lord Advocate, Sir William Rae, asked them, 'What should become of us all if he were not convicted?' Having heard the evidence, the jurors found Macleod guilty, but entered a plea for clemency. The presiding judge, Lord Pitmilly, rejected their plea, announcing that if the accused were not convicted, 'he could never lay his head on his pillow in peace again', and sentenced the editor to transportation for five years to Botany Bay. He arrived in Australia in 1820, and was joined by his wife and family, dying there around 1828.

The authorities were informed early in 1820 that a committee of 28 had been set up with the aim of establishing a provisional government to prepare for the creation of a separate Scottish Parliament and to declare a republic in Scotland. The government's response was to recruit more volunteer regiments throughout the Lowlands and in the Borders to deal with any rising, while government spies were used to infiltrate the radical associations. Local police forces encouraged members of radical groups to become informers, as in Ayr, where the secretary of the local Radical Committee, James Logan, became an agent of the police in February 1820.

When George III died on 29 January and was succeeded by the unpop-ular Prince Regent, he divided opinion in the country. The extravagant and licentious lifestyle of the new king was already a cause of gossip and scandal, and this came to a head in January 1820, when he refused to allow his wife, Queen Caroline of Brunswick, to attend his coronation and sought a divorce. The government, anxious to avoid bringing the monarchy into public ridicule, encouraged a low-profile approach, but the king demanded that the Lords pass a bill to allow him to divorce and remarry. *Cobbett's Register* carried news of the royal scandal and subsequently of the queen's trial, and the public eagerly read, or heard, the salacious reports in ale-houses throughout the country. Public sympathy was with Caroline, and the reputation of the monarchy diminished rapidly over the succeeding months, reaching a record low.

On 11 January 1820, the Lord Lieutenant of Lanarkshire, General Hamilton of Dalziel, convened a meeting of the 'Noblemen, Freeholders and Commissioners of Supply of the County' at Hamilton. At this meeting he proposed an address to the king assuring him of the loyalty of his subjects, and this was duly passed, but only by a majority of four, 90 of those present opposing the address. Even before the divorce scandal had become public knowledge, the reputation of the monarchy was questionable and it became worse as more details emerged. With respect declining for George IV, it became more problematic for the government to appeal to the people to support a king whose reputation had sunk so low, and, when disaffection became rife, the only course they could see was to meet it head-on with force.

In February, George Edwards proposed to a group of English radicals that they break into a house in Cato Street where the cabinet was supposed to meet for a dinner and kill them and then form a provisional government. Lord Liverpool's government, aware it was widely detested for the harsh measures that it had introduced, had been looking for some way to supress agitators opposing it, and the Cato Street Conspiracy offered a chance to be seen as victims of a 'Jacobin' plot. Edwards, it was later discovered, was a government agent and the plot had been hatched by Sidmouth and the Home Office, with the approval of the entire cabinet, which had agreed to release an announcement about a fictional dinner, to entrap the radicals.

On 23 February Bow Street Runners raided the house where the radicals were waiting to attack the cabinet and, after a scuffle in which one officer was killed and several injured, arrested the party. The leader, Arthur Thistlewood, and his companions were put on trial charged with treason. On 28 April, five of the conspirators were sentenced to death and another five to transportation for life.

In February 1820, there was a joint conference of English and Scottish radicals held in Nottingham. One of the Scottish delegates was John Neil from Paisley, who, on his return, informed his local committee that England was 'seething with revolt' and that '200,000 Radicals there were preparing to rise' on 1 April. Similar reports were presented to other groups in Scotland, and prepared the way for the revolt that month. After the insurrection, Neil was accused of being a government spy whose task was to encourage radicals to take up arms so that action could be taken against them. Neil denied the suggestion, but several writers have raised concern at the ease with which he and a number of other known radicals were able to travel to Nottingham and back without hindrance, and to the fact that the rising in England which they claimed was imminent, was without foundation.

The death of the king also triggered a general election due to be held in April 1820, and there was growing political dissent throughout central Scotland and increasing violence as the authorities sent military patrols to keep order in the streets. In mid-February, Colonel Northcott asked for magistrates to accompany troops on patrol in Glasgow, as his men had been 'insulted and pelted with stones.' As the date of the election due near there were reports of crowds heckling candidates and voters. On 16 March, Monteith was informed by George Napier that the Sheriff at Selkirk had been attacked and one of the voters assaulted.

> One Voter was taken hold of on Monday and carried off, and spirits in such a quantity pour'd down his throat that he was nearly killed – thinking him done for, they left him, but by timely Assistance, and the aid of a Surgeon he was so far recovered as to be carried to the Council Chambers just in time for the Elections.

Napier asked if the ringleaders 'should not be made an example of.' Two days later Andrew Lang, the Chief Magistrate at Selkirk wrote that he had not been badly injured but his servant had been 'chased for miles', and might have been killed had he not made his escape.

There was a lengthy correspondence between Glasgow's Lord Provost and Thomas Sharp, the Boroughreeve at Manchester, comparing the disturbances in the two cities. On 20 March, Sharp was anxious about the trial of the Peterloo radicals then taking place at York and suggested that this was the cause of much of the unrest, although he did comment that he believed the situation was worse in Glasgow.

The same day, rumours circulated that there was an immediate threat that Glasgow radicals were about to 'fire the City.' Monteith immediately informed the military, and troops were put on stand-by throughout Glasgow to deal with the trouble. In the event there was no attempted arson and the following days and nights passed off without incident.

Sharp and Monteith continued to send letters giving details of the events in their respective areas for several weeks after the troubles died down.

In Glasgow, John King, infiltrated the organising committee of an organisation planning the creation of a Scottish government, and discovered plans for a rising the following week. Captain Mitchell reported to Lord Sidmouth on 18 March that his informants had discovered a plot to overthrow the government.

> The Scottish Radicals have been making preparations for some little time now for a general rising in Scotland and to this end they have kept in close communication with the disaffected in England. Their plan is to set up a Scottish Assembly or Parliament in Edinburgh, likewise similar assemblies are to be set up by the disaffected in England and Ireland. As far as can be gathered by our informants they are imbibed with republican ideals… The bearer will present you with more detailed intelligence, especially in connection with a meeting of the organising committee of the rabble which is due in this vicinity in a few days hence.

This was at the same time, 16 to 30 March, as Henry Hunt and those arrested at Peterloo were facing charges at York Assizes of sedition and 'conspiring to Overthrow the Government', and Mitchell is clearly making a link between the Scottish radicals and those on trial in England. His inclusion of Ireland would seem a deliberate attempt to invoke memories of the Rising there in 1798 to overthrow British rule, and in which many of the commanders of volunteer units, including Samuel Hunter of the *Glasgow Herald*, had served. The police chief's letter makes it clear that the authorities were very aware of what was being planned; at times before the radicals themselves knew.

On 21 March 1820 the Committee for Organising a Provisional Government met in a Marshall's Tavern in Gallowgate. John King was present, but informed the members he had to leave at 9pm on other business and this was agreed, despite some claiming they should all leave together for security. Shortly after King left the meeting, Baillie Hunter, with a force of police and soldiers burst in and arrested the entire committee.

James Mitchell arranged for the arrests to be kept secret in the hope of luring other radicals into taking action that would enable the authorities to identify and apprehend them. He informed Kirkman Finlay and Lord Provost, Henry Monteith, on 29 March, that 'a week past we apprehended their committee of organisation, due solely to the efforts of an informant who has served his government well.' He suggested a scheme should be devised to bring radicals into the open.

> If some plan were conceived by which the disaffected could be lured out of their lairs – being made to think that the day of 'liberty' had come – we could catch them abroad and undefended ... Our informants have infiltrated the disaffected's committees and organisation, and in a few days you shall judge the results. It would, by the severity of their punishment, which must be harsh – quench all thought of patriotic pride and Radical feeling among the disaffected.

In his letter to Sidmouth about the arrests, he added the interesting, and very revealing comment that expose both his political aims and his fear that danger was near:

> My Lord, it is my earnest desire to serve Government to the extremes of my humble ability. I would strongly urge that action must be taken immediately to quench the treasonable ardours of the disaffected before they grow too strong.

The arrested radical leaders who were believed to be planning an insurrection were never brought to trial, and there is no surviving record of their arrest or of what became of them. This has led to speculation that they were really agents provocateur or spies, acting on behalf of the government, or Kirkman Finlay MP, or the Sheriff, or the Lord Provost, or the local authority, or the police, or a combination of any, or all, of these.

That Glasgow's Chief of Police wanted to force the radicals into action is clear from his correspondence with Kirkman Finlay, Lord Provost Monteith and Lord Sidmouth, and the appearance of a poster urging a general strike on Monday 3 April has been seen as a plot by Mitchell, perhaps in collusion with others, to do just that.

In the days following the arrests, two radicals. a tinsmith, Duncan Turner, and John King, who claimed to be a weaver but did not seem to work anywhere, were actively encouraging Glasgow workers to make arms. On 30 March, the authorities were informed. 'by persons unknown', that two smiths were making pike heads in a machine factory at the head of John Street. Led by a city magistrate, a body of troops raided the workshop, but made no arrests as 'the two men, who were the object of the search, made their escape through a window into the Grammar School grounds.' The Grammar School stood on George Street beside the machine shop.

The workers within the shop jeered and made fun of the soldiers, one even suggesting that if they were searching for radicals they would be as well arresting all of them. The news shocked the *Glasgow Herald* which seemed to believe that unrest was only due to industrial problems, as it ended its report of the raid by commenting,

The politics of the men employed in this work cannot be ascribed to the pressure of the times, as they have been in constant employment, and at very high wages.

4. GENERAL STRIKE 1820

On Saturday 1 April posters, claiming to be from the 'Committee of Reformation for Forming a Provisional Government' appeared throughout the industrial west and central Scotland, calling for a general strike on Monday 3 April, to draw attention to the demand for greater freedom for Scotland, and the right for worker's concerns to be heard.

ADDRESS
TO The Inhabitants of Great Britain & Ireland;

FRIENDS AND COUNTRYMEN:

ROUSED from that torpid state in which We have been sunk for so many years, We are, at length, compelled, from the extremity of our sufferings, and the contempt heaped upon our Petitions for redress, to assert our RIGHTS, at the hazard of our lives and proclaim to the world the real motives, which (if not misrepresented by designing men, would have United all ranks) have reduced us to take up ARMS for the redress of our Common Grievances.

The numerous Public Meetings held throughout the Country have demonstrated to you, that the interests of all Classes are the same. That the protection of Life and Property of the Rich Man, is the interest of the Poor Man, and in return, it is in the interest of the Rich to protect the Poor from the iron grasp of DESPOTISM; for when its victims are exhausted in the lower circles there are no assurance but that its ravages will be continued in the upper; For once set in motion, it will continue to move until a succession of Victims fall.

Our principles are few, and founded on the basis of our Constitution which was purchased with the DEAREST BLOOD of our ANCESTORS, and which we swear to transmit to posterity unsullied, or PERISH in the Attempt. Equality of Rights (not of Property) is the object for which we contend, and which we consider as the only security for our LIBERTIES and LIVES.

Let us show to the world that We are not that Lawless Sanguinary Rabble which Our Oppressors would persuade the higher circles we are --but a BRAVE and GENEROUS PEOPLE, determined to be FREE. LIBERTY or DEATH is our Motto, and We have sworn to return home in triumph - or return no more!

SOLDIERS:

Shall YOU, Countrymen, bound by the sacred obligation of an oath, to defend your Country and your King from enemies, whether foreign or domestic, plunge your Bayonets into the Bosoms of Fathers and Brothers at the unrelenting Orders of a Cruel Faction and sacrifice those feelings which hold in common with the rest of mankind? SOLDIERS, turn your eyes towards SPAIN, and there behold the happy effects resulting from the UNION of Soldiers and Citizens. Look to that quarter, and there behold the yoke of hated Despotism, broke by the Unanimous wish of the People and Soldiery, happily accomplished without Bloodshed. And shall You, who taught those Soldiers the principles of Liberty, refuse to spread them in your own Country? Forbid it Heaven! Come forward then at once, and FREE your Country and your King~ from the influence of those base maxims that have ruined our Country.

FRIENDS AND COUNTRYMEN: The eventful period has now arrived, where the Services of all will be required, for the forwarding of an object so universally wished, as just and equal Laws. Come forward, then, and countenance those who have begun the completion of so arduous a task, and support the laudable efforts which we are making to give to BRITONS those rights consecrated to them by the MAGNA CHARTA and the BILL OF RIGHTS and Sweep from our Shores that Corruption which has degraded us below the dignity of Man.

Owing to the misrepresentations which have gone abroad with regard to our intentions, we think it indispensably necessary to DECLARE inviolable all Public and Private Property. And, we hereby call upon all JUSTICES of the PEACE, and all others, to suppress OUTRAGE of every description; and to endeavour to secure those Guilty of such offences, that they may receive that Punishment which such violation of Justice demand.

In the present state of affairs, and during the continuation of so momentous a struggle, we earnestly request all to desist from their Labour from and after this day, the First of April, and attend wholly to the recovery of their Rights and consider it as the duty of every man not to recommence until he is in possession of those Rights which distinguishes the FREEMEN from the SLAVES, viz. That of giving consent to the laws by which he is governed. We, therefore, recommend to the Proprietors of Public Works, and all others, to Stop the one, and Shut up the other, until order is restored, as We will be accountable for no damages which may be sustained; and which after this Public Intimation, they can have no claim to.

And We hereby give notice to all those who shall be found guilty of PILLAGE OR PLUNDER that they shall meet with the severest Punishment, as we are determined by every means in our power, to prevent those evils of which we have ourselves so just reason to complain.

By order of the Committee of Reformation for Forming a Provisional Government, Glasgow 1st April, 1820.

Britons - God - Justice - The wishes of all good Men are with us. - Join together and make it one CAUSE and the Nations of the EARTH shall hail the day when the Principles of LIBERTY shall be those of our Native Soil.

It has been argued that the references to Magna Carta and the Bill of Rights would indicate that the writer was more familiar with English rather than Scottish history, and that Thomas (or Robert) Lees, a solicitor, who 'spoke with an English accent' and was particularly active in the distribution of the Address, was the likely author. However, as most history taught in Scottish schools was then and for very many years after mostly English history with scant, if any, reference to events north of the border, it would not have been unusual for an educated Scot to make reference to these 'British' documents. Thus, it is quite possible that the author was a Scot, perhaps, as has been suggested, Glasgow's Chief of Police, James Mitchell, since he had only days earlier, in his letter to the Home Office, suggested the idea of a plan to bring the reformers out into the open so that they could be identified and arrested.

The rough draft of the Address had been handed, late on Friday 31 March, to a writer named John Anderson by Duncan Turner who said he was an emissary from the Provisional Government. Anderson produced the final draft that was then taken to Duncan MacKenzie's print works in 20 Saltmarket, where two apprentices, Robert Fulton and John Hutchison, printed the document during the night: they later stated that the draft had been written on 'law paper', again pointing to Lees. The finished copies were collected in two batches, the first by Lees, the remainder by John Craig, early on Saturday morning, and within hours the proclamation was appearing on walls, lampposts and watchmen's huts throughout the city and beyond. Large crowds quickly gathered to read, and discuss the proclamation.

Robert Hamilton, a local radical, brought 300 copies of the proclamation to Strathaven, where most of the weavers had access to it. Urged by local leaders like Hamilton and John Stevenson, almost every worker in the area responded to the call and the strike brought industry in the surrounding area to a standstill on the following Monday.

In Glasgow, as the public surrounded the posters and engaged in animated discussion of its content, others were active in the crowds speaking to anyone who would listen. Lees, together with John King, who had left the meeting in Gallowgate just before the police raid that arrested the radical leaders eleven days earlier, accompanied by John Craig and Duncan Turner, were seen to be encouraging workers, not just to strike but to take up arms in defence of their rights. It was later claimed that they were working for the government as agitators to persuade radicals to move towards violence, and reveal themselves to the authorities, who were anxious for an excuse to take them into custody.

The same day, two men approached Richard Oswald of Auchencruive House in Ayr, who was 'a gentleman of extremely liberal opinions and an unflinching advocate of the people', to ask if he would take command the Radical Army in the rising that was planned. Oswald, who had formerly commanded the Ayrshire Yeomanry, gave them short shrift, but, believing they were being duped by others to entrap him, allowed them time to escape before he reported the incident to the authorities in Ayr. The local militia were called out and placed on stand-by, but no disturbances occurred and no arrests were made.

In Glasgow, copies of the Address attracted crowds interested in finding out what they said, and as workers discussed the content, a Lanarkshire Justice of the Peace, James Hardie, approached a group who were reading one of the posters on a watchman's box in Duke Street, and attempted to tear it down. He was stopped by a local weaver, Andrew Hardie, a member of the Castle Street Radical Union Society, who pushed him back from the box, causing him to stumble, and demanding to know his authority. When told that he was a justice, Andrew Hardie replied that rather than let him take it down, the justice later claimed, 'I will part with the last drop of my blood!' A surgeon, John Stirling, and a clerk, Hugh Macphunn, who were passing, saw the confrontation, and corroborated the justice's evidence at the trial in Stirling, to condemn Hardie and other radicals.

Informed of the Address, Lord Provost Monteith ordered that all copies be removed at once, as they were clearly the work of radicals who 'are evily disposed', and intent on causing greater agitation. Police and magistrates took to the streets to take down and destroy all the copies they could find, although many had been produced as leaflets and were in circulation well outside the city.

Convinced that the Address was the first step to a general rising, the authorities sought military help. On Sunday 2 April, a dispatch rider from the Rifle Brigade stationed in Gallowgate Barracks, was sent to Edinburgh to inform, Major-General Sir Thomas Bradford, Commander-in-Chief of the Army in Scotland that the west of Scotland had risen in rebellion, and that Glasgow was under siege. When he received the news just after lunch, Bradford immediately rode at the head of a squadron of the 10th Hussars, with his General Staff, to the relief of the city.

Passing through villages on their route, the Hussars were jeered, and at Airdrie stones were thrown at them, but the troops kept their discipline, and cantered past. Arriving in Glasgow, they found the streets quiet and there was no sign of the radical army they had been expecting. Never-the-less, Bradford set up his headquarters in the city and his troops moved into nearby barracks to await developments.

Industrial Stoppage

On Monday 3 April, an estimated sixty thousand workers went on strike throughout Central Scotland with support being strongest in, but not confined to weaving communities like Kilsyth, Neilston and the Calton in Glasgow. Alarming though this was to the authorities, their concern verged on panic when reports were received of men drilling at several locations in the city, and of troops having to be used to disperse large crowds at Balfron and Stewarton in Ayrshire. Even more worryingly, but confirming their suspicions, weapons were discovered at Kilbarchan in Renfrewshire. From Glasgow, the Lord Provost wrote to the Home Secretary that 'Almost the whole population of the working classes have obeyed the orders contained in the Treasonable Proclamation by striking work.'

The unnamed author of *The Late Rebellion in the West of Scotland* wrote that pikes and 'clegs' (spiked weapon shaped like a shuttlecock for throwing at horses) were being manufactured, and that in a house in the Anderston area cartridges and balls were discovered. He added that pikes were being openly sold for between 7d and a shilling, and gunpowder for 3d per pound, while large bodies of men were openly drilling in daylight on Glasgow Green, at Dalmarnock, Point House, and Tollcross.

However, the Glasgow authorities were not caught unawares, and by dawn had reinforced the regular garrison in the city. While eight artillery pieces covered the Clyde bridges, the 1st Battalion Rifle Brigade was stationed in Gallowgate, the Glasgow Yeomanry Cavalry Squadron in St Vincent Street, and Samuel Hunter's Glasgow Sharpshooters in St Enoch's Square. Hunter was the editor of the *Glasgow Herald* and having seen action in 1798 in Ireland firmly believed that parliamentary reform was dangerous, adopting the motto 'once a rebel, always a rebel' when referring to anyone who proposed any change to the constitution. The editor of the *Spirit of the Union* had, in November 1819, described Hunter as 'as dishonest a scribbler as ever stained paper for a periodical pension.'

General Sir Thomas Bradford anticipated a large-scale rebellion and requested supplies of arms and ammunition from Woolwich Arsenal, and ordered the 33rd and 80th Regiments from Edinburgh Castle to support the troops in Glasgow. By early morning, Glasgow was an armed camp with a dusk to dawn curfew imposed on the orders of the magistrates. This was the largest concentration of military forces ever seen in the city.

The Address had been placed on prominent buildings in Kilsyth, including the doors of the Parish Church and the Relief Church where it was read by almost the entire population of the town, and won their support for strike action. According to Matthew Stevenson, the Kilsyth Postmaster, in a report to his superior William Kerr, the Postmaster in Edinburgh, the local weavers 'laid down their shuttles and for several days paraded the streets.' His letter was passed to Lord Sidmouth at the Home Office who picked up on a comment that the local radicals were 'waiting on intelligence from England': confirming government suspicions that radical activity was being coordinated on both sides of the border. There were instances in Kilsyth of weavers who did not strike being threatened, and this led to condemnation from the pulpit as well as by the local authorities and employers.

Later that evening John Craig led a group of Glasgow radicals, armed with pikes, through the city towards the road leading to Falkirk. In Sauchiehall Street one of the men, unused to carrying a pike, accidently broke a street light and the noise attracted the attention of a group of police officers, who ran to the scene. When the radicals spotted the police, they scattered in all directions and only their leader was taken into custody. Craig was immediately taken to Anderston and brought before one of the magistrates, Mr Henry Holdsworth, who fined him five shillings, which he himself paid, and ordered the prisoner's release. It emerged shortly afterwards, that a troop of Hussars had been stationed at Port Dundas ready to ambush the radicals that they expected to pass that way. Clearly they were being led into a trap by Craig, and only the unexpected intervention of the police had frustrated this plan, and saved the radicals from arrest or worse.

In Paisley, where there was a strong radical tradition, the strike call was well supported and most mills were idle. While some radicals like James Spiers and John Lang were observed distributing copies of the Address and encouraging workers reluctant to lose a day's pay to join the strike, others were planning more militant action. John Parkhill and the Paisley Radical Committee met in the 'Smiddy' in Maxwellton Street to organise a raid for arms and powder in the surrounding area, and agreed to have the radicals gather at the Braes of Maxwellton later that evening.

The Provost of Paisley, Oliver Jamieson, was informed of the activities of the radicals and, fearing there would be a rising asked that troops be sent to keep order in the town. The Royal Veteran Battalion arrived from Ayr and was joined by the Port Glasgow Armed Association, the Kilbarchan Armed Association and two troops of the Ayrshire Yeomanry. By nightfall the town was patrolled by troops imposing the curfew ordered by Provost and magistrates. Despite the large military presence, a small group of radicals, led by Daniel Bell assembled at Maxwellton Hill that night and then approached and visited a number of houses in and around Ferguslie, where they collected four muskets and four fowling pieces from the inhabitants.

The following morning, the group attempted to get arms from Ross Robertson of Foxbar House, but Robertson and his son fired on the radicals, and another son, Alexander, who lived close by, arrived when he heard the shots and joined the fray, killing Adam Cochrane, a Paisley weaver, and wounding another named MacKenzie. Warned of the approach of a cavalry patrol, Bell and his men escaped, leaving their dead comrade behind. The *Glasgow Herald* reported the incident, identifying as the leader Cochrane, and noting that he 'was the more dangerous as he had been a soldier, he was fearless of danger, and in the prime of his life.'

Undeterred by the presence of troops, but avoiding them wherever possible, the Paisley radicals travelled to Neilston and Kilbarchan, but found little support as the local clergy had threatened 'eternal damnation' on anyone joining the rising, and attempts to make pikes were impossible without alerting the military.

On Tuesday morning, as a small military party was removing copies of the proclamation from streets in Paisley, stones were thrown at them, and the troops fired on the crowd wounding several people. One woman was shot in the neck and later died of her injuries. In response messages were sent to mills and factories ordering them to shut down, as the Provisional Government would not be responsible for any damage caused by the mob which was incensed by the reaction of the troops.

Later that day, a group of radicals gathered at Foxbar where there was a strong military presence, one Hussar officer estimating their number at between 300 and 400. Although the military saw the radical group, they did not attack them, and they soon dispersed, one of their leaders claiming because it was 'a rather stormy day.' Daniel Bell proposed that, in light of the strong military presence in the town, the armed group of radicals should disband and await developments elsewhere, which they did.

A person calling himself 'A British Subject' wrote to the Duke of Hamilton on 2 April with lurid details of the chaos the strike was causing throughout central Scotland, where 'almost all labouring population abandoned their work' and many were openly drilling in arms throughout the region.

> From Girvan to Stirling 70 miles from east to west and from Dunbarton to Lanark, 40 miles from north to south – the labouring population became or were thrown idle and prepared for the most desperate designs.

Paisley, he said, was 'thronged night and day by crowds waiting word from England to rebel', while armed men were seen at Tollcross and the Green in Glasgow, who refused to return to work until the government was changed, This had caused 'respectable families' from the surrounding area to flee into Glasgow to seek protection from the troops stationed in the city. These reports added to the government's paranoia, confirming, as it seemed, that there was to be a joint rising in England and Scotland.

In an attempt to restore order, the authorities ordered police and troops to search the houses of known radicals, but this produced few arrests as the men were not at home, and their wives and families disposed of any incriminating documents. Word was sent to the leaders to lie low and not return home until told it was safe to do so. The public was generally hostile to the military, and there were confrontations during which a number of people received bayonet wounds, and an elderly man named Campbell died of his wounds after troops charged a crowd in Lady Lane on Friday 7 April.

Anxious to keep the government fully informed of events in Glasgow and the surrounding district, and perhaps to prove to the Home Office that he was capable of dealing with the disturbances, Henry Monteith wrote to Lord Sidmouth on 5 April promising 'a daily letter to Whitehall.' Interestingly, he received a letter next day from John Hobhouse telling him that Lord Sidmouth had decided to replace Sir Richard Hussey Vivian as commander of the troops in Glasgow, with 'Major General Thomas Reynell, at once'. It seems that the government did not trust Sir Richard, the most highly regarded cavalry officer of his time, to deal with the radicals as effectively as Reynell.

Sir William Rae, the Lord Advocate, ordered a proclamation, on behalf of 'the Lord Provost, and Magistrates of the City of Glasgow, Sheriff of the County of Lanark, and Justices of the Peace of the Lower Ward of Lanarkshire', to be posted throughout Glasgow offering a reward of £300 to anyone revealing the identity of those involved in printing, publishing or distributing the 'most wicked, revolutionary and treasonable address.... openly proclaiming rebellion against Our Lord the King and the constitution of this realm.' It argued that the Address was an attempt by 'Wicked. Evil-disposed and Traitorous Persons' to 'compass or imagine the Death of Our Lord the King ... levy War ... and seduce soldiers from their duty': using the very same language as was to appear on the charges the leaders of the rising were to face when they came to trial later in the year. A direct appeal was also made to employers to prevent their workers taking part in the strike,

> We would particularly point out to all Proprietors of Public Works, Manufacturers etc that it is their indispensable duty by the allegiance which they owe their king to use all their exertions and influences with their Workmen to prevent them joining or continuing in the Strike of Work, and to prevent those dependent upon them assisting the purposes of the disloyal of their continuance of the present state of things.

On 7 April, Hobhouse again wrote to Monteith, expressing Sidmouth's approval of the strong action taken by the Lord Provost and agreeing to the offer of a reward to uncover the author of the Address. 'A proclamation may be issued with a view to discovering the author of the Treasonable Placard posted in Glasgow on Sunday last.'

The Yorkshire Revolt

Government suspicion that there was collusion for a coordinated radical rising in Scotland and England was strengthened when there was a general strike in Yorkshire on 1 April. This took place just as those arrested for organising the meeting in St Peter's Field, Manchester, were due to stand trial. As well as stopping work, around 2,000 armed men marched on Huddersfield with the apparent intention of taking over the town, taking captive the civic leaders and setting up an interim government. But the radicals dispersed on the outskirts and returned home: only four were later charged.

Thomas Sharp, the Manchester Boroughreeve, did not believe that there was a cross-border conspiracy. He was in possession of a copy of the Address, presumably sent by Monteith, and which he called 'the vilest of productions', and hence was well aware of what was happening in Scotland. Yet in his letter to the Lord Provost on 5 April he expressed the opinion that events in Huddersfield were 'probably not connected with the northern alarms.'

On 11 April, another group of three or four hundred approached Huddersfield carrying political banners and arms, but, after reaching Grange Moor, left when the military arrived, although 22 men were taken at Grange Moor. There were further disturbances in Sheffield, Halifax, Mirfield, Dewsbury the same day, and another crowd assemble at Wigan in Lancashire the following day, all with the same purpose in mind, it was claimed, although it has been argued that the main thrust of these demonstrations was, in fact, to protest against the trial of the Peterloo protestors.

Those arrested on 1 April were charged with treason. John Peacock and John Lindley were tried and sentenced to transportation, while Nathaniel Buckley and Thomas Blackburn were sent to prison, but released in 1822. The men captured at Grange Moor were initially sentenced to death, but this was commuted to transportation to Van Diemen's Land, and the names of eight of these are listed, along with Lindley and Peacock, as having been taken from 'York Gaol' and put aboard the *Lady Lindley,* which sailed for Van Diemen's Land on 4 January 1821: they were Richard Addy (weaver), John Burkinshaw (weaver), Joseph Chapiel (shoemaker),William Comstone (soldier), Joseph Firth (weaver), William Rice (cordwainer), Benjamin Rogers (linen weaver), and Charles Stamfield (weaver).

Like the Boroughreeve, the English radicals were aware of events in Scotland, as is obvious from the letter that the weaver John Burkinshaw sent to his wife of 10 August to reassure her that he expected that all would be well, in which he wrote, ' Don't be fearful of what will happen to me ... look at the special commission at Dumbarton – the president acquitted all the prisoners on one being found not guilty.' Unfortunately the jury at his trial found him guilty, and sentenced him to transportation. Soon after his arrival, he was joined in Australia by his wife and family, and they settled in Sydney when his sentence was finished, becoming a successful farmer by the time of his death at the age of 90.

It is likely that the English radicals later met up with their Scots comrades, if not in the hulks in London, or on the prison ship, almost certainly in the colony. We know, from research by the Macfarlanes in Australia that William Rice, one of the Grange Moore captives, gave lodgings in 1837 the Bonnymuir radical Robert Grey. It is unlikely that this was an isolated incident, and there was most likely contact between these men who had been transported for taking up arms in the same cause.

Highland Clearances

It is frequently overlooked that the disturbances in the industrial belt of Scotland coincided with militant activity in the Highlands, where clearances of people from the land to make way for sheep were facing resistance. Although regarded as a local issue, the fact that Highlanders were prepared to use physical force against landowners, forcing the government to send troops to enforce the clearances, added to government suspicions that the whole of Scotland was on the brink of a revolution, influenced by dangerous American and French ideas of 'democracy.'

The success of Patrick Sellar in clearing the Sutherland estates of people to make way for sheep which were more profitable, was seen by landowners as economic progress, and encouraged other landowners to follow suit. By 1819, several estates had seen their value increase tenfold as the result of turning them into sheep pasture. This led many Highland landowners to undertake 'improvement' and expel their tenants who were driven off the land and who made their way to the industrial belt, where they joined Irish immigrants, fleeing poverty in their country in swelling the numbers looking for work, and further depressing already low wages and increasing the strain on the Poor Law.

Hugh Munro of Novar announced a plan in February 1820 to clear the native population from Culrain to put the land under sheep, and sent agents to deliver writs of removal on the tenants. In the glen they were met by a hostile crowd and forced to run away. The Sheriff Depute wrote to the *Inverness Courier* that the agents had been 'threatened that if they returned their lives would be taken and themselves thrown into the Kyle', and asked the Lord Advocate to send 500 troops and three cannon to assist the clearance.

Sir William Rae sent forty police and twenty-five militiamen, and they, with a large body of armed local gentlemen, marched into the glen where they were confronted by a 'body of three or four hundred people, chiefly women', who rushed from behind a stone dyke and attacked them with sticks and stones. In the riot that followed, one woman was shot dead, a young boy shot in the leg, and a woman wounded 'in the mouth and eye by a bayonet.' Faced with this ferocious attack and believing armed men were about to come to assist the women, the police and troops fled. The carriage of the Sheriff Depute was overturned and his writs scattered and he ran the four miles to Ardgay pursued by the angry crowd.

The local minister went among the crowd and restored order, advising them of 'the madness and inutility of violence.' Having vented their anger, the people returned to their homes and were eventually driven from the land. Landowners and their factors realised that they were likely to face violence, and, despite a few confrontations in the following months, succeeded in clearing their lands, often by having military support to assist them.

To the government in Westminster, however, this was not seen as a local protest against eviction, but was regarded as part of a larger, and far more sinister, national plot to overthrow government authority. Coupled with the disturbances in the industrial areas, Lord Liverpool's administration believed that the only course open to them in order to preserve the constitution, was to clamp down on the 'rebels', using any method of identifying the leaders, and then inflicting the most severe punishment possible on those involved.

It has been argued that the general strike of 3 April 1820 marked the emergence of the working class as an organised social force in Scotland, and paved the way for the emergence of a socialist movement in the future. This is questionable, as the strike was intimately associated with the armed uprising that immediately followed it, and was the subject of condemnation from the press and the pulpit that put 'the fear of God' into many and made them reluctant to become involved in political agitation.

With the failure of the subsequent insurrection and faced with the repressive measures of government afterwards, the working class turned to more constitutional, and peaceful methods to achieve their ends. Once the working class disentangled political and radical popular action and clarified their objectives, the lesson of the general strike did, however, remain a potent factor in their campaigns.

5. THE RADICAL WAR

The Glasgow Rising

Early on the morning of Tuesday 4 April, Duncan Turner met with members of the Glasgow Radical Union, William Flanagan of Dobbie's Loan, Robert Walker of Rottenrow and William Maltman, on Glasgow Green. Flanagan later recorded that Turner told them the news from England was not good and that the radicals there had not risen, but were waiting for Glasgow to start the insurrection and they would take up arms to support them. He asked the three men to consult with their committee to find out how many would be prepared to turn out, and meet him again at 4pm.

Hearing that there was no English rising the Glasgow Committee split, with half the members expressing serious doubts about the whole plan, and the rest of them clinging to hope that events would improve in the southern cities. At the afternoon meeting, Turner claimed the he had received news from England that was more encouraging, and arranged a further meeting 'opposite the Catholic Chapel in Clyde Street' at 8pm, when he would have more information for them from the Select Committee.

When the delegates met as arranged near the Catholic church in Clyde Street, they decided to move to Port Eglinton for security, and there, Turner revealed the plan of action to the three delegates. He asked for 100 men who were, he said, to be joined by another 100 from Anderston, 'to go to Carron to secure a large quantity of arms and ammunition and three pieces of artillery.' The ironworks, he claimed, had been taken over by the workers who were ready to supply weapons to the radicals. He then ordered them to go straight away and bring their colleagues to Germiston Road, where he would join them to issue their final orders. Flanagan met with the Glasgow Union members in the Barony Kirk, where he called for volunteers for the raid to join him at Germiston Road. As Flanagan made his way to the meeting place with Dugald Smith the Glasgow radical commandant and Mr Bryson, the Drygate delegate to the committee, they met up with Andrew Hardie, a weaver from High Street, who asked to join them.

When only 60 Glasgow men turned up at Germiston Road and there was no sign of the Anderston contingent, the leaders wanted to call off the attack, pointing out that so few men stood little chance against any troops they might encounter. After a brief discussion and persuaded by Turner, around 30 men chose to carry on. Their usual leaders having decided not to participate in what they regarded as a doomed scheme, and Turner having explained that he had other duties to perform as part of the provisional Government the former soldier Andrew Hardie said he would take command of the Glasgow radical contingent.

As the men separated into two groups, those going home and those preparing to go to Falkirk standing on opposite sides of the street, Turner handed Hardie a card torn in half, telling him that the other half was in the hands of a man at Condorrat who would take command of the force and be their 'conductor to Carron.' Turner wished them well and, as Hardie led his men out at 1am on the Wednesday morning on the road to Falkirk, he left the scene and, like Craig, was never heard of again.

John King had meantime set out for Condorrat, and 'an honest but unsuspecting' Paisley weaver James Shields, had been sent by Lees to Strathaven, each was carrying credentials allegedly from the Provisional Government, and a message asking the Union leaders to raise the local radicals. Lees himself then went to Clydebank and met with the radical group there in an attempt to persuade them to march to Kirkintilloch where, he claimed, the radicals were in arms. But he was subjected to such rigorous questioning by the local leaders, who seemed to have doubts about him, that he left without convincing them to rise and like his fellow spies disappeared leaving no record of what became of him thereafter.

At 11pm the same night, a rain-soaked man calling himself 'John Andrews' arrived at the home of Robert Baird in Condorrat and asked Mrs Baird if he could speak with John Baird. He explained to the Baird brothers that he was a representative of the Provisional Government and informed them that strikers at Carron had taken over the ironworks and wanted to hand over arms to a radical army that was on the way from Glasgow. This group would take the weapons to the city, via Kilsyth, and give them to George Kinloch of Kinloch, who was camped with a large radical force on Cathkin Braes.

John Baird had served in Argentina and on the continent with the 95th Regiment (Rifle Brigade), and on leaving the army had returned to live with his brother, Robert and his wife, at Condorrat, working as a weaver. John King, now calling himself Andrews, asked Baird to raise the local radicals and take command of the group from Glasgow, whose leader would have the corresponding half of a card which he handed over. Robert Baird was sceptical, but John immediately set out to get together the local radicals while King was fed and rested in his bed.

Meanwhile, the authorities were fully aware of the activities of the radicals, as the Chief of Police in Glasgow sent reports of their activities to Kirkman Finlay and Lord Sidmouth. There is reason to believe that the spies Turner, King and Craig kept James Mitchell and Henry Monteith informed of events, and that they in turn passed the intelligence to the military, while keeping Whitehall up to date with events.

On Tuesday, before the Glasgow radicals were made aware of the plan for a rising, Major William Murray of Polmaise, Commander of the Stirlingshire Yeoman Cavalry, was aware of the radicals' movements and sent a despatch rider to Perth ordering a troop of the 10th Hussars, who were semi-permanently stationed in the town, to Stirling. There they were to stand ready to ride to Falkirk to defend the ironworks where, he informed them, an attack was expected on 5 April. Lieutenant Colonel Taylor quickly arranged for cavalry to be assembled, and Lieutenant Ellis Hodgson set out on a forced ride with his troop. But informed at Stirling that Carron was already protected by men from the 80th Regiment stationed inside the ironworks, and by troops from the Rifle Brigade in the surrounding area, his troop was diverted to Kilsyth, where the radicals were expected to go after the Carron attack.

After a 12 hour ride, his cavalry joined up with Lieutenant John James Davidson, the Edinburgh lawyer who commanded the Kilsyth Troop of the

Stirlingshire Yeomanry, who were stationed at the Duntreath Arms Hotel in Kilsyth, where they had been sent earlier to maintain order after the strike, and in anticipation of the arrival of a force of armed radicals.

Further west, Glasgow was rife with rumours of a large radical army approaching the city from Paisley to take advantage of the confusion caused by the strike, and which was expected on Wednesday 5 April. To reinforce the garrison already in the city, troops from the Dunbartonshire and Ayrshire Yeomanry Cavalry were sent there, although John Strang, in his history of the Waterloo Club in Glasgow, suggested their presence did not particularly impress the citizens.

> ... with such a disciplined and well-affected force, at once ready to act on any emergency, there was no fear felt on the part of anyone who could coolly reflect ... and they kept themselves steadily within their own habitations.

Aware of these rumours, the editor of the *Glasgow Herald*, Samuel Hunter, had, on 4 April, placed his Volunteer unit, the 'Glasgow Sharpshooters', on alert and at 5am on Wednesday they were summoned for action. One of the Volunteers later recorded the scene.

> As one of the Glasgow Sharpshooters, I leapt up at the sound of the Bugle at 5 o'clock ... and hastened to my regiment. I reached the square at 6 o'clock ... and I was among 500 bayonets ready to act at a moment's notice ... The Corps never appeared in better spirits, ready to rush, if need be, against the whole Radical pikes. It must, in justice be added, that there was not as yet a single hostile pike to put that courage to the test.

The Volunteers were not required to fight, as the action was elsewhere, but they were held in readiness for the rest of the day, lest the radicals succeeded and make an attack. Strang recorded that the day that had begun wet, and had worsened as 'the heavens opened and poured down such a torrent of rain as fairly cleared the streets.' He noted that 'by four o'clock, the redoubtable, Falstaffian army of Paisley malcontents had dispersed into thin air', although the troops were kept on alert until dawn, in what he lampooned as 'The Wet Radical Wednesday of the West.'

The Battle of Bonnymuir

At Condorrat King went on ahead to Falkirk claiming he was to rally the men there and bring them to join Baird and Hardie's force, and Baird had a Glasgow radical named Kean accompany him for protection, or, it has been suggested, to keep an eye on him. Baird, Hardie and their men set out at about the same time as the Glasgow Sharpshooters were called to arms, and arrived, soaked with rain and hungry, at Castlecary Bridge around 6am on the morning of the 5th where they stopped at the inn for food. Baird paid for the dozen two-penny loaves and porter from his own pocket, after the innkeeper, Archibald Buchanan, refused to accept a bill that was to be redeemed later by the Provisional Government of Scotland. Baird asked for a receipt, which he dictated: 'The party called, and paid for porter and bread, 7s 6d by cash. (Signed) Archd. Buchanan.' It seems that Baird expected that the Provisional Government would reimburse his expenses. During Baird's trial, the Lord Advocate claimed that in payment he had given the inn-keeper a bill to be redeemed in six months by the Provisional Government, but this was denied by Buchanan.

Shortly after leaving Castlecary, Buchanan, who was watching them, noted that Baird split his party into two groups for security and in the hope of linking with any radicals coming to join them. He led one of the groups along the tow-path of the Forth and Clyde Canal, while his second-in-command, Hardie, with 'four or five stout men' followed the turnpike road through Bonnybridge towards Falkirk, with the aim of re-joining Baird's group further on, at an underpass on the canal, now known as 'Radical Pend.'

At 7am, Hardie stopped at the toll-keeper's house at Catlecary, where his men took two muskets and some ammunition to augment their small supply of arms. When the toll-keeper, James Russell, protested, Hardie gave him a receipt on behalf of the Provisional Government. At Bonnymill, a local resident, William Grindlay, later testified that when the group was passing his house, one of the insurgents stole a pitchfork.

As they continued along the road on the outskirts of Bonnybridge, Hardie met an English traveller heading for Glasgow and warned him that he should turn back as the city was in the midst of a revolution. The man, confused at the news, rode on for a mile, and met Nicol Hugh Baird, a trooper from the Kilsyth Troop of the Yeomanry, and told him what Hardie had said. Trooper Baird did not reply to him, but turned his horse and raced to Kilsyth to warn Lt Davidson, although at the Stirling trial he said he had confronted 'a large body of Radicals' and driven them back, before heading to Kilsyth.

Meanwhile the traveller had decided to head back to Falkirk, and when passing the radicals on his return, thanked Hardie, telling him that he was heeding his advice and not going to Glasgow. No attempt was made to find this traveller by the prosecution, or the defence, during the trial, and it was not until 1832 that Peter Mackenzie, the historian who first published accounts of the rising when records became available, tracked him down and got his account of the incident, which differed greatly from that given by Private Baird, under oath, at Stirling.

At Bonnybridge, Hardie's men stopped Sergeant Cook of the 10th Hussars who was carrying despatches to Kilsyth. When he asked what they were doing, they stated they were seeking their rights and demanded that he hand over his weapons, but when he explained he was carrying no ammunition and expressed sympathy for their cause, they gave him a copy of the proclamation and allowed him to go. He immediately raced to Kilsyth to inform the troops there of a small armed band of radicals on the road to Falkirk. He arrived just as Nicol Baird finished telling how he had single-handedly fought off a large group of armed men before riding to Kilsyth with news of the uprising. Cook's story and the copy of the proclamation, which he showed to the officers, confirmed the presence of armed radicals on the road near Bonnybridge, and heading towards Falkirk. Lt Hodgson borrowed horses from the Yeomanry for his troops, whose mounts were exhausted after their ride from Perth, and set out with sixteen Hussars and sixteen Yeomanry to intercept the insurgents.

At 9am, shortly after Baird and Hardie's units had reunited, they were met by John King, who suggested that they should move off the road to rest in a field at Bonnymuir, while he went on ahead to bring the radical reinforcements that were gathering at Camelon. He was alone and claimed, when asked about his companion, that he and Kean had become separated while evading a military patrol; Kean was never heard of or seen again, leading to the suspicion that King had killed him and disposed of his body somewhere on the road to Bonnybridge.

Following his advice, the radicals moved up the slope and took shelter on the ridge to await the reinforcements, as Hardie recorded.

> The whole of us turned and went through the aqueduct bridge, and went up about a mile onto the moor, and sat down on the top of a hill and rested (I think) about an hour, when the Cavalry made their appearance.

As the radicals moved onto the muir, John King made his way into Bonnybridge, apparently to take the road to Falkirk. Although he was never seen again, some Camelon men did join Baird's group, as at least three can be identified as being engaged in the battle: one who was wounded and later escaped, and two who were tried at Stirling.

Shortly after 9am the Hussars and Yeomanry arrived and were heading for the Falkirk road, which ran past the muir where the radicals were located out of sight. But, after speaking with an unnamed person, who told Lt Hodgson that the insurgents were on the hill and were led by a man named Baird, he immediately turned and led his troops straight for their position.

On seeing the troops heading towards them, Hardie suggested forming a square to resist them, but Baird chose to move his force a little further down the hill to take up positions behind a five-foot wall which would offer some defence against a cavalry charge. Hardie later wrote that there was 'a slap in the dyke which we filled with pikemen', while those with muskets stood behind the wall itself and those who had no weapons remained behind. With a shout of 'Liberty or Death!' they cheered as they made ready to face the advancing cavalry.

The cavalry took a circular route across the muir and approached from a wood on the right of the radical position, and shots were fired, although neither side was clear who had fired first. Hodgson approached the wall and called on the insurgents to surrender and withdrew his men a short distance awaiting their reply, but receiving none drew his sabre and ordered the Hussars to charge, leaving the Yeomanry as a reserve. Making for the gap in the wall they were driven back, without casualties, by musket fire from the radicals. One Hussar made a lone charge at the gap where he shot and wounded a radical who had attempted to stab him. A second charge was no more successful as the troops could not force their way through the pikes protecting the gap in the dyke and Hodgson again called on the insurgents to surrender, at which one radical threw away his musket and ran into the nearby wood.

Hodgson then charged straight at the dyke, which his horse cleared and landed amongst the radicals. At the same time his cavalry pushed their way through the gap. The Lieutenant faced Baird, who aimed his empty weapon at the officer, threatening to shoot. Hodgson fired his pistol at Baird but it only flashed and did not go off. Baird used the butt of his musket to strike a Private on the thigh, and was fired at by Sergeant Saxelby, who missed. Baird then grabbed a pike and wounded the Sergeant in the right arm and side.

One of the insurgents thrust at Hodgson with a pike, wounding his hand and stabbing his horse, but he again called on the radicals to surrender, asking if their captain's name was Baird, leading Hardie, in his account of the battle, to comment,

> The officer of Hussars asked who was our Captain, and if his name was Baird, which made it evident that some person who knew him had given them information

That informant could only have been John King, as he had met with Baird in Condorrat, while Baird's group had encountered no one on the towpath, and the inn-keeper at Castlecary had not been contacted by Hodgson. It seems most likely that the 'unnamed man' who spoke with Hodgson and pointed the troops in the direction of the radicals was none other than John King/John Andrews, as he was the only person to know both the field where the men were waiting, and the name of their commander. After his appearance at Bonnybridge King, like the other spies, disappeared from the records. It has been conjectured that the government gave King, and the other agents, posts in the colonies, or set them up elsewhere with new identities, as a reward for their services to the Crown.

When Hodgson demanded unconditional surrender John Baird, after what the Lieutenant himself later described as 'stout resistance', ordered his men to lay down their weapons. Some of the radicals tried to escape, but were chased by troops from the Yeomanry who attempted to cut them down and then trample on the wounded: though as Hardie recorded of one such trooper, 'the horse had more humanity than his master.' Around a third of the force managed to get away, some, as Hardie explained had been standing apart from the main body as they had no weapons, and were better placed to evade capture.

On 7 April, the *Glasgow Herald* carried a report on the battle.

> …they advanced to a wall over which they commenced firing at the military. Some shots were then fired by the soldiers in return, and after some time the cavalry got through an opening in the wall and attacked the party, who resisted until overpowered by the troops, who succeeded in taking 19 of them prisoners, who are lodged in Stirling Castle… Lt Hodgson received a pike wound through the right hand and a sergeant of the 10th Hussar was seriously wounded by a shot in the right side and a pike … Four of the radicals were wounded. Five muskets, two pistols, eighteen pikes and about 100 ball cartridges were taken.

Among those taken by the Yeomanry were Alexander Hart, a cabinet-maker from Glasgow, who was slashed about the head, and a Glasgow weaver, Alexander Johnston, who was saved by Hodgson who ordered he be taken alive as a Yeoman trooper tried to cut him down. One of the radicals cut down and left for dead was a Glasgow printer named Black, and he was rescued by Alexander Robertson of Damhead farm, who took him to his home and sent for a doctor to treat his injuries. Robertson and the doctor refused to hand him over to troops who came to detain him, and later that night Black's uncle Robert MacClymont and his son James, came from Larbert and helped the wounded man to escape.

In all eighteen of the remaining insurgents were taken captive and the Yeomanry troops had to be prevented from attacking the prisoners by Hodgson, who had to use his sword to defend them. While Hodgson went to Bonnybridge to get a fresh horse to replace his, which had been killed, the wounded prisoners were loaded into a cart provided by a man from Denny, and set out for Stirling Castle. Hardie asked for water for the wounded, but Davidson refused, and began the journey with the exhausted prisoners. When Hodgson caught up with the convoy, he immediately gave water to them

At Stirling Castle the captured arms were taken to the armoury, where the armourer, James Murray and ordnance storekeeper, John Benson, recorded that there were five muskets, two pistols and eighteen pikes as well as a hundred rounds of ball cartridges, before placing them in two sealed chests and placing them in the ordnance store as evidence. The names of those detained were recorded as – John Baird (Condorrat), John Barr (Condorrat), William Clackson or Clarkson (Glasgow), James Clelland (Glasgow), Robert Grey (Glasgow), Andrew Hardie (Glasgow), Alexander Hart (Glasgow), Alexander Johnstone (Glasgow), Alexander Latimer (Glasgow), Thomas McCulloch (Glasgow), Thomas McFarlane (Condorrat), Benjamin Moir (Glasgow), Allan Murchie (Glasgow), Thomas Pike or Pink (Glasgow), William Smith (Condorrat), David Thompson (Glasgow), Andrew White (Glasgow), and James Wright (Glasgow). The prisoners were handed over to Fort-Major Peddie and then placed in a single room after being fed, except for John Baird, who was as Hardie recorded, 'taken away from us shortly after and put in a dungeon, and had about four or five stones of iron put on him.'

After the skirmish a troop of Stirlingshire Yeomanry, commanded by Captain Nicholson, searched the area for insurgents but found none, as most had made their way home. On arriving at Falkirk, a hostile crowd booed and hissed at the troopers, and some stones were thrown. Nicholson ordered his men to form a line and threatened to fire on the mob, which sullenly dispersed. The following day Major General Bradford, Commander-in-Chief of the Army in Scotland, wrote to Lord Sidmouth praising the actions of Hodgson and Davidson and their men for defeating and capturing the 'offenders', and seeking compensation for the owner of the horse that had been killed.

Fearing an attack on Glasgow, Lt-Colonel Northcott put his troops from the 1st Battalion Rifle Brigade on stand-by and was joined by Samuel Hunter's Glasgow Yeomanry (The Glasgow Sharpshooters), with his force of 1,128 men, while cannon were set up at bridges over the Clyde. Lord Elcho of Longniddry and the Midlothian Cavalry arrived in Glasgow to reinforce the garrison there, and the Royal Edinburgh Volunteers and Lothian Yeomanry were ordered to prepare for a forced march to Glasgow. But, apart from an incident when clegs were thrown at the Ayrshire Yeomanry, and house raids in Duntocher by the military to arrest suspected radicals, there were no serious disturbances.

With troops arriving in the city in great numbers, accommodation would have been a problem but for the actions of members of the gentry: men like James Edington of Queen Street Sugar House, who offered slated accommodation for 100 horses, and two houses for troops of the Edinburgh Cavalry who had been sent to Glasgow. Hotels and inns were commandeered, with the approval of the owners, to house the officers and stables and yards sought for the horses and men.

Throughout Wednesday the military stood to arms in Glasgow in anticipation of an attack that they had been told was planned for that day, and it was not until the evening that the Yeomanry were ordered to stand down, leaving the other, regular units on standby. But later that night they were recalled when news arrived that radicals were gathering in force at Bridgeton, and were parading under arms led by a drummer. Patrols were organised to search for the radicals from the Yeomanry headquarters in St George's Church, but they found nothing and were dismissed at 5am.

The Strathaven Rising

On Wednesday, Robert Lees, persuaded a Paisley weaver, James Shields, to carry a message allegedly from the Provisional Government, to the leaders of the Strathaven Radical Committee. This ordered the radicals there to take up arms and march to join forces assembling for an attack on Glasgow, where a large army under Kinloch of Kinloch was camped on Cathkin Brae, while another army was gathering on Campsie Braes to attack the city from two directions. Shields set out from Paisley the same afternoon to walk the fifteen miles to Strathaven in pouring rain. He arrived at the home of William Allan at High Bellgreen just before 6pm, and presented his credentials and passed on the intelligence provided by Lees.

Allan sent for the other local radical leaders, John Morrison, James Russell and John Stevenson, who questioned Shields about the proposed attack on Glasgow. Robert Hamilton, the Strathaven radical commandant, arrived and asked for Shields credentials and was handed a card which matched that given to him earlier by John King. This convinced Hamilton that the Paisley weaver was indeed an emissary from the Provisional Government and that his information could be trusted.

John Stevenson, in his account of the Insurrection, made it clear that many of the radicals anticipated a rising. He stressed that the local hand-loom weavers had 'grappled with the real difficulties of life – a profligate Court, a rapacious Ministry, that used the law to protect their interests', and,

> They knew if they could prove anything like the existence
> of a conspiracy among the sober and calculating tradesmen
> of Scotland, their hands would be strengthened by the

suspension of the Habeas Corpus Act and their capacity as sagacious statesmen, would be acknowledged by their Royal master, and the worthless minions who fatten and bask in the sunshine of the throne.

He added that there was an official intolerance of a free press, which combined with censorship to exclude 'carnaptious radicals' and prevent criticism of 'the glorious English revolution' and the Treaty of Union. The Anglo-Scottish ruling class, he claimed, wanted to exclude from university teaching posts and the law courts any who sought reform. Against this background, it would be easy for the Strathaven radicals to accept Shields' story that a rising was imminent.

The Strathaven leaders decided to seek the advice of 63 year-old James Wilson, who had been a member of the Society of Friends of the People, was familiar with the writings of most radical authors, and who had attended the Conventions of the Society in the 1790s. A well-respected member of the community, he was a father figure to local radicals who held him in high regard. After talking with Shields, Wilson stated that 'liberty is not worth having, if it is not worth fighting for', and agreed that the local men should gather arms and be ready to set out early the next day. He sent one of his neighbours, Matthew Rony, who had been active with the United Irishmen during the 1798 Rising and had entertained them with tales of that event, to Glasgow to inform the radicals there that the Strathaven men would 'be down by break of day.'

Throughout the night parties carried out arms raids on a number of properties to augment their small armoury, while Wilson sharpened and shafted pikes. During one raid the party decided to make fun of a local youth, James Fallow, who had been found hiding under his father's stairs and demanded that he accompany them as a prisoner. His clumsy attempts to escape as they went from house to house caused much amusement, before he eventually managed to get away when the party was demanding guns from another resident. Their 'fun' led to the authorities charging the Strathaven radicals with kidnap, in addition to the other charges at their later trials.

Where there had been almost a hundred men active during the night only 25 appeared at dawn on Thursday 6 April for the march to Campsie. Stevenson remarked that pleas by family and friends, together with reports that 'all was quiet in Glasgow, will account for the desertion of three-fourths of our number.' Attempts to raise the radicals in Glassford failed, and the depleted Strathaven contingent marched out, flying a banner that was carried by William Watson, which proclaimed, 'Scotland Free – Or a Desart', as James Wilson, with a sword resting on his shoulder, marched in the rear

At East Coldstream, near Chapelton, they met two men who told them that the Glasgow rising had failed and said they had no knowledge of a radical army on Cathkin Braes. Wilson expressed doubts about the enterprise, suggesting it could be a trap, and he and Hamilton questioned Shields who was marching with them armed with a musket and fifty rounds of ball, about the proposed attack on Glasgow. He maintained that he had told the truth and that the leader of the Anderston Committee (i.e. King) would confirm this, adding that if there was a problem and it was a trap, he was in as much trouble as they were. Stevenson, writing fifteen years later, stated that he had no reason not to believe Shields, and despite growing misgivings, the party decided to continue the march towards Cathkin.

When they arrived at East Kilbride they were told by local supporters that Captain Graham with a troop of the Kilbride Yeomanry Cavalry had been waiting for them and had only just been moved to Hamilton. This convinced Wilson that the alleged attack was a plot to entrap the radicals and he suggested that the entire company should return home to Strathaven.

John Morrison, who had seen service during the Peninsular War, urged the men to continue using, according to Stevenson, the struggles of Wallace and Bruce 'in the glorious cause of liberty' as examples to follow, adding,

> I am proud to see a few Scotsmen leave their homes to tread in the footsteps of such illustrious men, and if we were to perish, let us do it nobly, our names will be recorded among Scotland's patriotic sons.

Most still refused to believe that they had been betrayed and decided to press on. Wilson handed his sword to Robert Hamilton and wished the men good luck as the column continued on its way. He, however, decided to go to the home of a friend nearby to rest before returning to Strathaven.

The remaining 25 men arrived at the outskirts of Glasgow where they unfurled their banner on a hill near Rutherglen, but found that there was no radical army gathered there. They decided to wait for its arrival and sent two men into Rutherglen for supplies of food and to rouse the radicals there. Shields was again questioned about the Provisional Government and explained that his father was a prominent member of the Anderston Radical Committee, and that the Committee would vouch for him. They sent a messenger to Anderston to let the radicals there know the Strathaven men had arrived and to inquire about their location and that of the radical army.

At 9pm two Rutherglen radicals arrived and informed them of the defeat at Bonnymuir and that 'the bubble had burst.' They also reported that a rider had left Cathkin House heading for Glasgow, and they suspected he had seen the radical standard and was going to report to the military. Stevenson and MacIntyre organised the hiding of their weapons, with Shields being one of the last to give up his gun. Some of the men went into Rutherglen in ones and twos to have a meal at the inn, while others started to made their own way back to Strathaven. William MacIntyre was arrested three miles from home, and twelve others fell into the hands of the authorities before reaching Strathaven. Wilson did manage to get home, but he too was taken into custody by the military who had arrived in response to the messengers sent by 'prominent, well-disposed citizens' in Strathaven, many of whom had armed themselves as soon as the radical column had left the village that morning.

The prisoners were held in Hamilton Barracks for a few days before being sent to Glasgow, where they were placed in the Bridewell to await trial. Many of the radicals who had managed to evade the authorities made their way to ports to seek ships to take them to Canada and America.

A little further north there appears to have been some support for the radical cause. At Airdrie late on 5 April, Private Thurtell of the 10th Hussars, who was carrying despatches to the town, reported that a shot had been fired at him as he approached the outskirts, but his attackers had managed to escape. The Procurator Fiscal offered a £200 reward for information leading to the arrest and conviction of the perpetrators of the offence, but this did not produce any results. In spite of these incidents, the authorities seem to have regarded Airdrie as less of a problem and transferred line troops elsewhere, replacing them there and at Hamilton with troops from the Middle Ward cavalry

On the same day, and to the south, the Ayrshire Yeomanry, carried out raids on suspected radical houses, and took thirty suspected radicals into custody at Mauchline, where they also found arms and ammunition, while a raid in Ayr uncovered a number of pikes.

'The Battle of the Bellows'

There had been radical activity reported in the Dumbarton area, particularly at Duntocher in the immediate aftermath of the general strike, with stories of pike-making and drilling by men whose numbers were variously reported as in the hundreds and in the thousands. With news of events in Glasgow, alarm spread among the population who feared an insurrection in their area.

Early on Thursday 6 April, information was received by the authorities that a large radical force from Duntocher was planning to seize the Castle, and the Dumbarton Volunteers were called to arms. John Glen in his *History of the Town and Castle of Dumbarton*, published in 1847, gives an account of their first task being to carry coal up the 365 steps into the Castle, adding that they 'did not altogether relish this first duty in their campaign against the Radicals.' When ordered to prepare for action, many of the Volunteers guarding the castle were so afraid that they did not load their muskets properly, putting the ball into their muskets before the powder. After they were organised and a detachment sent to guard the road from Glasgow, they formed up and marched away to carry out raids on the homes of the known radicals.

Led by the County Fiscal, troops surrounded Duntocher at dawn and arrested a number of men known to have expressed support for reform. Robert and George Munroe, William Blair, Patrick McDevitt, Richard Thompson and William McPhie were taken along with William Smith, Matthew Bennet and James Hamilton: two of whom are believed to have become informers and were not charged, although all three of this last group were released before the trial. As the captives were taken to the Castle, a raid on a smith's shop resulted in the seizure of a pair of black-smith's bellows and a number of pikes, which were bundled into carts and taken to the castle, as Glen recorded.

> The result of this campaign was the capturing of a few rude-made pikes, with two pairs of large smiths' bellows, which were carted through the burgh in triumph, at the head of the regiment, as the only trophies of their victory. This half-serious half-ludicrous affair was ever afterwards face-tiously called 'The Battle of the Bellows' by Dumbartonians.

In the following days warrants were issued for the arrest of Alexander Lindsay, Archibald McLaren, Daniel McNab, John Stewart, Robert Mc Kinley, William Roney and Robert Sinclair, but they were not found, appar-ently having made their escape when alerted to the warrants having been issued. Raids produced further arrests, and another eight radical prisoners were brought to the cells in the Castle. When John Rankin, Hugh Pollock, William Lochier, Robert Macintyre, and Robert Neil, were released without charge on 9 June, they wrote a letter thanking the Lieutenant Governor, General Ferrier, for 'the many favours we have received from you.'

It is doubtful if there ever was a plan for the radicals in Dunbartonshire to take part in the rising, and the numbers involved in radical activities there was grossly exaggerated, both by informers and by a public that was on the verge of panic. The pre-emptive strike by the authorities certainly prevented Dumbarton becoming involved in the insurrection, but was later to create a problem for prosecutors who attempted to have those arrested there charged with treason.

Government Claims of Success

Highly exaggerated reports of victory over a large revolutionary force in a 'great and bloody battle' at Bonnymuir were sent to Lord Sidmouth, who personally told the king of the triumph of his forces in saving the country from revolution. The news then circulated throughout central Scotland on Thursday 6 April, with sections of the press claiming 'perfect tranquillity' had been restored, which was greeted with relief and rejoicing by the propertied classes. That day was a religious fast day and many people attended church, where they were subjected to sermons that condemned the 'wicked and treasonable' radicals who had attempted to destroy the natural order and whose eternal damnation was assured.

The Established Church regarded what it saw as the attempted overthrow of the constitution as not just a crime, but a heinous sin. The minister at Kilsyth, the learned and highly respected Rev Robert Rennie, wrote to Murray of Polmaise, on 26 April demanding that the trial of 'those taken at Bonny Muir' be conducted with solemnity and 'their executions be a display of military force.' There is no record of a reply, but Murray, it seemed, preferred to await the outcome of the trials. In New Monklands Church, Rev Dr Begg denounced the rising as 'an attempt by the scum of the earth to become the masters of the nation.'

In Hugo Miller's *History of Cumbernauld*, writing about Cumbernauld at the time of the Rising, he noted that when Baird and Hardie left Condorrat they passed the village, but were not joined by the local workers who were 'too law-abiding' to take part in the rising. But, and significantly, he added 'one suspects that the hand of the Kirk was strong upon them.' The local minister, John Watson, was not noted for reformist views, and the minutes of the meetings in the parish church make no reference to anything of note in April, concentrating instead on the moral behaviour of the congregation, and the internal affairs of the kirk.

James Lapslie, the minister at Campsie, who had been a member of the Friends of the People and knew Thomas Muir, expressed horror at the actions of the radicals. He had even opposed Sunday Schools on the grounds they might encourage reformist ideas. When he learned that there had been men drilling with arms in the area around Kirkintilloch, he roundly condemned their 'evil' actions, and later, on a visit to James Wilson in Glasgow Jail was thrown out by the radical when he threatened that divine retribution awaited radicals.

The Established Church disapproved strongly of anything that disturbed the 'natural order', although it was noted in some contemporary accounts that the Relief Church was more favourably inclined to reform but preferred peaceful means. The Catholic Church was reluctant to be seen as favouring reform, partly as most of their flock where Irish and it feared association with the 'rebels of '98', and feared that support for parliamentary reform would almost certainly jeopardise government plans to consider Catholic Emancipation.

In addition to criticism by the Kirk, the Establishment and the press, radicals were lampooned in the press and in books, becoming the subject of versifiers determined to bring them and their aims into contempt. One such verse that appeared soon after the rising had collapsed was entitled 'A Radical's Character.'

A Radical's character's easy to draw -

He hates to obey, but would govern the law;

In manners unsocial, in temper unkind

A rebel in conduct, a tyrant in mind.

Malignant, implacable, incurably sour,

He hates every man who has riches and power;

So imprisoned himself, he would gladly destroy

The comforts and blessings which others enjoy.

6. MILITARY RULE

Within hours of the battle at Bonnymuir the commander of the troops at Falkirk, Captain Nicholson, sent a despatch to Murray of Polmaise with the suggestion that raids to arrest radicals should be immediately begun, even if there was no evidence against the persons arrested.

> … the principal blackguards and most notorious characters should at least be taken up. I am sure from what I have seen today that it would have an excellent effect to take up at least six fellows here and as many at Camelon, no matter whether anything eventually be actually proved. The fright of being taken to Stirling Castle should have great effect.

The idea of using the military as part of a campaign of terror and intimidation was not one viewed with approval by the regular forces, but seems, from what happened, to have appealed to the Yeomanry Cavalry. Although there is no evidence that Murray approved the plan, individual local commanders may have chosen to act on their own initiative, as many towns and villages experienced raids by police and military units in the weeks following the capture of the armed militants.

At midnight William Gardner of Kilsyth was ordered to sound his bugle in the town, and the Kilsyth Yeomanry assembled at the Cross, from where they spread out to raid the homes of known radicals. Several men were taken into custody, including Gardner's father Robert, and transported to Stirling Castle. Robert was the manager of two shops and ran the mill at Tak-Ma-Doon Road, and was not a radical, although he was known as a 'Democrat' who advocated peaceful constitutional change. His family believe that he was reported to the military as a reprisal for having won a court case against the factor of the Edmonstone estate at Colzium. He was held for nine weeks before being released, and immediately upon his return to Kilsyth made plans to leave Scotland and sailed for Canada seven weeks later. A few years later the family moved to Utah, where his descendants played a major role on building mills, canals and bridges, and became prominent members of the Church of Latter Day Saints.

That same Thursday evening, a group of radicals marched to the Forth and Clyde Canal at Kirkintilloch, but hid their arms before dispersing when no support was forthcoming: the arms were later discovered by a party of troops. The *Edinburgh Weekly Journal* noted on 14 April that at Kirkintilloch 'the men had generally the appearance of factory men.' Later the same night, troops from the Rifle Brigade and a troop of Hussars raided Duntocher and seized a quantity of arms and ammunition, arresting ten men and wounding another who tried to escape.

In a display of military strength Major-General Thomas Bradford held a review of troops from the Rifle Brigade, Glasgow and Dumbarton Yeomanry and artillery gunners in George Square on the rainy morning of 6 April. After a short survey, he thanked the assembled troops before he and his staff left for lunch in the Star Hotel. His Deputy, Quarter-Master General James Douglas, issued a General Order stating that the General was impressed by their turnout and felt they were well 'qualified for the duties for which they have been formed.'

After Bradford's departure, Samuel Hunter ordered the entire parade to march to Buchanan Street, and at Queen Street divided them into two columns, one going to Anderston and the other to Bridgeton where they carried out raids on the homes of suspects looking for arms. They found a few mostly old weapons and some ammunition, and seized 'a trunk containing papers.' A number of arrests were made, among them it was reported 'three of the principal Radical leaders', George Washington, David Graham and William Graham. Having delivered their captives to the Tolbooth, the wet and dirty soldiers returned to their quarters and were dismissed at 3.30pm.

Despite the widespread belief that the insurgency was over, General Bradford had concerns about the possibility of another attempt to take munitions from Carron Ironworks. As a precaution, he ordered the removal of armaments from Carron, sending them along the Forth to Grangemouth and from there to Leith, where they were secured in the Fort. On 21 April, the *Dundee Advertiser* reported,

> About sixty carronades, and a considerable quantity of ammunition were lately brought down from Carron, and safely lodged in Leith Fort, beyond the reach of the radicals.

The following day, Friday 7 April, Captain Brown and fifteen coaches of men from the Edinburgh City Police arrived in Glasgow 'to aid the civil and military authorities in that city.' Captain Mitchell and his officers joined them to carry out a mopping-up operation that lasted for two days. The Edinburgh officers returned to the capital late on Saturday night and were commended, on 13 April, for having 'rendered very essential service in ... searching for arms, etc, at Glasgow, Airdrie and Kirkintilloch.'

One of those taken into custody during the raids, was John Anderson Junior, arrested on a Sheriff's warrant charging him with 'circulating, publishing and posting up the above treasonable Address.' Taken to Glasgow Jail, he wrote directly to Lord Sidmouth explaining how Duncan Turner had persuaded him to print the address. By a special Home Office warrant of 21 April he was to be held in custody 'till liberated in due course of the law.' It is believed that this was ordered by Sidmouth, who feared that if Anderson was brought to trial his evidence would uncover the use of spies by the government. On 4 August Anderson was released and escorted to a ship that took him to the East indies, where he was employed by the government.

On 7 April the *Glasgow Herald* announced the end of the rising, stating that 'We believe we may congratulate the public on the prospect of a speedy termination to our revolutionary outrages.' With the defeat of the radicals at Bonnymuir the establishment felt that the danger was now past, and their thoughts turned to how they could prevent further militancy. Forty-nine prominent citizens wrote to Lord Provost Henry Monteith asking for a public meeting to discuss 'the future employment of those who have obeyed the command of a Treasonable Confederacy to desist from their ordinary labour.' He agreed and announced that a meeting had been arranged for Tuesday 11 April.

The Saturday edition of the *London Gazette* carried news that Lord Sidmouth had assured George IV that the threat was ended and the conspirators were being sought, and that the king was offering a reward of £500 for the discovery of the radical leaders who had produced the Address, promising,

> ... our most gracious pardon to any person concerned in the Affixing and Publishing the same, except the Authors and Printers thereof, who shall give such information to one of our Principal Secretaries of State, or to our Advocate of Scotland, or to the Lord Provost of Glasgow, as shall lead to the Detection of the Authors or Printers thereof.

The same day, fifteen of the Bonnymuir prisoners were taken by steamboat to Newhaven and then in six coaches to Edinburgh Castle. Three, Hart, MacFarlane and Clarkson, were too badly wounded to travel and remained in Stirling until 28 April when they too were transported to Edinburgh. They were taken to the castle dungeons, and detained there for interrogation until 21 June, when they were returned to Stirling to await trial on charges of high treason.

Greenock Incidents

Despite an influx to Greenock of people, some of them fleeing radicals seeking passage to Canada and America after the disturbances in central Scotland, the town had remined relatively quiet during the insurrection. There had been no demonstrations or riots during the troubles, yet it was to become the focus of the worst bloodshed during the insurrection, resulting in the killing and the maiming of civilians.

Colonel John Dunlop and the 120 men of the Port Glasgow Armed Association had been stationed in Paisley from Monday 3 April to maintain order there, and by Friday it was decided that, as the town was quiet, the unit should return home on Saturday. That morning Provost Jamieson asked Dunlop to take five radical prisoners to Greenock Jail as the prison at Paisley was overcrowded and the Colonel agreed. It is highly likely that the five sent to Greenock were James Walker, a weaver from Johnstone, Robert Parker a Johnstone shoemaker, Robert Smellie and James Nixon, weavers from Elderslie, and John Young, whose occupation and place of residence is not given, as they were cited for trial but were noted as being 'not in custody' at the time of the Paisley Grand Jury trial on 1 July: writs of capias were issued for their arrest, but they were never found.

As the Colonel was remaining in the town where he had a meeting later that morning with General Bradford, he sent two officers, Carswell and Cleland, to escort the cart in which the prisoners were carried, together with a strong body of 80 men as he feared an attempt might be made to free them. The rest of the Association force remained with him.

Leaving Paisley at noon the detachment approached Greenock at 5pm, where the Chief Magistrate, James Dennistoun, had made no arrangements for the arrival of the prisoners. A large crowd had been gathering from 4pm when there were rumours that many radical prisoners were on their way. There was a long-standing rivalry between the two towns that dated back to 1754, when Glasgow merchants had created Port Glasgow to avoid paying taxes on goods arriving at the port of Greenock, and this added to the anger of the crowd, who resented the presence of troops from the rival town. Led by a fife and drum band, the soldiers made their way through the jeering, hostile crowd and safely delivered their charges to the Bridewell, leaving half their number to secure the gates to the prison where a large hostile crowd had gathered.

Dennistoun ordered the crowd to disperse but was ignored and stones were thrown at the troops as they started to march out of the town. At Cathcart Street, concerned at the growing hostility, Carswell ordered his men to fire over the heads of the crowd, but two people were wounded. At this the crowd began stoning the soldiers in earnest, injuring several of them. In response, the troops, when they reached Rue End, fired indiscriminately into the crowd, killing three and wounding eighteen, five of whom later died of their injuries.

The April edition of the *Scots Magazine* listed the casualties: killed, or who died of their injuries, were John Boyce (aged 33), Adam Clephane (48), Archibald Drummond (20), James Kerr (17), William Lindsay (15), James MacGilp (8), Archibald McKinnon (17) and John MacWhinnie (65). There were ten who were wounded: Peter Cameron (14), flesh wound; Gilbert MacArthur (18), slight wound; John Patrick (30), John Gunn (24), flesh wounds; David MacBride (14), slight wound; John Patrick (30), slight wound; Hugh Paterson (14), leg amputated; Robert Spence (11), slight wound; George Tillery (25), slight wound; Mrs Catherine Turner (65), leg amputated.

It is clear from the injuries inflicted that the shots were not aimed but fired in panic, indicating the troops had lost all discipline. The now-incensed crowd followed them to the outskirts of Port Glasgow but then headed back to the prison in Greenock to free the radical prisoners.

After the departure of the troops, the crowd, some now armed with guns and swords, made its way to the prison as Dennistoun gathered a small group of police to defend the jail. At 7pm the angry crowd launched a barrage of stones at the defenders who quickly retreated and the victors broke into the jail and released the radicals, but left the other prisoners in their cells. Of the escapees, only one was later found and sent to Ayr prison, but there is no record of him having been brought to trial there and his name does not appear among those brought before the court on 9 August. By 10pm, the town was quiet.

Later that night, Dennistoun summoned a meeting with the town's officials in Greenock Council Chambers and they issued a proclamation condemning the 'outrageous assault made this evening on the Prison of Greenock, and the rescue therefrom of five prisoners confined on a charge of High Treason.' A reward of fifty guineas was offered for information leading to the recapture of the released men, with a warning that military aid had been summoned to the town and that anyone who attacked or molested the troops 'have themselves alone to blame for the consequences.' They got no response to the reward.

At 1am on Sunday, troops from the 10th and 7th Hussars, followed by a body of the Renfrewshire Militia, entered Greenock to find the streets empty and the town peaceful. During the day the homes of suspected radicals were raided, but nothing to incriminate the occupants was discovered. Later in the day Lord Blantyre and Sir Michael Shaw Stewart, with companies of the Rifle Brigade and Sir Thomas Bradford's 3th Regiment of Foot, arrived and congratulated the Port Glasgow Armed Association for the 'very excellent conduct of all the individuals of the corps.' Comments that were endorsed by Oliver Jamieson of Paisley.

Although there was little evidence to identify those who had actually broken into the jail and released the radicals, eight men who were known to hold radical views were arrested. Fearing that Greenock Jail was not secure, the Lord Advocate wrote to the Lord Justice Clerk on 14 April, seeking warrants to have the arrested men taken to the more secure location of Dumbarton Castle. Archibald Campbell Lord Succoth, granted the warrant the next day, and John Cameron, a currier, Edward McGown, labourer, Alexander Foster, shoemaker, Dugald McAuley, smith, Darby Canning, labourer, John Sinnet, hatter, Robert Bole, joiner, and John Calder, smith, were taken under a heavy escort of dragoons and placed in the custody of Major General Ilay Ferrier at Dumbarton Castle.

One of the eight taken, the leather-merchant John Cameron, was highly respected in the town and known for his opposition to violence but was thought by the authorities to be one of the radical leaders. Like the others, he was held in isolation in the castle dungeons, and had no communication with the outside world. The editor of the *Greenock Advertiser* published a short article in defence of Cameron, stressing his good reputation.

> His politics, whatever they might be, were kept to himself; nor did he, like many, seek to vent his spleen on every person with whom he came in contact, who chose to be of a different way of thinking from himself. We hope and trust, therefore, that he will ultimately be found innocent of any serious breach of the laws.

Mrs Cameron cut the article from the paper and had it smuggled into the castle in a sandwich she was delivering for him, to let him know that there were people were working on his behalf in the town to have him freed. He was released without charge at the end of the month.

Less fortunate were the other seven arrested men, who were held on charges of treason until the end of July, when, after the collapse of the case against the Duntocher prisoners, they were released without explanation.

On 12 July Sir Thomas Bradford, with the Lord Advocate, Sir William Rae, and the Deputy Lord Advocate, John Hope, joined Lord Blantyre, the Lord Lieutenant of Renfrewshire, to investigate the events at the prison, claiming some of the otherwise 'respectable population' had been seduced by a few radicals from Paisley. Their report blamed the actions of the towns-people for provoking the militia, and not only exonerated, but praised, Carswell and his men for their actions.

On 30 July, in the early hours of the morning, several other Greenock residents were shot at by a group of drunken troops from the 13th (1st Somersetshire) Regiment. The troops had become engaged in a brawl with some sailors outside the inn at Shennans Close where they were residing, and had dragged one man into the public house and given him a beating. The landlord and his wife called for help and when a crowd gathered, the troops retreated upstairs and fired on a group of people in the street killing a young sailor, Archibald Morrison. Police arrived and demanded entry to the premises but the troops shot and killed two of them, Robert Simpson and Henry Pearson. Only the arrival of armed troops from the guard ended the confrontation and the seven drunken soldiers were handed over to the civil authorities.

Privates John Dempsey, Robert Surrage, John Beck, Joseph Elliot, Malachi Clinton and Patrick Lynch, were tried for the murder of the two police officers on 7 November in Edinburgh. It appears that the killing of young Morrison was not deemed murder. They claimed that they did not know that Pearson and Simpson were police, and fired on the crowd out of fear for their lives. The jury acquitted four of the accused but found two guilty of murder. Both were sentenced to death and Dempsey's body sent to Dr Alexander Munro for dissection at the university medical school. Robert Surrage's sentence was commuted to transportation for life, and he sailed for New South Wales aboard the *Countess of Harcourt* on 8 April 1821.

Four days after the shootings, the commander of the Somersetshire Regiment, Lt-Colonel Williams sent a letter to Mr Dennistoun, the Chief Magistrate, apologising for the conduct of the troops, particularly that of 'two soldiers' who had 'fired on the people', apparently aware who had fired the deadly shots He transferred £100 to the town as a 'donation to the relatives of the deceased.' Within weeks the regiment, which had become the most hated English unit in the country, was transferred to Edinburgh and later sent to Ireland.

The news of these events made headlines throughout the United Kingdom, and it was revealed that militant radical activity was not confined to Scotland as there had been abortive risings in West Yorkshire, as was reported in *Blackwood's Magazine*.

> In at least three places, the King's standard is assaulted by rebels, prepared for a singular campaign. We write on 19 April 1820, and allude to Bonnymuir, Greenock and Huddersfield.

Continuing Repression

On Sunday 9 April troops of the 7th and 10th Hussars and the Rifle Brigade were ordered by Sir William Rae, the Lord Advocate, and the Sheriff and magistrates of Glasgow to raid the homes of suspected radicals. Over 100 people were arrested, including some prominent citizens, and taken to Glasgow Jail, the Bridewell, and others were held in cells in the police office.

James Turner of Thrushgrove was in bed when the Procurator Fiscal, Mr Salmond, and Sheriff Officer, Alexander Calder, entered his home under warrant to search for incriminating evidence. They found only a letter from members of the public asking permission to hold a meeting on his land to discuss their grievances, and a copy of a letter Turner had sent to Lord Sidmouth. Turner was arrested and taken, under armed guard, to Bridewell, where he was locked in a cell until Friday evening, when he was questioned by John Hope, the Advocate Depute, who told him he faced charges of treason. It was not until late on Wednesday the 19th that he was freed on £150 bail, which was not returned when all the charges were later dropped.

By Monday 10 April, a week after the strike, and five days after the Bonnymuir confrontation, there appears to have been a feeling that the worst was over and order restored. Certainly Lord Sidmouth seem to have thought so, as Hobhouse sent a congratulatory letter to Monteith telling him that 'His Lordship highly approves of the rigourous measures resorted to for suppressing the daring Spirit of Insurrection.' Another letter, undated and filed with earlier correspondence, suggested that the Lord Provost could show his gratitude to the Sharpshooters for their service by making 'every one a Freeman of the City' and is signed, 'A Sharpshooter.' From the tone of the letter it is clear the author believed that what he termed the 'rebellion' was over.

On Monday, two justices of the peace, James Hardie and Thomas Hopkirk, with military assistance, raided the printer William Lang's house in Bell Street and carried away a collection of books and papers. It was later discovered that Sheriff Officer Alexander Calder had offered one of Lang's apprentices £300 to testify that his master had printed the proclamation of the Provisional Government, despite the printer actually having been identified on 3 April. Glasgow police chief, James Mitchell, and the Procurator Fiscal Salmond had hired William Reid of the *Glasgow Chronicle*, the printer Robert Chapman, and an engraver, James Haldane, to check the print on the Proclamation against the type of all the printers in the city, and they had concluded it had been printed by Duncan MacKenzie of 20 Saltmarket. Clearly the local authorities were determined to secure Lang's conviction, even where there was no evidence against him.

Two men were arrested in Ayr for taking part in radical arms raids and stealing guns. Tried at the Ayr Circuit, Joseph MacGheer was acquitted, but John Forran was found guilty and sentenced to fourteen years' transportation, with the judge, Lord Meadowbank warning those involved in 'instances of insurrection', that 'vengeance would be terrible. Let those misguided men not delude themselves. They have no chance of success.'

Many radicals, and even moderate reformers, made their way to ports and fled the country to avoid arrest, and the *Glasgow Herald* noted that 'a number of persons have disappeared not previously suspected of taking part in the revolution.' Many were warned of their impending arrest by some in authority who were sympathetic to reform or who wanted to save those they knew from being arrested. At the unveiling of a memorial erected at Thrushgrove in 1832 to the memory of the three executed radicals, Robert Baird, brother of the leader of the Bonnymuir men, proposed a toast to Rear Admiral Charles Fleming of Cumbernauld House, who had warned several of the radicals of plans for their arrest, and so given them time to escape.

The meeting that Henry Monteith had promised was held in Glasgow Town Hall on Tuesday 11 April,

> … for the purpose of considering what steps it may be proper to take regarding the future employment of those who have obeyed the command of a Treasonable Confederacy to desist from their ordinary labour.

Kirkman Finlay MP reminded the gathering of prominent citizens that a large armed force had been gathering to attack the city, and that only their divisions had prevented 'bloodshed and crimes.' He suggested that striking workers had given support to this 'Desperate and Unprecedented Resistance to all Lawful Authority' and proposed,

> We, therefore, hereby declare our fixed purpose and determination to be, not to employ in future any persons who may have already joined, or who shall hereafter join, the promoters of this treasonable confederacy, who may have taken up arms, or lent aid and encouragement to it by his presence or his countenance.

James Oswald an officer with the Glasgow Yeomanry, agreed that employers should take a firm stance as he believed the 'lower classes were contaminated and ready to enter any plan of rebellion.' When James Ewing suggested leniency towards workers who had been intimidated into striking, another employer and member of the Yeomanry, Charles Stirling, insisted that people could not be seduced into committing treason, and all who had taken part in the strike should be treated the same. The resolution was passed unanimously and it was agreed that it be published in the newspapers.

At another meeting, later that day, forty-five employers accepted the resolution, but added a stipulation that they would not employ a member of any secret society that did not accept employers as members. Three days later, General Spens sacked all his employees that he suspected of having radical sympathies. Robert Rennie, the minister at Kilsyth, in a second letter to Murray of Polmaise on 26 April, wanted employers to go further and only offer employment to those who informed on the 'deluded fools.'

> I think the Resolutions of the Mercantile interest in Glasgow are defective, however Prudent and Proper in every other Point. Might they not have held out the offer of Employment to all such, who not only delivered up their arms, but make a full disclosure of the Names of those desperate villains, who deluded them? And might it not be prudent, that you, as Vice Lieutenant, or the Sheriff, or even his Majesty, should hold out the olive branch to such (excepting always the Printers etc of the Treasonable address and the Instigators and Ringleaders of the Radicals) as gave a full and detailed account of the whole Plot (which they all know) and the Names, Residence etc of the Ringleaders so as to bring them to condign Punishment?

There is no trace of Major Murray ever having replied, nor indeed, of his having taken the advice so charitably offered by the minister about the welfare of his flock.

On Tuesday night Alexander Boswell of Auchinleck wrote to Lord Sidmouth to let him know of the actions of his troops in rounding up radicals in Galston.

> We secured all the avenues leading to the dwelling of those against whom there were warrants, but we took only one man, the Radicals having somehow got notice. I go tonight (or rather tomorrow, at three) to seize the Preses, the secretary and two delegates of a Union Society and I hope we may succeed as I have taken precautions to prevent alarm.

On 18 April, the Home Secretary replied, congratulating the Ayrshire Yeomanry for 'their part in crushing the insipient Rebellion' and urging continual vigilance to preserve order.

Similar military raids were being conducted throughout central Scotland and caused panic among the population. Men, women and children fled their homes in Cambuslang at night to seek refuge in the glens and fields, and those on the Duke of Hamilton's estate, many of them Irish immigrants with experience of such raids in 1798, literally took to the hills to avoid the troops. At the same time, there were Yeomanry units on stand-by who had not been called into action and were feeling frustrated, as Mr Gilfillan of St Andrews Drive, Glasgow explained. Writing to Monteith on 14 April, he said that the Voluntary Corps of which he was a member was 'growing restive' at not being deployed, and that some 'gentlemen of property and known religious principles' had left to join the Sharpshooters, although sixty were 'left still.'

By Wednesday 18 April, General Bradford felt the situation was sufficiently under control that he could return to Edinburgh with his staff, leaving Major-General Reynell as commander of the 'South Western military district of Scotland.' On his return he issued a General Order congratulating troops of the line, Yeomanry and Volunteer corps,

> ... who were employed on the late occasion, particularly those who repelled an attack of rebels, on the 5th inst.

between Kilsyth and Falkirk, and made a great proportion of the assailants captive, that His Majesty has been graciously pleased to express his entire approbation of their conduct.

Kirkman Finlay reported to Sidmouth that order had been restored and the city was returning to normal, a belief echoed by the *Glasgow Herald* which reported on 10 April, that 'We continue to enjoy perfect tranquillity here.'

'Perfect Tranquility'?

During a raid in Glasgow on 17th, two police officers were beaten up at Barrowfield by two men, who were later arrested. Two days later troops escorting an ammunition convey from the city to Airdrie were attacked several times as far as Baillieston. There were further police raids in Kilmarnock and Galston.

The town of Paisley had been relatively quiet during the first days of April, due to the presence of large numbers of troops and Yeomanry patrolling the streets, although many of the town's textile workers did strike. The homes of suspected radicals were raided, but raids there seem to have been carried out in a calm and mannerly way and no attempt seems to have been made to prevent the suspects being given advance warning, This appears to have been the case when the home of David Gilmour's family was visited by the Sheriff Depute, Alexander Campbell of Barnhill.

Two soldiers rode through the entry, and, drawing swords, stood guard there; two stood in front of the house in a similar position, to prevent egress; and Mr Campbell came inside and told his business, but said he regretted the necessity of his visit.

Finding nothing after a brief, almost cursory, search, Mr Campbell thanked Mrs Gilmour and left: David's older brother had thrown a number of documents down the well as they had been warned of the raid. Most of the leading members of the Paisley radicals, like Arthur Sneddon and John Dickie, realising that the authorities sought them, had escaped from the town before the raids began.

James Spiers, the Johnstone radical, evaded capture and travelled south to Ecclefechan in Dumfries, where he started working as a weaver. Anxious to let his wife know that he was safe, he wrote to John Fraser, the schoolmaster at Johnstone, at the end of April, asking him to inform her that all was well with him. Miss Hodgart ran the Post office in the Black Bull Inn, and she allowed her lawyer nephew, William, to steam open the letter and give it to the authorities, who promptly prepared to arrest both Spiers and Fraser.

The Sheriff and a troop of cavalry were sent to Ecclefechan to take Spiers into custody while Mr Brown, the Paisley Fiscal, and Mr Hodgart senior, accompanied by a court officer with drawn sword arrested John Fraser in his home on a charge of High Treason. A troop of Scots Greys escorted him to the jail in Paisley, where he was later joined by Spiers and held until their trial in August.

Sylvia Clark, in her history of Paisley, noted that three years after Spiers was tried, the treasurer of a church building fund absconded with money from his business partner. The latter opened a letter addressed to the thief, and was imprisoned for six months for doing so. She pointed out that no such action was taken against William Hodgart for his similar breach of the law by interfering with the mail.

Held in Paisley Tolbooth in a room near Laing, Fraser and John Neill, who had attended the great radical meeting held in Nottingham in December 1819, Spiers passed messages of support to them with the assistance of a sympathetic under-jailer.

On 17 April, after Chapman, Haldane and Reid had reported that the evidence proved the proclamation had been printed by Duncan MacKenzie, the police abandoned their attempt to blame William Lang, and arrested MacKenzie. The same day Monteith noted that a Robert Falconer of 32 Drygate had 'provided information relating to the Seditious Placard of 1 April.' It would seem that this intelligence, combined with the report by the experts, was enough to have the charges against Lang dropped. A reward of £300 was offered for information leading to the arrest of his two apprentices, 18 year-old Robert Fulton, and 20 year-old John Hutchison. This failed as both men had evaded capture and were safely on their way to the United States. Fulton later wrote to William Lang giving full details about the printing of the notorious document and implicating Turner and Lees, information that, had it been revealed in court, would have embarrassed the government. For the escapees and the government, it was probably in both their interests that the apprentices had made good their escape.

By the last weeks of April, the country seemed quiet At the State Opening of Parliament on 17 April, George IV indirectly referred to the rising and expressed his satisfaction that it had been suppressed and that the laws had 'greatly contributed to restore confidence throughout the Kingdom', adding that he looked forward to the removal of the distress 'that unhappily prevails among many of the labouring classes.' About the same time, the Lord Advocate received a letter from Lord Sidmouth thanking him for restoring peace in Scotland, as he and the other MPs for Scotland prepared to make their way to Westminster for the opening of Parliament on the 21st.

The collapse of the insurrection, while welcomed by middle and upper class citizens, also led to them contemplating what might have happened and why the rising failed. The *Ayr Chronicle*, welcomed the insurrection as it had given the authorities the opportunity to crush radical hopes of reform through the use of force.

> We are glad that the Radicals have made the long threat-
> ened attempt at a general rising, because it has taught them
> several lessons which they could not otherwise learn.

On Friday 21 April, Samuel Hunter's *Glasgow Herald,* expressed the view that although the insurrection had been suppressed, its failure was at least partly due to weaknesses within the radical movement,

> We are now enjoying the most perfect quiet in this part of
> the country and a great number of those arrested on suspi-
> cion of being implicated in the late transactions have been
> liberated, either simply, or on a bail so trifling as to imply no

heavy supposition of guilt. ... we have all along acknowledged that our safety was owing – the want of leaders, among the ranks of the disaffected.

Contrary to the apparent leniency seen by Samuel Hunter, when he claimed that the bail payments, including that of £150 on James Turner, were 'trifling', it amounted to more than twice the annual wage of a weaver, and, as bail sums were non-refundable, imposed a severe financial penalty on the released men, forming a type of punishment in itself.

Despite the 'most perfect quiet' and 'restored confidence', the authorities were still anxious to apprehend radical activists, particularly those associated with the Provisional Government. On 24 April the *Greenock Advertiser* reported that two days earlier police had apprehended William Watson, the Strathaven weaver who had carried the banner 'Scotland Free – Or A Desart' on the march to 'make a second Bannockburn of the field of Bonnymuir': failing to realise that he had not been at Bonnymuir but carried the banner as he marched at the head of the Strathaven radicals when they set out for Glasgow. He and a female companion, 'presumably his wife' according to the press, had taken refuge in Dalrymple Street, Greenock, waiting for a ship in order to escape to the United States. On their way to the jail, he persuaded one of the two officers into go to a nearby spirit shop to get them a drink, and then made off as the woman grappled with the other officer. More police arrived and Watson was quickly recaptured, but again made his escape when a group of workers came to his assistance and attacked the police. He got safely away.

There were sporadic attacks on employers in several industrial areas, particularly on the owners of cotton spinning mills who had implemented Finlay's resolution and sacked workers that they thought had radical sympathies. In Glasgow in the early hours of 30 April, police came upon a group of armed men about to attack the home of one such mill owner and in the ensuing melee, shots were fired before the attackers made their escape. The same day, the 10th Hussars were ordered to leave Glasgow for London, and were replaced by troops of the 7th Dragoon Guards from Preston who were to maintain a military presence in the city in preparation for the trials of the radicals, during which the government anticipated further trouble.

Periodic raids by the military continued into May. At a house in Stewarton a party of troops led by Sheriff Deputy A Bell, arrested three suspected radicals on 3 May and took them to Ayr, but they were released soon after for lack of evidence. Two days later eleven men were taken into custody by 7th Hussars and sent to Paisley. On Friday 12 May, the Condorrat radical John Allan was arrested and sent to Stirling Castle. Even as late as 30 May raids were being carried out to find arms, and at least one was successful, as in the cellar of a house in Bridgeton troops discovered a number of pikes, wrapped in copies of the *Black Dwarf*; 'a most appropriate wrapper' according to one of the justices involved.

Writing to Lord Sidmouth on 19 May, D Dick of Glensheil informed him that shots had been fired at his house that morning, his boat smashed, and three of his horses killed. He added that 'I am afraid it is not confined to the lower classes but to some of the better sort of the old tenants.' By the end of the first week of June the Loudoun Factor to the Marquis of Hastings, John Hamilton noted that there had been an increase in employment and a slight increase in wages, and that together with an improved supply of food, this seemed to have reduced grievances with a consequent decline in radical activity. The following week, Sidmouth wrote to Boswell, 'The rising is certainly smothered; and, I trust, it may 'ere long be extinguished, but we must all be vigilant.'

As late as July there were violent incidents that emphasised the need for such vigilance and increased official concern. On 30 July, as the trials of the radicals were in progress. James Murray attempted to assassinate the Duke of Atholl at Dunkeld House on 30 July, but was overpowered by the Duke and his servants, and later sentenced to transportation. The attempt was made on the same day that drunken troops fired on the public in Greenock, killing a sailor and two police officers.

7. OYER AND TERMINER

On 1 May it was announced that the radical prisoners were to be tried on charges of High Treason, but not by the law of the land where the offences took place. Government was concerned about ensuring guilty verdicts against the accused and decided, notwithstanding the Treaty of Union, that the trials were to be held under English Law, and set up a Special Commission of Oyer and Terminer which it was felt was more likely to find against the radicals. Under the seal of the Privy Council and signed by Lord Bathurst the legal papers, one in Latin the other in English, were sent to the Lord Justice General, James Graham Duke of Montrose, naming all the Scottish judges and authorising trials under the terms of the Commission of all those arrested for radical activities in early 1820.

All the judges from the Scottish Court of Justiciary were eligible to serve on the Commission, and it was ordained that each panel of judges for the trials was to consist of the Lord President of the Court of Session, the Lord Justice Clerk and two other judges. The Lord Chief Baron of the Exchequer, Sir Samuel Shepherd, a former Solicitor General for England and Wales and MP for Dorchester from 1814 to 1819, was appointed as advisor on English Law to the judges hearing the cases. A leading English barrister, Mr John Hullock, Serjeant at Law, was appointed to lead the prosecution team. Even the Clerk of Arraigns to the Commission was not qualified in Scots Law, but an English official, Thomas Knapp of Haberdashers Hall, London.

Also provided was a very detailed list of the charges faced by each of the radicals at each of the individual trials, the only difference between the documents being the name of the accused. These bulky documents are held by the National Records of Scotland in Edinburgh, along with the Writ of Certiorari, signed 'D Boyle' and 'S Shepherd' confirming their 'Authority to conduct trials for Treason and Misprision of Treason as was used in England.' This writ was noted and signed by 'T G Knapp, Clerk to the Special Commission' and dated 7 November 1820, confirming that the trials had been satisfactorily completed.

There was some public and legal concern in Scotland that persons were to be tried for actions undertaken there, before a panel of Scotland's most senior judges, but under English Law. At the time Scots were regarded as aliens in English Law: although the government agreed to repel the legislation in 1707, the Aliens Act was not formally repealed until 1869, making it difficult to understand how the accused could be tried by a foreign system. Lord President, Charles Hope, stated this was justified as the offences threatened all of the United Kingdom, adding that Scots Law was not as well-equipped as English Law to deal with treason, since in England the offence had been clearly defined from the time of Edward III (1327-77). However, at the Stirling Grand Jury hearing on 23 June, he let slip that the Scots Statute of 1695 was 'little different' from the then current English Law of treason.

Grand Juries

Under English Law it was required that a Grand Jury in each place where a trial was to take place should examine the evidence to determine if true bills for high treason had been found against the accused men, and to ask each accused how he was to plead. The Grand Jury was not a part of Scottish legal proceedings and the jurors and judges were led through the procedure by Lord Chief Baron, Sir Samuel Shepherd. Grand Juries, of 23 members, were summoned at Stirling on 23 June, Glasgow on 27th, Dumbarton on 29th, Paisley on 1 July, and at Ayr on 4 July, to decide if there was a case against the accused men in each location. (Appendix II) The Commission was read to them and each jury was given the same formal statement by Lord Hope, who explained the development of the English Law of Treason and how it applied in the cases that they were to examine.

The lead prosecutor was to be an English barrister, Mr Serjeant John Hullock, who had led the prosecution against Henry Hunt at Manchester in March 1820, and was later knighted and became a judge in 1823. At each Grand Jury trial, Thomas Knapp of Haberdasher's Hall, London, was appointed Clerk of Arraigns to the Commission.

The accused each faced four counts of High Treason, with three of these counts each containing 19 overt acts, defined in great detail, any one of which, if proved, it was stated was sufficient to prove treason. Two of the counts (1 and 2) were under the 1351 Treason Act (25 Ed III), which had only ever applied to England, and two (3 and 4) under the Treasonable and Seditious Practices Act of 1795 (36 Geo III): this last had originally been a temporary measure during the French wars and had applied to the whole of the United Kingdom, but was made permanent in 1817.

Count 1:	Compassing and Imagining the Death of the King.
Overt Act	1. Conspiring to devise Plans to subvert the Constitution.
	2. Conspiring to levy War and to subvert the Constitution.
	3. For the publishing and posting up a Treasonable Address to the Inhabitants of Great Britain and Ireland, to incite Soldiers of the King and other Subjects to Rebellion.
	4. For the publishing and posting up of Printed Addresses to the Inhabitants of Great Britain and Ireland, stating the substance only of such Addresses, with similar intent as in the third Overt Act.
	5. For composing, and printing, and posting up divers Addresses, containing solicitations to the Troops and Subjects of levy War.
	6. For assembling together, and, whilst so assembled, making speeches to incite the Subjects to Rebellion.
	7. For purchasing and providing Arms, in order to attack the Soldiers of the King, and to make War against the King.
	8. For assembling and parading with Arms, and attacking the Houses of divers Subjects, and taking

therefrom Arms and Ammunition, with similar intent as in the last Overt Act.

9. For manufacturing Arms, with similar intent.

10. For training and drilling themselves and others, with similar intent.

11. For levying War.

12. For endeavouring to seduce the Troops of the King from their allegiance.

13. For detaining and imprisoning divers Subjects, with intent, by duress, to compel them to join in levying War.

14. For forcing divers Subjects to discharge and turn off their Workmen.

15. For striking Work, and compelling and persuading others to do the same.

16. For sending Persons to England, to incite the liege Subjects of the King there to acts of Treason.

17. For subscribing Money for the purpose of procuring Arms.

18. For exhorting and persuading certain of the liege Subjects of the King to procure Arms, to be employed in Rebellion.

19. For giving notice of Meetings to be held for the purpose of consulting as to the means of raising War.

Count 2:	Levying War
Count 3;	Compassing and Intending to Depose the King from the style, honour, and kingly name of the Imperial Crown of the Realm. With the same Overt Acts.
Count 4:	Compassing to levy War against the King, in order to compel him to change his measures. With same Overt Acts.

The Accused:
At Stirling the accused were grouped into four separate cases:
The Bonnymuir Case; Thomas MacCulloch, Andrew Hardie, Benjamin Moir, Allan Murchie, Alexander Latimer, Alexander Johnston, Andrew White, David Thomson, James Wright, William Clackson (or Clarkson), Thomas Pike (or Pink), Robert Gray, James Clelland and Alexander Hart, all from Glasgow, together with John Baird, John Barr, William Smith and Thomas MacFarlane, from Condorrat, and who had been taken after the battle there.
St Ninian's Case: James Anderson, James Rait and George Lennox.
Balfron Case: William Crawford, George Gillies, Moses Gilfillan, Andrew Reid, Andrew MacFarlane, James Gunn, Robert Drew, and Joseph Gettie.
Camelon Case: John MacMillan, James Burt, Andrew Burt Junior, Daniel Turner, James Aitken (grocer) of Falkirk, James Aitken (wright) of Falkirk and Andrew Dawson: at the request of the Grand Jury, John Johnson was added to this list.
At Glasgow there were again four groups arraigned before the Grand Jury

1. Strathaven Case: James Wilson, William McIntyre; together with William Robinson and William Watson, who were not in custody
2. Strathaven Case: John Walters: together with John Stevenson, William Howat, Peter Macallum, Robert Hamilton and John Morrison (not in custody).
3   Anderston Case: William Campbell, and George Allan: with Alexander Cameron, Walter Provan, Peter Ferguson & Matthew Logan (not in custody).
4. Parkhead Case: John May, Alexander Graham, and Matthew Bogle: with Andrew Kirkland, William McCracken, John McAllister & David Sharp (not in custody)

The Dumbarton Grand Jury on 29 June heard the evidence against Patrick MacDevitt, William Blair, Robert Munroe, George Munroe, Richard Thompson and William MacPhie from Duntocher, together with those not in custody, Robert MacKinlay, William Rowney, Robert Sinclair, John Stewart, Daniel MacNab, Archibald MacLean and Alexander Lindsay.

On 1 July, the prisoners arraigned at Paisley were James Spiers, John Lang, John Fraser, John Neil, and Alexander Thomson. Also named were James Walker, Robert Parker, John Young, Robert Smellie and James Nixon, who were not in custody: it is highly probable that last five named were the prisoners taken to Greenock Jail and released by the crowd that attacked the prison on 8 April.

At Ayr on 4 July, four Mauchline men, Thomas MacKay, Andrew Wyllie, Hugh Wallace and John Dickie were arraigned, and the names of others who were not in custody recorded: William Orr, John Dunlop, James Wyllie, Robert Kerr, James Rayburn, from Stewarton; John Goldie, Joseph Abbott, Alexander Roxburgh, James Roxburgh, Andrew Adamson, and Alexander Wilson, from Galston; James Nisbett of Loudonkirk.

Writs of capias, ordering the arrest and detention of those who were not in custody, were issued, in the hope that they would be detained if discovered in another part of Scotland. Most, however, had already made their way furth of Scotland to evade capture, and if they returned later kept a very low profile.

The Hearings

At the Grand Jury hearing in the Tolbooth at Stirling on 23 June, Thomas MacCulloch was the first to be asked how he pled. His lawyer, Archibald Hope Cullen, intervened to say his client could not plead until an issue vital to the case had been clarified. He then read the indictment which stated that the offence (ie the Bonnymuir engagement) was committed 'at the parish of Falkirk, in the county of Stirling.' He pointed out that the law in both countries stipulated that the location of the place where the offence was committed had to be precise and required the identification of the townland (vill) nearest the site of the offence. As this did not appear in the indictment, he argued, citing several examples from 'learned opinion' in England, the indictment should be quashed.

Mr Serjeant Hullock rejected this, stating that such a requirement had been abandoned in all cases in England and thus did not support the argument for quashing the indictment. He further argued that the concept of a 'vill' did not exist in England, and that in Scotland the existence of hamlets of 'a mere five or six households' was insufficient to qualify as a 'vill.' At the same time he was dismissive of some of the opinions Mr Cullen had cited, claiming they 'are not to be considered as authorities.'

After much discussion of the opinion of various learned authorities on the matter, the Lord President and the presiding judges agreed with Hullock and declared that the indictments were valid. Mr Cullen accepted the ruling and withdrew his objection, and Thomas MacCulloch, and the other Bonnymuir prisoners then entered pleas of 'Not Guilty.'

That MacCulloch was the first of the Bonnymuir contingent to be arraigned is perhaps significant. He was not one of the leaders, nor is there any evidence that he had an official role in the Glasgow Radical Union, or that he had been particularly prominent in the action at Bonnymuir. But what may have been significant was that he was Irish. Having been born in County Down in 1787, and although too young to have been involved in the United Irish Rising in that county in 1798, the government may have used his nationality to make a connection with the Irish insurrection in the hope of influencing jurors against all of the accused. Charles Stirling, and the editor of the *Glasgow Herald*, Samuel Hunter, who had served in the campaign in Ireland in 1798, spoke for many when he claimed 'once a rebel, always a rebel.'

The members of the Grand Jury, comprising mostly landowners, were then presented with the Crown case. After having had the list of charges read out, the Declaration was read to them and several witnesses testified as to the events involving the accused. After a short retiral to consider their verdict, the jurors found true bills against each of the accused. The date for the trial was set for 13 July.

At each of the subsequent hearings, the same procedure was followed and the Grand Juries confirmed the charges of treason against each of the accused. The opening dates for the sessions at which the different groups of prisoners were to face arraignment for trial were confirmed as, 29 June in Dumbarton, 4 July in Ayr, 6 July in Stirling, 8 July in Glasgow, and 1 August in Paisley.

The Stirlingshire Trial

The eighteen radicals taken at Bonnymuir, Thomas McCulloch, Andrew Hardie, Benjamin Moir, Allan Murchie, Alexander Latimer, Alexander Johnston, Andrew White, David Thomson, James Wright, William Clarkson, Thomas Pink, Robert Gray, James Clelland, Alexander Hart, all from Glasgow, together with John Baird, John Barr, William Smith, and Thomas McFarlane, from Condorrat, were arraigned at Stirling on 13 July.

The panel of judges were Lord President of the Court of Session Charles Hope, Lord Justice Clerk David Boyle, with Lord Chief Commissioner of the Jury Court William Adam, and two Commissioners, Lord Adam Gillies, and George Ferguson, Lord Hermand; also present was Lord Chief Baron of the Exchequer, Sir Samuel Shepherd as advisor to the Scottish judges on English Law.

In accordance with English legal procedure, a twelve-man jury was sworn in: Andrew Hutton (writer) as foreman, James Bryce (bookseller), John Wright (writer), Alexander Wilson (carpet manufacturer), William McFarlane (baker), William Glass (timber merchant), Allan Johnston (architect), Alexander Bowie (mason), James Reid (timber merchant), John Stewart of Corntoun (portioner: i.e. a small landholder), John Burd Esq of Seafield, and John Wilson (carpet manufacturer).

Presenting the case for the Crown were Sir William Rae, the Lord Advocate, with Mr Serjeant John Hullock and the Solicitor General James Wedderburn, assisted by Mr Henry Drummond, Mr Alexander Maconochie and Mr John Hope. Francis Jeffrey and Mr A Hope Cullen represented the accused.

In the opening session on 13 July before the jury took its place, defence council Francis Jeffrey, questioned the right of John Hullock to plead in a Scottish court, pointing out that although he was a highly respected English barrister, he was not qualified to appear in a Scottish court. Hullock's response was so slighting about Jeffrey, the Scots and Scotland in general that Sir Ranald MacDonald, the Tory High Sheriff of Stirlingshire, is said to have passed a note to Jeffrey offering to be his second if he were to challenge Hullock (actually' the bastard') to a duel, 'outside this country' (ie not in Stirlingshire). When Jeffrey leaned over the table to shake Sir Ranald's hand, Lord President Hope, sensing the tension, even on the prosecution benches and anxious to allow the trial to continue, persuaded Hullock to amend his statement and to apologise to Jeffrey. The judge then ruled that in the case of high treason it was Great Britain was threatened, not just Scotland, and consequently a lawyer qualified in English Law could appear before the Scottish bar. They dismissed Jeffrey's further objection that warrants had not been issued in accordance with the conditions of Scots Law, and that Hardie's statement after his arrest was inadmissible under the same law.

When the trial began, it was announced that each of the accused was to be tried separately, and that there was to be no reports published until after all the trials throughout Scotland had finished;

> I have to announce to all persons concerned that no part of the proceedings of this trial, and more especially the speeches of counsel, that no part of the evidence be published till this and all the trials in this and other countries, included in this Commission, be brought to a conclusion, otherwise the severest punishments that this court can inflict will be pronounced against them.

Andrew Hardie was the first to be tried, with the other prisoners lined up behind him. The Solicitor General detailed the charges against the accused and then read out the Address, explaining to jurors its seditious content and showing that this demonstrated the intent of the radicals to rise in rebellion. He reminded them that under English law, being guilty of only one overt act was sufficient proof of High Treason.

Sergeant John Hullock led the examination of the witnesses and several from the Castlecary and Bonnybridge area were called and they all identified Hardie as the leader of the men who had seized their weapons as the radicals made their way to Bonnymuir, and others gave brief accounts of seeing, from a distance, the radicals fire of the troops when the cavalry arrived from Kilsyth.

Also called as a witness was James Hardie, a Justice of the Peace in Lanarkshire, who told how the accused had physically prevented him removing the 'seditious publication' from a watchman's box in Duke Street in the city. He testified that Andrew Hardie had been reading from the publication when he had tried to intervene, and that Hardie had pushed him off the pavement, warning him that he would 'part with the last drop of his blood' before he would allow the paper to be taken down. Two other witnesses from Glasgow, John Stirling and Hugh Macphunn, corroborated the justice's evidence.

James Murray, the armourer, and John Benson, the ordnance store-keeper at Stirling Castle, identified the weapons that had been taken from the radicals. And James Russell identified the weapon that had been taken from him by Hardie's men.

Trooper Nicol Baird gave a colourful account of his bravery in confronting the 'large party' of radicals near Bonnybridge, and presenting his pistol to deter them, before making for Kilsyth to raise the alarm – to the amazement of Hardie who later recorded that he and his men had never encountered the trooper. Lt Hodgson gave a precise account of the confrontation at Bonnymuir, mentioning being directed to the radicals' position by a 'gentleman.' He surprised the court , and particularly Hullock, by expressing his admiration for the bravery of the radicals and for the stout resistance they put up. Lt Davidson confirmed most of what Hodgson had said, although without any praise for the actions of the radicals. Each of the military witnesses identified the individuals that they had confronted on the muir.

When the prosecution rested its case, Jeffrey announced that the witnesses for the defence were to testify as to the history and character of the accused, but the prosecution case was such that their testimony was rendered irrel-evant, and it had been agreed not to call any witnesses. He then made his address to the jury, explaining that the men had been led into a trap by persons unknown, and that they were the victims, rather than perpetrators of the insurrection. He argued that although the evidence that had been presented might prove criminal intent, it was not sufficient to prove treason.

...the question is, whether you have evidence sufficient ... to compel you to say, that there is no doubt that the prisoner has committed the specific and aggravated offence of High Treason.

He concluded by reminding the jury that the nature of the charge was flexible and they should withhold a conviction if they entertained any doubts.

The Solicitor General, James Wedderburn, summing up for the prosecution stressed that the evidence of the witnesses proved the charges, and reminding jurors that the evidence of two 'credible witnesses' was all that was required for a guilty verdict. He then emphasised that being guilty of one overt act was all that was required to find the accused guilty of treason. Having read out the 1351 statute of Edward III, which he claimed 'is now embodied into the law of Scotland', he detailed how Hardie was guilty under each of the nineteen overt acts.

Summing up, the Lord President drew particular attention to the evidence of the magistrate James Hardie and that of Private Nicol Hugh Baird, which together with that of Lt Hodgson was, he instructed them, sufficient to show treasonable intent. Referring to the defence case, he stated that the declarations made by Hardie when he was questioned after his arrest, and which he disputed, were 'unfortunate for the prisoner', and then calling attention to the absence of any witnesses for the defence. He sent them to consider their verdict with the advice, 'it is the facts of which you are to judge.'

The jury retired at 12.55am to consider their verdict and after twenty minutes returned to the court with a finding of 'Guilty on the second and fourth Counts of the Indictment, and Not Guilty upon the first and third Counts', ie. Guilty of 'levying war', and of 'compassing to levy war against the King in order to compel him to change his measure.'

The court retired at 1am and was ordered to resume at 10am the same morning for the remaining trials.

When the court reconvened, John Baird was brought to the bar and the other untried prisoners lined behind him, and a new jury sworn in. The jurors again came principally from the merchant and business class (nine) with three being landowners: James Mitchell (tanner) foreman, Thomas Smart (tanner), James Hodge (baker), Peter Bell (merchant), William Stone (writer), Alexander Munro (writer), Alexander Dallas (gentleman), James Buchan of Corntoun (portioner), James Buchan of Berryhill (gentleman), James Ewing (seedsman) Robert Bulloch (grazier), and John Shaw (land surveyor).

After being given the same opening speech by the Solicitor-General, the jury heard the evidence of the previous witnesses, including the magistrate James Hardie, who repeated his testimony that Andrew Hardie had prevented the removal of proclamation, despite the defence protesting about its relevance to the charges against John Baird.

The only new evidence came from the Castlecary innkeeper, Archibald Buchanan, who identified Baird as the leader of the insurgent 'army', and stated that some of the men carried pikes, with a few having muskets and swords, and there was one pistol. He testified that the bill had come to eight shillings, but charged only seven shillings and six pence, as the leader only had a note and he did not have change and the bill for payment by the Provisional Government that he was offered was not due for payment for six months. Baird, he said, then asked for a receipt, which he dictated and Buchanan signed, and the witness identified the document when Hullock handed it to him in court. When asked about other members of the party, he was unable to identify Hardie as one of those at the inn.

Again calling no witness, Jeffrey for the defence attempted to show the influence of spies and agents provocateur as a factor in bringing about the march to Carron, as he 'addressed the jury at length with that eloquence of which he is master', according to the *Glasgow Herald*.

The Lord Justice Clerk, David Boyle, repeated the summing up he had delivered for Hardie before sending out the jury, instructing them not to consider charges under the first and third count but only those of levying war and of compassing to levy war (counts three and four). Again, the jury refused to accept the defence arguments and after retiring for an hour and three quarters returned at 2.05am with a verdict of guilty on the second count, 'compassing to levy war.'

Jeffrey realised there was little prospect of acquittal for the remaining prisoners, and advised them to offer guilty pleas and hope for clemency. After spending some time in discussions with the other accused radicals, they all eventually accepted his proposal and the next day he announced that the other prisoners had changed their plea and threw themselves on the mercy of the court.

The trial of the men from Camelon was arranged for Friday 4 August, and the court reassembled in the Tolbooth. However the prisoners and their counsel, together with the potential jurors, were kept waiting until after twelve noon. Lord President Hope explained that the judges had been delayed after the trial at Paisley, and required time to prepare for the new trial. He was assisted on the bench by Lord Pitmilly and Sir Samuel Shepherd. When Andrew Dawson and John McMillan were put to the bar, J P Grant announced that the prisoners had chosen to plead guilty and throw themselves on the mercy of the court.

A jury was sworn and, instructed by the court, pronounced the remaining prisoners, James Aitkin (wright), Andrew Burt junior, James Burt, James Aitken (grocer), John Johnstone, and Daniel Turner, not guilty, and they were released.

Later on 4 August the court assembled again at Stirling for the sentencing of the Bonnymuir men. Lord President Hope accepted the guilty pleas of the remaining prisoners, and agreed that clemency should be shown but that it was not in the power of the court to do more than advise mercy. He then expressed his regret that it was necessary to make an example of the leaders, and that they should expect the capital penalty. He then sentenced them all to death.

> That you, and each of you, be taken to the place from whence you came, and that you be drawn on a hurdle to the place of execution, and there be hung by the neck until you are dead, and afterwards, your head severed from your body, and your body divided into quarters, to be disposed of as His Majesty may direct – and may God, in His infinite goodness, have mercy on your souls

Baird and Hardie were executed, but the king showed mercy and the other Bonnymuir men had their death sentences commuted to transportation to the penal colony in New South Wales for periods of fourteen years to life. Lord Advocate Rae successfully appealed directly to Lord Sidmouth for mercy for Cleland, who only learned of his reprieve days before his execution date. It is, perhaps significant that Baird, Hardie and Cleland had previously been soldiers, and seen active service in the French and Napoleonic Wars, and were thus likely to be regarded as more of a threat than the others. Despite their service to the country, their deaths were to serve as a warning to others who might be inclined to take up arms to change the constitution.

The Lanarkshire Trial

With the conclusion of the trial of the radicals taken at Bonnymuir, the judges moved to Glasgow where the trial of the twelve Strathaven insurgents opened on 20 July. The court met at nine o' clock, under Charles Hope, the Lord President of the Court of Session, together with Lord Justice Clerk Boyle, Lord Chief Baron Sir Samuel Shepherd, Sir William Adam the Lord Chief Commissioner of the Jury Court, and Lord Pitmilly.

Prosecuting for the Crown were the Lord Advocate, the Solicitor General and Mr. Serjeant Hullock, with H.H. Drummond and Mr. Maconochie, the Lord Advocate's Deputes; Mr. Menzies, and Mr. James Arnot W.S., agent. The Clerk of Arraigns was again Thomas Knapp.

The accused were represented by Mr. John Archibald Murray, Mr Robert Graham, Mr A E Montieth, Mr. Pyper, Mr. Cullen, Mr. Miller, and Erskine Douglas Sandford, Advocates. Agents for the defence were Messrs. Fleming and Strang of Glasgow, with, as adviser on English Law, James Harmer the English Attorney who had defended the Cato Street conspirators in the trials that had taken place earlier at the Old Bailey in London.

James Wilson was the first of the Strathaven prisoners put to the bar, having been brought from Bridewell. The Clerk of Arraigns called over the list of the petit jury, consisting of 200 names, which took a considerable time. After many challenges on the part of the prisoner, and one on that of the Crown, the following were chosen to try the case,

David Laird of Balornock (foreman); Thomas Muir of Muir Park; John Lochhead of Govan; Robert Grandberry Baillie; Thomas Sommerville, younger of Carnwrath; Andrew Smith of Auldhouse; James Howison of Douglas; James Gilchrist of Gilfoot; George Rowan of Holmfauldhead; Thomas Douglas of Moss; John Woddrop of Dalmarnock; and James Ewing (merchant) Glasgow.

The *Glasgow Herald* reported that the Lord President had prohibited,

> in the most positive manner, the publication of the evidence, or the speeches of the Counsel; in the case of Wilson or any of the other trials which are to take place in Glasgow or elsewhere, until the whole proceedings against the persons accused of High Treason are finished; his Lordship observing, that the cases were all in some degree connected together as part of one grand conspiracy, and that it would be inconsistent with public justice, if the witnesses in one trial could read in the newspapers, previous to their own examination, the evidence of other witnesses.

He then warned that violation of his prohibition would 'bring down on the heads of violators the severest penalties of the law.'

The case for the prosecution opened on July 20, and John Hullock again led the prosecution team. When James Wilson was brought before the court, the indictment was read by the Clerk of Arraigns, charging the prisoner with sticking up in various places, and acting upon the recommendation of, the Glasgow Treasonable Address of the 1 April, which was read as part of the indictment. He was further charged with

> procuring arms and ammunition for the purpose of levying war against our Lord the King, and, along with others, marching in military array, with arms in their hands, for the purpose of making war on the soldiers of the King;

with appointing commanders to lead them against the troops of the country; with imprisoning various subjects of the King, for the purpose of forcing them to accompany them in levying war against the government of the country, and arraying themselves in military order in the parish of Avondale, on or about the 6th April, with Arms in their hands, for the avowed purpose of assisting to overthrow the constitution.

The full Indictment took two hours to be read.

Lord Hope then stated to the Jury the main charges of the several Counts of the indictment and the overt acts under each main count, and charging the prisoner with levying war against the King and constitution, and of imagining the death of the king.

Twenty-eight witnesses were examined on the part of the Crown. These testified that Wilson was the acknowledged leader of the radicals in Strathaven and had a long history of involvement in that cause, having been actively associated with the Friends of the People and the United Scotsmen. Several stated that they were aware that he had owned and read, often to others, suspect publications like *The Spirit of Union* and *The Black Dwarf,* as well as the *Manchester Observer* and *Cobbett's Register*. It is interesting to note that one of the chief witnesses against Wilson was Sheriff Substitute William Aiton of Hamilton, who had confessed to having attempted to bribe men into forging pikes so that they should be liable for arrest on charges of high treason. Although at the trial he merely testified that he had taken a declaration from Wilson at Hamilton shortly after his arrest, and advised him to be truthful.

Some of the witnesses claimed that Wilson had been the initial instigator of the Strathaven Rising, persuading the men to take up arms, and then leading them out of the village when they set out for Glasgow. It was further alleged that he was seen directing the insurgents to several houses where they could find weapons, and others told of how they had been intimidated into handing over firearms. James Fallow testified that the radicals had taken him prisoner and forced him to go with them. Seen as a joke by the radicals, the court viewed it more seriously and when this was mentioned, Lord President Hope interjected to state that the radicals had clearly 'abducted' the youth involved, adding kidnap to their other crimes. When it was revealed that Wilson had, in fact, marched in the rear of the insurgent force with a drawn sword, witnesses claimed that rather than showing reluctance on his part, he had done so to prevent an attack by loyal villagers.

In a bizarre move, the prosecution produced James Hardie, the justice who had been prevented by Andrew Hardie from removing the proclamation in Glasgow. Despite this being irrelevant to the case against James Wilson, he repeated the evidence he had given as a witness at Stirling, but had nothing to say about the accused or the events at Strathaven. In his concluding speech, A J Murray was scathing about the relevance of the magistrate's account of events in Glasgow, commenting 'I have might as well have said Edinburgh, because it has as little connexion with the one as the other.'

The court adjourned at twelve o' clock, and was ordered to return again at ten the next day.

Resuming the hearing on Friday 21 July, the court listened to the examination of exculpatory witnesses. J A Murray, leading for the defence, opened by raising a legal point. He indicated that the indictment served on Wilson had made no reference to the actual charges, or to the precise location where the alleged offences had taken place, as was a requirement of Scots Law. Mr Hullock rose to explain, with some annoyance, that it was not necessary to make such detailed charges. Murray ignored the interruption, but was advised by Lord Hope that under English Law such detail was not required and was forced to withdraw his objection.

Thirty-two witnesses were called by the defence, most making reference to James Wilson's radical background and to the events of April. Dealing with the issue of the publications that prosecution witnesses testified to seeing him read, Mr Murray pointed out that this was not evidence of treason as there was no proof that these books or papers were bad in themselves, or that they had contained anything improper or seditious.

Some of the defence witnesses said they believed that Wilson had been reluctant to take part in the rising, even arguing with those who wanted to fight but had been pressurised into going along with them. It was claimed that his marching in the rear of the column rather than at its head, where the leader would be expected to march, indicated his lack of enthusiasm, and Murray pointed out that his turning back at Kilbride was further evidence that his client was not the eager rebel the prosecution had portrayed.

After both sides had presented lengthy concluding statements, Lord President Hope instructed the jury on how the evidence related to the law, and they retired at seven o' clock. Having spent two hours considering the evidence, the twelve men returned to the court with their verdict, finding Wilson guilty on the 4th count - 'compassing to levy war against the King, in order to compel him to change his measures', and not guilty on all other counts. The foreman, speaking in the name of the entire jury, recommended Wilson to the mercy of the crown.

When the trial resumed on Monday 24 July, Sir William Rae, the Lord Advocate, announced that the crown was not pursuing the charges against the remaining prisoners as they had not been 'the leaders in the late disturbances.' The trial of the other prisoners at Glasgow, William McIntyre, Mathew Boyle, Alex. Graham, John Walters (husband of Wilson's daughter Lilly), John May, William Campbell, and George Allen, continued before new juries. They were all formally found not guilty, and immediately set at liberty.

Later on Monday 24 July, the court resumed for sentencing and, after Wilson had stated his belief that the trial was a 'mummery', and would not prevent the success of his cause, Lord Hope pronounced sentence:

> The sentence of the law is - To be drawn on a hurdle to the place of execution on the 30th August, and after being hung by the neck till you be dead, that your head be severed from your body, and your body cut in quarters at the disposal of the King; and the Lord have mercy upon your soul.

After the sentence was passed, the *Glasgow Herald* reported on 1 September that 'the prisoner was then taken from the court without showing any signs of agitation and taken to one of the iron rooms of Glasgow Jail.' There he was held until the day of execution.

The Lord President concluded the proceedings by expressing his hope that the people would come to their senses and return to their allegiance to the king, obey the law, and respect 'this glorious constitution.' He urged employers to 'be vigorous and strong' in dismissing 'disaffected' employees, and in assisting the authorities in putting down such dangerous disaffection.

8. THE LAST TRIALS

Dumbarton

On Wednesday 12 July, the prisoners arrested at Duntocher were brought from the castle to Dumbarton Church to be formally charged with treason. The Lord Advocate, Sir William Rae, and the Solicitor General, assisted by Mr Sergeant Hullock led for the prosecution, while John Peter Grant and Erskine Douglas Sandford represented the accused: Peter McDevitt (a smith), William Blair, Robert Munroe, George Munroe, Richard Thompson and William McPhie (all cotton spinners): not in custody were Robert McKinley (a tailor), William Roney (a labourer) and the cotton spinners, Robert Sinclair, John Stewart, Daniel Mc Nab, Archibald McLean and Alexander Lindsay. After hearing their pleas of not guilty, their trial was set for 26 July.

The court reassembled on 26 July, with Lord President Hope, Lord Justice Clerk Boyle and Lord Pitmilly, and Lord Chief Baron Shepherd present. The first to be put to the bar was Robert Munroe, but, before the jury could be selected, J P Grant raised a question relating to the qualification of one of the potential jurors. He pointed out that by giving up his property. he had forfeited his right, under Scots Law, to serve on a jury. Sir Samuel Shepherd and John Hullock engaged Grant in a discussion about this, but agreed to have the man questioned. James Ewing admitted he had sold an interest in his property, but claimed he still had a right to be called as a juror. After further discussion, Mr Grant challenged the witness and he was rejected as a potential juror.

The final group of twelve jurors to hear the evidence was made up of Archibald McLachlan (gentleman) the foreman of the jury; William McFarlane (gentleman); John McFarlane (grocer); Parlane McFarlane (farmer); Robert McHutcheon (miller); David Napier (smith); John Latta (portioner); Robert Denny (farmer); James Lang (portioner); Donald

McFarlane (grazier); James Smith (farmer), and Walter Colquhoun Esq.

As the Duntocher men had not taken part in the rising, the evidence against them was that they had been on strike and that they had been at a site where pikes were being made. Several witnesses testified to having seen some of the accused at the forge, but were uncertain about whether they had been involved in making pikes or just talking with others there. Hullock frequently badgered the witnesses insisting they accept his interpretation of the facts, and Grant several times complained to the judges about leading questions being asked, but was overruled each time. Lord Chief Baron Shepherd stepped outside his purely advisory role on a number of occasions by intervening to seek clarification of certain points and to seek amplification of witnesses' evidence. Throughout the evidence not one witness testified to having seen Munroe handling, making or talking about arms.

Much of the evidence centred on the strike, and Hugh Wilson, clerk to Duntocher Cotton Mill, testified that most the men had taken part in the strike, which he said had passed off without trouble. Cross-examined by E D Sandford about the cotton spinners in the dock Wilson stated, 'I would trust my life ... in the hands of those four.' The mill owner, William Dunn, testified that he had had a 'remarkable talk' about wages with Munroe shortly after the strike. He explained that the men had returned to work the day after the strike and had resumed normal working, although he admitted, under questioning that other employers had refused to allow the men back until the following week.

The court adjourned until 10 am the next day, when the Mr Sandford opened the defence case. He questioned a number of witnesses about the Address and the strike, asking what they had seen, and why they had taken part. Most testified that they had read the Address which was posted in several places in the town and in the mill, and that they had gone on strike in response to it. There was some confusion over who had brought the address into the mill, with one naming prosecution witnesses. Under cross-examination by Mr Hullock, a few agreed to his suggestion that they had struck out of fear of retribution if they had failed to come out along with the others, but most denied having been threatened.

Mr Grant then attempted to introduce further character witnesses, but was interrupted by the Lord President, who said this was not necessary as Crown witnesses had already given Munroe a 'good character.' Grant then moved to his closing address in which he explained the law of treason and how it did not apply to the accused, arguing that the Crown had not produced evidence that Munroe had done anything wrong. He highlighted that even the prosecution witnesses had shown that such charges were out of character for the man.

Serjeant Hullock replied by stressing that the Act of Edward III made it clear that a person's actions showed their intent and that by reading the Address the accused had been guilty of treason, and by striking had 'compassed the death of the king.' He then added that Munroe had 'taken up pikes', at which Grant protested that no such evidence had been provided. But Hullock ignored the interruption, arguing that being part of a group where pikes had been made, or talking with persons who were making pikes, meant he was involved and urged the jury to find the accused guilty.

Summing up, Lord President Hope repeated the points of law that reading the Address was treasonable, and that striking to make the king and his minsters change their measures was also treasonable. He added that associating with those who were making pikes meant that the accused was guilty of 'levying war against the king' according to the Act of Edward III. But then added,

> ... a great deal of Treason was committed in the forge on that day: but the doubt will be, whether that is brought home to the prisoner, and I think ... you will consider that the evidence is in my mind very doubtful, and therefore you will form your opinion upon it.

The jury retired at 6pm to consider their verdict and returned after only twenty five minutes to declare Robert Munroe 'Not Guilty.' Lord Advocate William Rae rose and addressed the judges, asking that the charges against the remaining prisoners be dropped.

It must be obvious that I have no proof to offer against them, which has not been adduced against their companion, and as they were all charged with the self-same acts I could not expect but a repetition of that evidence to alter the opinion of the Court or the jury.

Lord President Hope told him 'I think you have, on the present occasion, acted with prudence and discretion.' He then had the other prisoners brought to the bar and told them that all charges against them were withdrawn and they were free to go.

Shortly after this trial John Hullock returned to London and took no further part in the subsequent trials. It has been suggested that the verdict of the jury at Dumbarton annoyed him and he left to avoid further defeat. However, having secured convictions in Stirling and Glasgow, he may have sensed a change in the mood in Scotland. The public reaction to the verdicts had been hostile and with his aggressive attitude towards witnesses and disparaging remarks about Scotland and its law, he won no friends in Scottish legal circles. Lord Hope's summing up in this trial had amounted to a questioning of the way in which the law was being used to treat lesser offences as treason, and Hullock may have realized that opinion was turning towards leniency, and decided that he should leave as there was less chance of further convictions.

As the judges and their entourage left, with a military escort for Paisley, the Lord Advocate authorized the release of seven men from Greenock held at Dumbarton on charges of aiding the escape of the radical prisoners from Greenock Jail on 8 April, and they were released from the castle and turned home. Travelling across the Clyde by ferry, the judicial party landed at Renfrew, where Oliver Jamieson and the Paisley authorities met them with an escort of Hussars and brought them to the Tontine Hotel in Paisley.

The Renfrewshire Trial

On Tuesday 1 August, the court assemble at Paisley for the trial of the radicals held there. Finding there was no other large accommodation for the trial, St George's Church in George Street was converted into a courtroom, with the public being admitted to the lower floor, while admission to the gallery was by ticket only. The presiding judges were those who had been at the Dumbarton trial and the prosecution team was led by Lord Advocate William Rae, in the absence of John Hullock. The accused were represented by Erskine Sandford, in place of Francis Jeffrey, and John Archibald Murray, in place of John Peter Grant.

James Speirs and John Lang were brought from the jail in manacles by a troop of Hussars, and had the indictment read to them. Although not directly involved in the rising, they were charged with treason for having read copies of the Address and having been on strike on 3 April. Both entered pleas of not guilty. It was agreed that James Speirs should be tried first, but this led to a discussion as to whether John Laing should be in court during this trial as the prosecution wished to call him as a witness against Speirs. It was agreed that he should be removed from the bar and held outside the court, but close enough to be called without causing delay to the proceedings, although there is no record of him having been called.

The first duty of the court was to select a petit jury from the list returned by the Sheriff. From this three were rejected as not being freeholders in the county, ten were excused and the remaining 72 were examined. The prisoner rejected 35 and the Crown 25, before the required twelve men were sworn: Sir Michael Shaw Stewart, Bart, to be foreman of the jury, Allan Ker (merchant), John McNaught (merchant), Robert Hunter (merchant), James Coats (manufacturer), Matthew Rodger (farmer), Alexander Leiper (merchant), Gavin Browning (druggist), David Trail (dyer), John Gibson (cotton-yarn merchant), Thomas Wright (perfumer) and James Wilson (merchant).

After the usual admonition about not publishing details of the trial, James Spiers was brought to the bar and the Solicitor-General read out the indictment, explaining that actions,

> intended against the person of the King, be it to dethrone
> or imprison him, or to oblige him to alter his measures of

government, or to remove evil counsellors … all amount to levying war within the statute.'

He elaborated on this by stating that any attempt to change one or other of the Houses of Parliament was a threat to the constitution and thus treasonable. Distributing the Proclamation, he claimed, was likely to incite a demand for change and so constituted an attempt to levy war. The only proof required to have an offender 'deemed, declared and adjudged a traitor' was the oaths of two 'lawful and credible witnesses.'

He then read in full, at the insistence of the jury after he had attempted to select only parts of it, the Proclamation, pointing out that sections of it fulfilled all the requirements to be regarded as inciting treason, adding that mere possession of the document was itself sufficient proof of the charge. Quoting the judge in the trial of the Spa Field rioters in March 1820 that 'any act manifesting the criminal intention, and tending toward the accomplishment of the criminal object, is, in the language of the law, an overt act', he charged the jury that they consider two points:

1. Whether there was a general purpose and conspiracy to levy war for altering any part of the constitution, 'however minute.'

2. Whether the prisoner acted in obedience to the Address and cooperated with others to accomplish 'the purposes therein named.'

The Lord Advocate, Sir William Rae opened the case for the prosecution by outlining the law of treason and the importance of attending closely to the evidence. He reminded them that if two credible witnesses agreed on a point of evidence that they must consider that point to be proved.

The first witness was the mill owner William Houston, who stated that he had been told to close his mill by Speirs and Watson, but failed to identify Speirs in court as the man who spoke to him at School Green, claiming that he did not look like the man he had spoken to. His honesty won the admiration of radicals in the town. Other witnesses, including Andrew Logan and Thomas Watt, who were partners in a neighbouring mill, agreed that they had seen Speirs and Walker and were certain that Speirs had been the spokesman for the group of weavers. Some testified that they had seen, but not heard what Speirs said at the meeting or that they had not been paying attention to his words. A number of other witnesses testified that Speirs had been on strike during the first week in April and had been seen distributing copies of 'a document' at various locations in Paisley, including 'in the vicinity of the chapel.'

One witness, John Fraser, school master in Johnstone, had been held in prison with another suspect, John Neil, for three months before the trial, and, before taking the oath demanded to know why he had been imprisoned and what was planned for him. After some discussion among the prosecution legal team he was told by Sir Samuel Shepherd that he had been held as an important witness and that no charges were to be brought against him. He took the oath and gave his evidence, which amounted to merely having seen Speirs with some leaflets and, despite badgering by Sir William Rae, produced no damaging evidence against the accused. Mrs Marjory Fraser was called next and again in spite of bullying by the prosecution, particularly Samuel Shepherd, merely corroborated her husband's testimony. As the couple left court there was cheering and Lord Hope announced that 'firm action' would be taken if this was repeated.

The account of the trial shows that many of the Crown witnesses were reluctant to give evidence and that much of the information had to be extracted by prolonged questioning. This was particularly so in the case of Archibald McInnis, who, it was alleged, had been involved in getting pikes near the canal, whose responses to questions verged on the monosyllabic.

Did you get staves there?

Yes.

What kind of staves were they?

Middling long.

. . . .

Q. You say you bought that stick – was there anything upon the end of it when you bought it?

A. Yes, there was.

Q. What was it?

A. I cannot say particularly what it was; there was a thing at it.

Q. What kind of thing was it?

A. I could not tell what it was made of.

Q. Was it iron?

A. I could not particularly tell.

Q. Was it metal?

A. It was some kind of metal.

Q. How long was the piece of metal?

A. Not quite a foot long.

Q. Was it sharp?

A. Middling.

Evidence of the widespread nature of the strike was provided by James Brown, the police superintendent, who testified that 'the operatives generally struck on Monday' and that 'weavers of Paisley were a great many of them in the streets, and appeared to be totally idle.'

A declaration signed by Speirs under questioning, to the effect that he had been involved in organising strikes and distributing copies of the Proclamation was introduced by the poet William Motherwell, Sheriff-Clerk Depute, who had served as a special constable during the 1819 riots.

His attempt to introduce this document was objected to by the defence, as it was not clear if the accused had signed the original or a copy and Motherwell was unable to confirm which had been signed. Two further witnesses, Alexander Campbell, Sheriff-Substitute and Andrew Caldwell stressed that Speirs had given his statement freely under questioning. Mr Grant and Mr Sandford argued that as no such procedure existed under English Law which did not accept declarations made under interrogation and thus the declaration was inadmissible in this trial The Lord Chief Baron countered that an examination does not oblige a person to speak, and if he chose to do so it was voluntary making their statements admissible. The judges agreed with Sir Samuel Shepherd and allowed the declaration.

Speirs statement was read and indicated that he had overheard Mr Houston and another man talk about a stoppage of work at Cartside Mill. He claimed that a copy of the Address had been left with his wife while he was out and that he had later read it and had given it to another person who had sent for it. He said that he had seen a further copy in a shop window.

After a sheriff-officer testified that he had served a subpoena on Alexander Cairdie, who had failed to appear, the prosecution closed its case and the court adjourned until 10 am the following day.

The trial resumed on Wednesday 2 August, when Erskine Sandford opened the case for the defence. His main argument was that English Law distinguished between levying war against the person of the king and actions to obtain a specific object, and 'compassing or imagining' which were an 'internal act ... could not possibly fall under any judicial cognizance, but of God alone.'

The first six defence witnesses all testified that they knew Speirs, and had seen him at Houston's Old Mill and at the meeting in School Green in Johnstone, but swore that he had taken no active part in the demonstrations. At Old Mill he had been invited to become preses (president), but had declined, and the Address was read by Robert Parker, with Speirs being little more than a spectator. As Grant was questioning the second witness, William Clark, he was interrupted by Sir Samuel Shepherd who asked that he put the questions in a different manner, but Grant refused to comply. Under cross-examination by the Solicitor General and Shepherd, who behaved more like the chief prosecutor than the adviser to the judges, all the witnesses stuck to their stories.

The Johnstone weaver Alexander Thomson was in the witness box longer than any other. He said he did not know Speirs and only learned Lang's name later but testified that Speirs had been critical of those who had shouted down Mr Houston and that when the Address had been read out he had not heard all the words due to the noise of the crowd.

When the Deputy Lord Advocate, John Hope, asked Thomson about being present at the meeting at Quarrellstone, Mr Grant intervened asking the court to 'put the witness on his guard' in case he incriminated himself. The witness was asked to leave the court and there was a furious legal argument, as Hope claimed that Grant had no authority to warn the witness as that was the job of the court.

Grant replied, 'I shall not submit to the orders of my learned Friends – to the Court I bow.' Shepherd joined in, arguing that to warn the witness might interfere with the course of justice, and that any caution should be given after the question had been put. The Lord Justice Clerk brought the confrontation to an end, and issued a ruling that Hope's question about the witness's presence at Quarrellstone was valid, but if he went on to question him about drilling there Thomson was not obliged to answer, and would be so cautioned by the court.

Resuming the stand Thomson steadfastly denied, under aggressive questioning by the Lord Chief Baron, that drilling had taken place. When asked if, as a member of the volunteers, he had drilled the men, he denied the suggestion but admitted he had organised the men to get them 'walking in order' and to 'do a facing or so.' When Shepherd commented that he had just admitted to drilling the men, Thomson rejected the suggestion. Angered at Thomson's obduracy Sir Samuel dismissed him and concluded,

… in the presence of a Jury of this country, and, I am sorry to say, in the face of your God, you have sworn to tell the truth as you shall answer at the day of judgement, yet hesitate to say that it was drilling. I hope to God I will never make such a figure again in a Court.

After a further two witnesses testified that Speirs had been little more than a spectator at the meetings, Malcolm Fraser, a former Sergeant-Major in the 26th Regiment was sworn. He testified that he had served with Speirs for six years in the regiment, and that Speirs had been promoted to Sergeant. When Grant produced Speirs' certificate of discharge, Sir Samuel Shepherd complained that it was irrelevant, but, at the insistence of the jury the court agreed to it being read out as evidence of the character of the accused. The witness identified the signature on the certificate as that of his former commanding officer, Captain Hall, who had written that Speirs had 'merited approbation.'

After concluding statements and summing up by the Lord President, the jury retired to consider the evidence and after two hours returned with a verdict of 'Guilty on one overt act', that of being on strike, and declared Spiers Not Guilty on all other counts. Asked by the Lord President if that meant guilty on the main charge, the foreman Sir Michael Shaw Stewart replied that they had found no evidence of treason.

Lord Hope was unhappy with the this and Sir Samuel Shepherd was called to explain the law, and he stated that if part of the charges had been proven then the main charge of treason was also proved. Sir Michael and several jurors engaged in exchanges with Sir Samuel over the evidence and indicated that they felt he was trying to pressurise them into reaching a verdict that did not arise from the evidence presented. One juror actually stated that it was for the jury to decide, not the judges.

They were told to retire and reconsider their decision, and twice more returned with the same verdict, giving the explanation that it was a 'special verdict.' Lord Hope and Sir Samuel Shepherd, clearly irritated by the jury's persistence in sticking to their original verdict, ordered them to retire yet again. After a short deliberation the jurors returned to the courtroom and Sir Michael announced that they found Spiers 'Not Guilty on all counts.'

As Spiers was told he was free to leave the court, members of the public began to cheer and one man was arrested for contempt of court. Another was arrested outside the building, but Lord President Hope ordered his release. Shepherd then threatened to have anyone else who celebrated the verdict arrested.

John Lang was then brought to the bar and the Lord Advocate rose to announce that all charges against him and all the other defendants elsewhere in Scotland were withdrawn.

> From the proceedings which have taken place in the last trial, it appears, that while the whole facts are admitted to have been proved, yet a jury of this country have by their verdict, been pleased to find that those do not constitute the crime of treason. I should not feel myself justified in occupying the time of the Court by again laying the same evidence before another Jury.

Lang was told he could leave a free man, and the authorities abandoned the case against all outstanding accused, although the court was obliged to convene at the remaining trials to formally discharge the prisoners.

The Ayrshire Trial

The Lord Justice Clerk, accompanied by Lord Pitmilly and the Lord Chief Baron, travelled to Ayr for the final trial, which should have been a formality after the Lord Advocate's decision not to pursue further convictions, and all the prisoners having entered pleas of not guilty at the Grand Jury. That they regarded the trial as a simple procedural exercise is clear from the reduced number of judges that had been stipulated by the Commission.

Proceedings opened on Wednesday 9 August in the New Church, and the prisoners, John Dickie, Thomas MacKay, Hugh Wallace and Andrew Wyllie, were taken from the town jail to face the judges.

Thomas MacKay was the first to be brought before the court and, to the astonishment A J Grant and E D Sandford, who were defending the group, and the judges, changed his plea to guilty. That this was unexpected is clear from the reports in the press.

To none did MacKay's cause more surprise than to Mr Grant, the counsel, who had been engaged to defend him and the others. He turned quickly round and looked at the prisoner sternly in the face as if to reproach him for recklessly throwing his life away.

James Howie, in his history of Ayr, claimed that 'there was not sufficient evidence to prove the charges' against the Stewarton men, and anxious to secure at least one conviction, the Commissioners resorted to trickery. The authorities in Ayr tried to persuade MacKay to plead guilty promising 'a free and unconditional pardon' if he did so. Although reluctant at first, under pressure from his family and friends, who had been told that this was the only way he could save his life, he eventually agreed to change his plea.

The jurors chosen for the hearing were, Sir David Hunter Bart, as foreman, with Alexander Hamilton Esq, John Logan Esq, Patrick Campbell Esq, William Montgomery Esq, James Warner Esq, John Crawford (thread manufacturer), Hugh Crawford (thread manufacturer), Robert Faulds (banker), James Faulds (manufacturer), John Shedden (grocer), and Robert Houston. Their role was merely to confirm the pleas and hear the sentences.

After the others were brought before the jury and were freed after pleading not guilty, MacKay faced the judges fully expecting to be pardoned, but instead Lord Boyle pronounced sentence,

> You be taken from thence to the place whence you came, and that you be drawn on a hurdle to the place of execution, and there be hanged by the neck until you are dead, and that afterwards your head be severed from your body, and your body divided into four quarters to be disposed of as His Majesty shall direct, and may God have mercy upon your soul.

The stunned prisoner was led away to jail, and held there before being sent to New South Wales when his sentence, along with that of most of the other condemned radicals, was commuted to transportation.

The Commissioners had got their last victim, although MacKay was according to some accounts granted a reprieve and released on 23 August: certainly his name does not appear of the list of prisoners sent to Sheerness on 11 October, nor is he among those sent to New South Wales in 1821, which would tend to support the belief that he was indeed set free.

Conclusion

Thomas Knapp received a letter from John Hobhouse thanking him for his account of the trials at Stirling and Glasgow and adding 'I am sorry to perceive that the subsequent prosecutions have not terminated so prosperously as the earlier ones.' Knapp had started collecting the trial documents but was ordered to bring these to Whitehall where he could collate them before they were deposited in either Edinburgh or Westminster, or as was 'finally determined.'

The decision to abandon the outstanding prosecutions after the failure to obtain guilty verdicts at Dumbarton and Paisley has raised questions about the motives for so doing. It would appear that the trial at Ayr was seen as a formality as the panel of judges was reduced to two, the Justice Clerk and Lord Pitmilly rather than four as had been stipulated in the Commission. That Thomas MacKay was sentenced to death at Ayr was solely due to him having changed his plea from not guilty, leaving the Lord Justice Clerk no option other than of pronouncing the death sentence.

Of the eighty-eight Radicals charges with high treason, twenty five had been found guilty and sentenced to death, although only three suffered the ultimate penalty, and the remaining twenty two were transported to New South Wales. While Sidmouth and Hobhouse seem to have regarded this as too few, many in Scotland saw the punishments as very severe, and great public sympathy was expressed for the victims. It is not unreasonable to conclude that public opinion felt that justice had been done and that any further prosecutions would have been counter-productive.

It is very likely that the government and local authorities were aware that prolonging the legal process would result in massive publicity for the radicals and their cause, when the ban on reporting the trials was lifted. As those found guilty had been sentenced to death there was likely to be a wave of sympathy for the accused accompanied with criticism of the harshness of the sentences imposed by the establishment. The last thing the government wanted was to create a pantheon of political martyrs and abandoning the remaining trials, and showing mercy by commuting the sentences of all bar the ringleaders, would allow them to portray the king and themselves as merciful.

Equally, the Scottish legal establishment may have seen an opportunity to bring proceedings under an alien legal system to a conclusion. Some may have, like Ranald MacDonald, Sheriff of Stirling, become irritated by the overbearing and sneering posture of John Hullock, who showed contempt for all things Scottish, including Scots Law. Equally, Sir Samuel Shepherd, who had been appointed as adviser to the judges, by his interference in the examination of witnesses and his attempts to bully witnesses and jurors, particularly during the trial in Paisley, where he acted more like the lead prosecutor than an adviser did not help relations with the Scottish legal establishment. Lord Hope's summing up at Dumbarton, and Sir William Rae's speedy abandonment of the remaining trials after the refusal of the Paisley jurors to be intimidated by Sheherd, would indicate that the Scottish legal establishment had had enough. To many, even those on the prosecution benches, the end of the trials must have come as a relief.

Thomas Knapp was ordered by Lord Sidmouth to return to London where he completed writing up his account of the trials while attending to other duties. The Home Secretary told him that a decision on where the records were to be held would be made when he had completed them. There was some early doubt about the eventual location of the documents. The National Records Office in Edinburgh holds the Commission and the prisoners' indictments, together with a few writs of capias, but Knapp's written record of the trials have yet to be found.

Over many years researchers have sought these records in the National Archives of Scotland and England, and in government and legal archives, as well as major depositories throughout the country, but no trace of them has been found. Ellis and Mac a'Ghobhainn noted that the official record of such trials, *A Complete Collection of State Trials and Proceedings for High Treason* has no mention of the above trials. They did point out that the relevant volume for the period 1817 to 20, No. 33, does state that some proceedings had been omitted as they 'did not appear to be of sufficient importance', although a number of trials for the lesser charge of sedition are included, leading some to conclude the Scottish trial documents were destroyed on official orders.

An account of the proceedings was published in three volumes in 1825 by Manners and Miller of 92 Prince's Street Edinburgh. This record is based on the notes of the journalist C J Green, 'taken in short-hand' during the trials. They are an almost complete transcript, but as the trials went on into the early hours of the morning and the only light in the court was from the candles at the judges table the record of the proceeding after dark had to be done from memory, as recording them at the time would have been almost impossible. Thanks to Green, however, we have been given a glimpse of the happenings in the courtrooms during the trials of the Scots radicals.

9. EXECUTIONS

James Wilson

There was considerable public sympathy for Wilson, and shortly after he had been sentenced to death a public petition seeking clemency was organised and collected many signatures. His reputation as a long-time radical was widespread throughout central Scotland, while many who may not have shared his political views were reluctant to see a man of his advanced years, he was sixty-three, suffer the indignity of the English capital sentence, which was more severe than that of Scotland. The petition was given to Lord Provost Henry Monteith to be presented before the House of Commons but he refused to accept it or to send it on, and later attended the execution in his official capacity.

In an attempt to discredit Wilson in the eyes of the public, a rumour was circulated and carried in the press that he had burnt his Bible and denounced the Christian religion. He was known to have been a free-thinker on matters of religion and the authorities believed that in a staunchly Christian country like Scotland the rumour would cause many to see him as deserving his fate, or at least lose respect and sympathy for him. The ploy failed, partly as few believed it to be true and partly as Wilson made a point of carrying a Bible when attending a religious service before making his way to the gallows.

On Sunday 20 August, Wilson attended a religious service in Glasgow Jail and was seen to be carrying a Bible, thus giving the lie to the story of his rejecting Christianity. During the service the minister, Rev Dr Greville Ewing told him he was a base criminal and damned in the eyes of God, to which he made no reply. He was later visited in his cell by Rev James Lapslie of Campsie, a former member of the Friends of the People who had become a government informer, and famously opposed Sunday Schools arguing that they encouraged the spread of democratic ideas. The minister tried to get Wilson to confess to his crimes and launched into a tirade against radicalism threatening him with 'eternal damnation' for his 'heinous crime', at which Wilson physically ejected him from his cell and told the jailer not to allow 'any of his ilk' to visit him again.

On the evening of 29 August, the day before his execution, James Wilson's family was allowed to visit him for a short time in the Iron Room at Glasgow Jail. His wife, and daughter, Mrs Walter, with his grandchildren spoke with him through the grated door of his cell, while the turnkey was present to observe them. When they left, a group of 'pious persons' stayed with him throughout the night, spending the time in prayer.

In 1834, a paper, allegedly given by Wilson to his wife during this visit, was found in Lennoxtown, which stated that he died a 'true patriot for the cause of freedom', but claiming that he had been forced to go with the radicals for fear of his life. (Appendix V) It was denounced by his grandson, who was present at the meeting in Glasgow Jail, and declared that the family spoke to Wilson through a grilled door, and that no paper was passed to his grandmother. Both the author and purpose of this document are still a mystery: opinion ranges from it being an attempt to show that he and the other radicals were the gullible pawns of others, to it being an attack on the character and integrity of James Wilson.

From early on Wednesday 30 August, large crowds had begun assembling on the execution ground at Glasgow Green and in the streets from there to the Jail, but the mood was one of sullen silence rather than the usual festive atmosphere at executions. By noon it was estimated there were 20,000 people assembled in the area and the military commander, Major-General Reynell, became alarmed at the possibility of trouble. His fears seemed justified by the appearance of posters stating:

May the ghost of the butchered Wilson, haunt the pillows of his relentless jurors

– Murder! Murder! Murder!

His response was to order Lt-Col. Northcott to deploy the 1st Battalion of the Rifle Brigade in the streets around the execution ground, with Col. Elphinstone's 33rd Regiment of Foot to reinforce the 3rd Dragoon Guards already there. It was the largest military presence ever seen at an execution in the country.

Before being taken to the gallows erected beside the Clyde, Wilson attend a public religious service at 2.05pm in the County Court Buildings, sitting in front of the Lord Provost, Henry Monteith, the magistrates and the Sheriff. During the service Rev Dr Ewing told the public that the man before them was to be hanged as an object lesson to others with evil designs. After prayers by Dr Daniel Dewar of Tron Church, Wilson drank the traditional glass of wine and, after the public and officials left, was escorted to the south door while the executioner made his way from the Jail, via an underground passageway.

In addition to the city hangman there was the executioner who was to behead Wilson; a 20-year-old medical student, Thomas Moore, who had volunteered for the job. When Wilson, his arms tied behind him, was assisted into the cart, Moore, dressed in grey and his face masked in black crepe, sat opposite him holding the axe with its blade facing the condemned man and with a knife in his left hand. Surrounded by a group of 3rd Dragoon Guards, with drawn swords resting on their shoulders, and followed by the City officials the cart set out for the Green. As the procession moved slowly between the crowds along the route, Wilson was heard to remark to the hangman, Thomas Young 'Did y'ever see sic a crowd, Tammas?'

At 2.55pm the cart arrived at the Green, where a coffin and block were placed beside the gallows. When the hood had been placed over Wilson's head and the city hangman adjusted the noose round his neck, the crowd shouted 'Murder! Murder!' When Wilson dropped a handkerchief to show he was ready and the trapdoor opened there were angry shouts from the crowd, followed by screams as an officer of the Dragoon Guards led a party of troops into a section of the crowd to try to disperse them, as he thought the mob was about to try to free Wilson. Order was quickly restored when it became clear that the crowd was voicing their disapproval and had no intention of taking other action.

It was reported that Wilson's body convulsed for about five minutes and 'some blood appeared through the cap opposite the ears, but upon the whole he appeared to die very easily.' After half an hour his body was taken down and placed on supports across the open coffin with the head on a block. Moore then stepped forward and 'with most determined coolness', according to the *Glasgow Herald*, severed the head with one blow. As he lifted the head to show it to the crowd, proclaiming 'This is the head of a traitor!', the crowd responded with shouts of 'He is a murdered man?' and 'He is a martyr!' The *Glasgow Herald* reported,

> The whole ceremony of decapitation did not occupy above a minute, and at four o'clock the ground was clear, without any material accident having happened.

The remains of James Wilson were placed in the coffin and taken by Alexander Calder, the Sheriff's Office and an escort, to the 'pauper's ground' beside the High Church, where it was buried in a shallow grave without ceremony. This shocked Wilson's family who had been led to believe his body would be given to them for burial at Strathaven. When members of the family tried speak with the authorities they refused to meet them, so Wilson's daughter, Mrs Walters, and her niece, Mrs Ritchie, hired a coach, and with the assistance of a couple of friends disinterred the body from the 'pauper's ground' at midnight, with the possible collusion of the cemetery officials, and transported it home in a coach to Stathaven.

There the local minister conducted a service and buried James Wilson in the churchyard opposite the house where he had been born and where he had lived his entire life. Fearing the authorities might attempt to retrieve his body he was laid to rest in an unmarked grave to keep the location secret. The authorities were angered but did not take action against either the relatives or the minister who had flouted their design by having held a short burial service. Had they attempted to disinter Wilson's body a second time, solely to deny him a dignified burial, there would have been public outrage, and quite possibly ecclesiastical condemnation. Letting sleeping corpses lie was deemed the sensible option.

John Baird and Andrew Hardie

At Stirling Castle John Baird, Andrew Hardie and James Clelland were told that the other prisoners from Bonnymuir had had their sentences commuted to transportation, but that their executions were scheduled for Friday 8 September. On 26 August they were separated from the others and placed in the same cell to await execution.

Over the next two weeks Baird and Hardie wrote letters to their friends and received letters in return. (Appendix V) Andrew Hardie was able to write an account of the Radical Revolt which was smuggled out of the castle by 'Granny Duncan' and her daughter, who brought food in for the prisoners and hid the papers in the pot containing their porridge. This eyewitness account of the Rising was sent to Rutherglen, where P Walsh published it at the end of 1820. The two women attended the condemned men up to the day of their execution, and thanks to their bravery and cunning, the story of the events at Bonnymuir from the perspective of the radicals has survived. (Appendix IV)

The letters of both men are full of religious references and express forgiveness to James Hardie and Private Nicol Baird for their perjury during the trial. John Baird wrote to his brother and sister during his time in prison urging them to lead their lives to the full and to think kindly of him. In his letter to Daniel Taylor of Kilsyth on 4 September, he stated his belief that he was a political martyr,

> I resign my life without the least reluctance, knowing that it is for the cause of truth and justice. I die a martyr … I hope you will keep in your remembrance the cause for which Baird, Hardie and Cleland died on the scaffold.

James Clelland, as Baird noted in a postscript to the letter, had his sentence commuted to transportation for life the day after, i.e. 5 September.

Hardie in addition to penning his account of the events at Bonnymuir, wrote several letters to his mother and family members, as well as to a number of friends. In these he explained why he had been part of the rising and how he felt that his 'poor, suffering country' demanded change and that he had answered her call.

In a moving letter to his fiancée, Margaret McKeigh, he wrote that he hoped his death would not dishonour her as he died for his 'distressed, wronged, suffering and insulted country.' He ended by expressing the hope that rather than instill terror in his fellow Scots, his execution the following day 'will awaken my countrymen – my poor, suffering, countrymen, from that lethargy which has so overclouded them!' In another letter, written on the day of his execution, to Isabella Condy of Stirling who had nursed the wounded from Bonnymuir, he wrote that he fell 'a martyr to the cause of truth and justice on the 8th of September, 1820.'

On the Thursday, friends and relatives of the condemned men were permitted to visit them in prison. Baird's two brothers, three sisters and two brothers-in-law, together with his 80-year-old father and a friend, Mr Bruce, spent some time with him, during which he told them of his hopes for Scotland. As they were leaving, he gave his father a home-made snuff box as a memento.

A small group of friends, including Mr Bruce and two ministers, Rev Dr Wright and Rev Dr Small spent the night with the two condemned radicals, praying and engaging them in conversations. They slept from 4 to 6am before washing and dressing. After brief prayers and reading the Bible they were escorted by the Fort Major, W Peddie into the courtyard to say farewell to their Bonnymuir comrades, where they told them that although they were condemned 'right was on their side and that the cause which they championed would in the end prevail.' They embraced each of the prisoners in turn before being led back to their cell to await the escort that would take them to the place of execution.

The scaffold had been erected in Broad Street, opposite the Jail, with two coffins set beside the headsman's block on the platform. Sir Walter Scott, writing in the *Edinburgh Annual Register*, gave an account of the scene,

> During last night the usual apparatus was erected in front
> of the stair leading to the Townhouse, and in the morning

exhibited two decently ornamented coffins on the platform, with a dark-coloured wooden block.

Two troops of the 8th Dragoon Guards arrived from Falkirk at noon and formed a square in front of the castle, where they were joined at 1pm by the Sheriff, Sir Ranald MacDonald of Staffa, and the Stirling magistrates. The two prisoners, each carrying a New Testament, were placed in a hurdle and were joined by the medical student Moore dressed in the executioner's black gown and hood, who sat facing them holding his axe. A group of Dragoons marched at the front of the procession to clear the way and another in the rear, while Rev Dr Wright and Rev Dr Small, with a group of relatives and two sheriff's officers, walked beside the cart as it passed through a silent and sullen crowd. Hardie was heard to say 'God bless you' to some weeping women on the roadway.

At the Tollboth the ministers held a short service and Mr Bruce recited the 13th Psalm, 'Out of the depths have I cried to thee, O Lord.' After the prayers Baird and Hardie were given the customary glass of wine and their arms were tied. Hardie then expressed his thanks to General Graham and Major Peddie for treating the prisoners with humanity, before they were led out to the scaffold at 2.45pm.

As the prisoners appeared on the scaffold the crowd cheered and John Baird stepped forward to address them, saying he did not fear facing God and advising them always to venerate the Bible.

> Friends and countrymen, I dare say you well expect me to say something to you of the cause which has brought me here; but on that I do not mean to say much, only that what I have hitherto done, and which brought me here, was for the cause of truth and justice. I declare I never gave my consent to anything inconsistent with truth and justice.

Andrew Hardie then spoke telling the crowd to return home and think of God, adding, 'I die a martyr to the cause of truth and justice...' At this the crowd roared its approval, which led an officer to order his men to present arms, causing panic in a section of the crowd for a few moments before it became clear to them that the troops were not preparing to open fire. The Sheriff, Sir Ranald MacDonald of Staffa, told Hardie he would not allow him to continue his speech and Hardie bowed and spoke out to the crowd saying,

> My friends, I hope none of you have been hurt. Please, after this is over, go quietly to your homes and read your Bibles, remembering the fate of Baird and Hardie.

The execution caps were placed on the heads of the men and they said farewell to each other before the noose was placed round their necks. Hardie gave the signal and they dropped to their death with a struggle. The bodies were taken down after half an hour and placed on the spokes laid over the coffins for the beheading. When the executioner stepped forward toward the bodies the crowd, which had been silent during the hanging, greeted him with hisses and shouts of 'Murderer!' Unlike in Glasgow, Moore seemed unnerved and hesitant. He twice raised the axe and lowered it before striking at Hardie and it took three strokes to cut off his head, before he presented it to the public.

Turning to Baird, his first stroke only nicked the neck and stuck in the wooden block. Prising the axe out he again hacked at the neck and finally severed it and held it aloft proclaiming, 'This is the head of a traitor!' The crowd yelled their disapproval and anger and only when troops were given the order to present arms did the crowd sullenly quieten and order was restored. The spectators muttered their condemnation of the 'murders' but slowly and murmuring began to disperse, leaving the sheriff's officers to seal the coffins and escort them to the pauper's graveyard.

Scott, who was vehemently opposed to the radicals, was determined to down-play the crowds that had gathered to express sympathy with the condemned men. In his account of the executions, he claimed that they did not attract any great crowd and that few inhabitants of Stirling showed any interest in the proceedings.

To the credit of the humanity of the inhabitants of this place, very few attended the execution. The crowd seemed almost entirely composed of people from the country, this being the market-day. Females of any respectability there seemed none, and scarcely any spectators occupied the neighbouring windows.

Ranald MacDonald of Staffa turned to the officials and remarked, 'And that, gentlemen, completes the business.'

Far from being over, there was further trouble. That night an armed mob attacked the home of the Glasgow justice, James Hardie, and ransacked it when they found he was not there, although his servants were unharmed. Over the next two days attacks were made on witnesses in Stirling and strikes took place at Usherwood and Milngavie mills, and an attempt was made to set fire to the latter. This series of events led Francis Jeffrey to assess the situation in a letter to a friend,

I am very much ashamed of the Commons, and have little now to say against the Radical Reformers; if any reform is worth the risk of such an experiment. The particular question upon which every man should be making up his mind, is, whether he is for tyranny or revolution.

The *Edinburgh Review in 1832,* was more forthright in describing the events of 1820 as, 'a war of the rich against the poor – of the Government and soldiery against the people.'

10. THE TRANSPORTED RADICALS

After the trials in which those found guilty were sentenced to death, the government commuted the sentences of nineteen of the Bonnymuir radicals to transportation. John Anderson (Camelon) for life, John Barr (Condorrat) 14 years, William Clarkson (Glasgow) 14 years, James Clelland (Glasgow) Life, Andrew Dawson (Camelon) Life, Robert Gray (Glasgow) Life, Alexander Hart (Glasgow) 14years, Alexander Johnston (Glasgow) 14years, Alexander Latimer (Glasgow) 14 yaers, Thomas McCulloch (Glasgow) 14 years, Thomas McFarlane (Condorrat) Life, John McMillan (Camelon) Life, Benjamin Moir (Glasgow) 14 years, Allan Murchie (Glasgow) Life, Thomas Pike (Glasgow) 14 years, William Smith (Glasgow) 14 years, David Thompson (Glasgow) 14 years, Andrew White (Glasgow) 14 years, James Wright (Glasgow) 14 years

Australia

After the loss of the American colonies in 1783, Britain turned to Botany Bay as a new penal settlement. It had the advantage that it was a base for naval vessels in the eastern seas and as a point for economic expansion in the area. The first convicts arrived in January 1788 and in the succeeding years 150,000 arrived, among them 8,207 Scots (mostly women). Other settlers were soldiers sent to guard the convicts, and many of these troops, like the 73rd Regt., were Scottish. Officers took a role in administration and a Scot, Lachlan Macquarie, became Governor.

Appointed Governor in 1809, in place of William Bligh (of *Bounty* mutiny fame), Macquarie saw the potential of the convict settlement to become a flourishing colony and introduced a programme of town planning and began economic development that, by 1822 had sponsored over 200 schemes, and he introduced the colony's own currency. When Captain John MacArthur suggested that the colony was ideal for sheep farming, agriculture and wine production, the Governor helped introduce sheep, and opened the territory for cultivation by granting pardons to convicts, especially those who dug roads through the Blue Mountains to open the interior of the continent for settlement.

The arrival of literate and skilled craftsmen like the Scottish radicals provided an opportunity to develop the industrial base of Sydney and attract others to settle there. He made use of skilled convicts, encouraging them to work hard, often in new industrial shops he had set up to help develop the area, to lay the basis of a new country, and rewarded them with grants of around 200 acres of land, to encourage them to settle in the colony once they had served their sentences.

This was not appreciated by the government at Westminster, where members believed the settlement was to be used solely as a place of punishment, and that the new governor was not sufficiently punishing the criminals sent there. Some MPs even went so far as to claim that he was rewarding them for their crimes. As a result, in November 1821, Macquarie was replaced as Governor by another Scot, Sir Thomas Brisbane, but was not rewarded with a peerage, as was the custom: he is the only Governor not to have been given recognition for his service in New South Wales.

His replacement arrived late in 1821; Thomas McCulloch writing to his wife on 12 October to ask her to join him in Sydney, mentioned that Sir Thomas Brisbane had 'arrived here two days ago.' Soon after his arrival, the new Governor, rather than turning the settlement back to being a penal colony as was intended by politicians at home, continued his predecessor's policy and encouraged agriculture and industry, and encouraged convicts, who had served their sentence, particularly those with skills, to settle in Sydney and develop the colony.

Arrival of the Radicals

After sentencing, the radicals had been held in prison in Scotland before being sent from Edinburgh to Sheerness on 11 October to await transportation. There they were kept for some weeks on the prison hulk *Bellerephon,* the ship on which Napoleon had surrendered. During this time, they were allowed to write to their relatives, and Alexander Hart wrote to his brother on 11 December, from the convict ship *Speke,* before leaving for Australia, giving him idetails about their conditions. The radicals were well-regarded by their captors and, unusually for convicts, it was noted that most attended church services. Their behaviour was commended to Captain Peter McPherson of the *Speke,* the vessel that was to transport them to Australia. The Bonnymuir radicals were kept in two groups, of 9 and 10, in different parts of the hulk prior to boarding the *Speke* on 9 December.

The *Speke* set sail on 22 December with the Scots radicals as part of a group of 156 male convicts being transported. There were also a few free passengers, including Dr Henry Grattan Douglass, Assistant Surgeon of the medical establishment in the colony, and Mr and Mrs Mulgrave, who had been sent to found a system of education in Van Diemen's Land. The ship's manifest shows that also on board were two Maori chiefs, named 'Whycato' and 'Shungie', who were travelling home to New Zealand from London, along with Rev. Thomas Kendall of the Church Missionary Society. These chiefs, native names Hongi Hika and Waikato, had accompanied Rev. Kendall when he visited the capital and were presented to George IV: they had helped the missionary to compile the Maori alphabet and grammar.

The prisoners were accompanied by a body of troops from the 30th, 34th and 89th Regiments under Lt Sutherland, and they had been freed from their irons before reaching Tenerife, making their long voyage less arduous. One prisoner wrote that 'a gentleman who was going out to settle' promised to help them, and he and a clergyman, (probably Rev Thomas Kendall), gave religious instruction to the convicts. It is not without significance that some of the Scots radicals from the *Speke* were assigned to Dr Douglass and Mr Mulgrave, and served them loyally during their sentences.

The ship arrived at Port Jackson on 18 May 1821, but the convicts were not allowed to go ashore until Wednesday 23rd, after the other passengers had disembarked. As the radical prisoners prepared to leave the ship, both the ship's and the military officers commended them for their 'exemplary behaviour', and the radicals in return thanked the Captain, Peter MacPherson, and the ship's surgeon, Edward Coates, for their attention during the voyage. The convicts were then inspected by the Lieutenant

Governor, James Erskine, and examined by doctors, before disembarking on the 26th and being allocated to places of employment in the colony. The *Sydney Gazette* reported that they had 'a healthy and satisfactory appearance.'

Erskine addressed the convicts and promised that if they behaved well during their captivity, and worked hard, they would be welcome to remain in the colony and given land to work as free men. The Scottish arrivals had two advantages over the majority of those transported, they were literate, and most had skills that could be put to use to develop the economy of New South Wales. It was their and Australia's, good fortune that they arrived at a time when the Governor, Lachlan Macquarie, and his successor Thomas Brisbane, were anxious to develop the economic potential of the penal settlement to transform it into a thriving colony. Several of the Scots radicals were given appointments in government posts due to their skills, and most remained to build successful lives, and founded families in their new home.

Brief Biographies

Over the years since the radicals settled in their new home, their descendants have taken pride in their 'convict' and radical ancestors, regarding them as the founding fathers of Australia. In 1981, Margaret and Alastair Macfarlane, themselves related to the Condorrat radical Thomas Macfarlane, one of the men transported after the failed insurrection, produced a history of the Bonnymuir Radicals, entitled *The Scottish Radicals: Tried and transported to Australia for Treason in 1820* (Stevenage, 1981). The authors used the records available in Australia to trace the movement of the transportees in their time as convicts, and, where information was found, their later lives as settlers.

The following is a very brief summary of their account of the lives of the men transported after the Radical War.

John Anderson (1793-1858)

Anderson was a weaver in Camelon, near Falkirk in Stirlingshire, who had been arrested after Bonnymuir, but had not taken part in the skirmish there, and had been given a life sentence. Despite his skill as a weaver, he was sent as a servant to Simeon Lord before being appointed, in 1823, as the teacher at the Ebenezer Presbyterian School at Portland Head and, on account of his good singing voice, became Precentor at Ebenezer Church. As a teacher, he was given a salary of £40, and an expenses payment of another £40, but slept on the floor of the church, which also served as the schoolroom. His sister joined him in 1834 as his housekeeper, and she later become a nurse to the Wilson family at Port Macquarrie.

He married Lucy Watson in 1854 and they moved into the accommodation provided in the school building that had been constructed in 1840. They had no children. Unlike the other radical prisoners, he was given a separate Royal Pardon 1836. In 1855, the *Sydney Morning Herald* reported that he had been presented with an address and gift of money for services to the local community. He died shortly after.

John Barr (1793-1862)

Although he had been born in Glasgow, John Barr had moved to Condorrat where he worked as a weaver. He was one of the radicals taken in arms after the defeat at Bonnymuir and whose death sentence had been commuted to fourteen years in New South Wales. While awaiting trial, and transportation he wrote a number of letters to his brother which have survived, and which trace the movements of the prisoners. (Appendix V)

Employed at first by Sir John Jamieson, he moved in 1825 to the Male Factory at Paramatta as a weaver. In 1828 he was granted a Certificate of Freedom and set up as 'a woollen man.'

In 1831, he married Margaret Harrington, a convict, in St John's Church, Paramatta. There is no record of them having children. He was admitted to the Benevolent Society of New South Wales twice before his death there October 1862. There is no mention of his wife in the Society's documents, and it is presumed that she was already dead.

William Clarkson (aka Clackson)

A Glasgow shoe-maker, he was one of the three radicals seriously wounded at Bonnymuir. In his account of the battle, Andrew Hardie reported that one was 'dreadfully wounded in the head ... in four places, and shot through the arm' and, from other sources describing the wounds of the other two wounded, it is clear that Clarkson was this casualty.

He was employed, along with John Anderson, as a servant by Simeon Lord. Having gained his Certificate of Freedom on 18 December 1827, he appears in the 1828 census as a shoemaker and living with his wife, Margaret, whom he married in 1825. No record exists of him after 1828, and his age is problematic as the date of his birth is not known.

James Clelland (1785- ?)

Born in Edinburgh, Clelland had served in the 7th Dragoon Guards during the French Wars and, after his discharge, settled in Glasgow where he became a locksmith. There he became involved in radical politics and was one of the men Hardie led from Glasgow to Bonnymuir.

Like the other two former soldiers taken at Bonnymuir, Baird and Hardie. he had been sentenced to death, but after correspondence with Lord Sidmouth, Sir William Rae, the Lord Advocate, persuaded the Home Secretary to commute the sentence to transportation for life: he was only told of his reprieve three days before the scheduled execution.

In Australia his skills were utilised and he was employed as locksmith in government service. In 1828 he was staying with Alexander and Mary Johnston at Clarence Street, Sydney. But thereafter there is no record of what became of him, and his Absolute Pardon was never collected, leading to the presumption that he had died before 1850.

Andrew Dawson (1782-1839)

Dawson was born in Stirlingshire and was a weaver, but in other records he is described as being a blacksmith and nailer. Although he was not at Bonnymuir he was one of the radicals arrested in the aftermath of the Bonnymuir battle, as the *History of Stirlingshire* put it he was 'picked up ... out of Camelon.'

At Stirling he was among the last of the eight prisoners convicted, and together with another Camelon man, John McMillan, his death sentence was reduced to transportation for life.

He was employed in Sydney, becoming 'Govt. Overseer' in 1822, and in 1825 as Principal Overseer of the Works at Newcastle, with a salary of £54 15/- a year. In 1822 he asked for his family to join him, but to date no record of their arrival has been found. It is believed that his wife Janet died before July 1834, as he married Agnes Mercer at Maitland, and died with no assets and in debt in 1839.

Robert Grey (1791- ?)

Born in Berwickshire, he was working in Glasgow as a weaver in 1820, when he joined the march to Carron. He was sentenced to transportation for life, and on his arrival in Australia, was employed as a servant to P A Mulgrave, along with Alexander Latimer. But in 1823 it was recorded that he was employed by Public Works and was also a schoolmaster in Hobart. Pardoned in 1828, he wrote to the Colonial Secretary in 1836, asking for a copy of his royal pardon.

Writing to John McMillan in March 1837, he complained about a lack of money, and took lodgings with William Rice, one of the York radicals who had been sent to New South Wales. The letter mentions he was about to 'leave for the Huon', but gives no further details. This could mean he moved to Tasmania, but there is no trace of him thereafter, nor is there any record of him having married or, indeed, of his death.

Alexander Hart (1794-1876)

Born at Old Kilpatrick, he became a cabinet-maker. At Bonnymuir he was wounded by a sabre cut that permanently scarred his forehead. On 2 September 1820, he wrote to his brother John in Glasgow, 'from Edinburgh Gaole', asking that he send him his tool-chest and drawing papers, so that he could take them to Australia with him.

He was employed, along with Andrew White, as a servant to Dr Henry Gratton Douglass, Superintendent of the General Hospital at Paramatta.' In May 1822, he married Bridget O'Heara, a convict, at St John's Parramatta, with Andrew White as a witness. In June 1825 he was granted a Ticket of Leave 'on the special order of the Governor.' This was later replaced by his Certificate of Freedom in December 1827.

The census of 1828 shows him working as a cabinet-maker in Sydney, with his wife, who was still listed as a convict. By 1831 he had a servant and stated he was happy to remain in Australia, and later lived at several addresses in Sydney. His niece, Margaret, arrived there in in 1841 and she later married a George Brown, and it was at their home in Elger Street, Glebe, that Alexander died on 28 March 1876, his wife having been admitted to the home for destitute women run by the Benevolent Society of New South Wales in 1860.

On his death in 1876, Rev John Dunmore Lang claimed he was the "last of the Bonnymuir Radicals of 1820." However, at that time John McMillan, who had been sentenced along with Hart, was still alive, but Lang was, it seems, drawing a distinction between those taken in arms at Bonnymuir and those, like McMillan, later arrested as being associated with the rising.

Alexander Johnston (1804-1867)

This Lanarkshire weaver who was working in Glasgow was only fifteen when he took part in the insurrection. His stiff resistance during the fight at Bonnymuir greatly impressed Lt Hodgson, who ordered a Yeoman who was trying to cut him down, to spare his life. At the trial at Stirling, his age did not save him and he was sentenced to death, later reduced to transportation for fourteen years.

In the Colony, he was assigned as a servant to the Commissary-General, Mr William Wemyss. By 1824 he was with George Lang of Parramatta, and a year later was assigned to William Lang of Sydney, and was there when he was granted a Ticket of Leave by the new Governor, Sir Thomas Brisbane in 1826,

Two years later he married Mary Newland, with Andrew Lang as a witness. His association with the Lang family was extensive: George and Andrew, along with Rev John Dunmore Lang, were the sons of William, and another of the Lang brothers had been Johnston's teacher in Lanarkshire.

By 1828 he was working as a carpenter in Sydney, where he and Mary brought up their family of seven sons and four daughters. In 1845, he is recorded as an innkeeper at Falbrook, Hunter's River, Sydney. Three years later the family had moved to Scone, where they ran the Woolpack Inn, and were all active in the Presbyterian church there. Alexander became Treasurer of the Committee of Management of the Benevolent Association of Scone.

In 1856 he bought a part of the St Aubins Estate, Scone, and became wealthy when he sold some of the properties. He gave land for the building of the Presbyterian Church and manse there. Despite his declining health, his wife and family helped him run the inn, and he secured a good education for his large family. His descendants were prominent in law, and two became judges, and one of them, David Gilbert Ferguson, was knighted in 1934. Gilbert had married Alexander's daughter Elizabeth, and his grandfather had, ironically, been a guard at Stirling Castle when the radicals were held there.

Alexander Johnston died at St Aubins, Scone on 21 May 1867.

Alexander Latimer (1795- ?)

A 25 year old Glasgow weaver, he was captured at Bonnymuir and sentenced to fourteen years transportation. He became a servant to P A Mulgrave in Sydney, together with Robert Gray.

They went with Mulgrave in 1821 when he moved to Hobart, and were recorded as being with him there in 1823. Thereafter, nothing else is known about him, and his pardon in 1839 was not collected, leading to the conclusion that he may have died before then.

Thomas McCulloch (1787-1863)

Born in Co. Down, Ireland, his family moved to Glasgow where he became a stocking maker. Many Presbyterians who had been involved in the Society of United Irishmen made their way to Scotland after the failure of the 1798 Rising: and Down had been one of the areas that had been prominent in the movement. While there is no evidence his family had been involved, the prosecution may have been trying to make such a connection by having him produced as the first of the 'rebels' at the Grand Jury at Stirling. He had marched to Bonnymuir with the other Glasgow radicals, where he was captured, and taken to Stirling Castle.

Sentenced to fourteen years, he became a servant to Captain Irwin, and wrote to his wife that he, and the other Radicals, were highly regarded by the people in the colony, and asking her to join him there. After writing an appeal to Lord Brisbane, he had his wife Sarah, and 2 sons, Thomas and Andrew Hardie, brought to Australia in 1823, and a daughter and another son were born there.

In 1833 he became the licensee of the Sydney Arms and began acquiring land in the area. In 1863 he died very wealthy, fulfilling his promise to his wife, when he had asked her to join him in the colony, that 'a steady man and woman can do well, as they are very rare articles found here.' His descendants became prominent in Australian society: Nea MacCulloch is a member of the Scottish Australian Heritage Council.

Thomas McFarlane (1775-1851?)

He was the oldest of the group and had been born in Glasgow and became a weaver. He married Elizabeth Baird and was living in Kilsyth when their first three children were born. A further three sons were born in Glasgow, but by 1809 when another son was born, the family had moved to Condorrat. Having been involved in radical politics from the 1790's, he joined John Baird on the march to Carron.

Severely wounded in the face by a sabre at Bonnymuir, he was sentenced to the colony for life. Assigned as a servant to Ensign McIntosh of the 73rd Regiment, he later moved to Simeon Lord and then became a labourer. Little is known about his life in Australia, other than he gained his pardon in 1839 and returned to Scotland soon after, where the 1841 census records a Thomas MacFarlane living with William MacFarlane at Condorrat. It seems that his wife died before he left New South Wales, and he returned home, where he resumed his trade, while living with his son.

The *Stirling Observer* reported that Airdrie Working Men's Association marched to Glenmavis to fete him, on 15 January 1840, soon after his return, because of his involvement in the rising and for his radical politics 'back to the days of Muir, Palmer and Gerald' and for his association with the Society of United Scotsmen. The following year, he sat beside Fergus O'Connor as guest of honour at he Chartist rally in Glasgow, and was present, 'with his sabre wound' as a reminder of the sacrifice of the men of 1820 as Gordon Pentland has pointed out, at the erection of the monument to the Radical Martyrs at Sighthill in 1847.

On his death about 1851, he was buried in Cumbernauld Parish churchyard, but there is no note of his burial in the church records, although there is a record of a Thomas MacFarlane aged 90, being buried in 1861, making identifying an accurate date of death problematic, and with reconstruction of the graveyard later in the century identifying his grave is impossible.

John McMillan (1793-1877)

Born in Falkirk he was living with his wife and family in Camelon, where he was working as a blacksmith and nailer. He was one of the eight radicals who were arrested there in the aftermath of the Bonnymuir campaign. At Stirling he was sentenced to transportation for life

As a skilled craftsman, he was employed in government service and on gaining his Certificate of Freedom set up business in Sydney. In 1832 he wrote to his wife advising her to prepare to move to New South Wales, where she would have servants, telling her that he had just bought 'another house' for £100 and employed three free men and two convicts. He warned her to trust no one, and to let the Scottish authorities know that 'I Would not Return to their Storm Guted Country if they Was to Mack Me Sheriff of Stirling.'

His wife Jane and daughters Jane and Mary left aboard the *Diana* on 11 December 1832 and joined him on 27 May 1833. His business grew and he expanded into other branches of metal-working, as well as becoming a publican. He wrote several letters to the Governor and Colonial Secretary, Sir George Gipps, pestering them to send the absolute pardon documents, and these were sent soon after. He was very active in the church, and particularly interested in education, becoming a trustee of the St Peter's Presbyterian Church School.

Having read Peter Mackenzie's exposure of the spy system, perhaps brought out to Australia by his wife, he sent his journal to Mackenzie, together with shackles, 'Radical Boots' as he called them, on 17 August 1834 for his information. Indeed as a collection of Peter Mackenzie's letters held in the William Patrick Library Kirkintilloch prove, he maintained contact with the historian for a number of years, sending him copies of documents, including the letter of Absolute Pardon granted to the Bonnymuir radicals.

In later life he bought land, one estate he named Thrushgrove, after the radical meeting place in Glasgow. In addition to a variety of business interests that included letting property, he farmed successfully living on his estate at Comely Park and cultivating the recently introduced oranges. He died on 28 August 1877 at the age of 84, his wife having died twenty-one years earlier, and he was buried in Devonshire Street Cemetery (later all the bodies were reinterred at Rookwood Cemetery).

He was the last of the radicals of 1820 to die.

Benjamin Moir (1786- ?)

Originally from Stirling, he was working as a labourer in Glasgow, where he stayed with his wife and two daughters in Green Street in the Calton. He was part of the Glasgow contingent that set out for Carron ironwork and was taken at Bonnymuir after the confrontation with the cavalry. Originally sentenced to death, his sentence was commuted to fourteen years transportation.

Assigned first to Sir John Jamieson he was later assigned to Dr H G Douglass, along with his wife, who had joined him in 1823, and they were employed to run a dairy for Douglass. They left his employ in October 1824, apparently owed money by his employer, and Benjamin was assigned to his wife Jane, who as a free woman could be assigned convicts as servants.

It seems that the former convict joined the police, as in August 1828 he was appointed as the constable at Windsor by the Governor. He is listed in this capacity in directories between 1834 and in 1837, but there is no record of him, or his family, thereafter.

Allan Barbour Murchie (1796-1866)

Originally from Dunfermline, he had moved to Glasgow where he worked as a blacksmith. Having fought at Bonnymuir, he was given a life sentence. While in prison in Stirling Castle, he wrote the song *Bonnymuir* that was sung to the tune *Hey! Johnnie Cope* by the prisoners. (see Appendix VI)

His father had his tools and some books sent to Australia in 1821, when he was working for the government in Emu Plains. His fiancé, Elizabeth Marshall, joined him in 1823 and they married in St James's Church, Sydney. They had seven children with two of the girls inheriting their father's writing abilities.

Originally a blacksmith, he is variously recorded over the years as baker, a dealer selling a range of goods, and a publican with two licenced premises in Sydney. Like other radicals sent to New South Wales, he turned misfortune into success, and by the time of his death in 1866 was a well-respected member of the community.

Thomas Pike (Pink) (1799- ?)

A Glasgow man, he is recorded as being a weaver or a muslin slinger. For his part in the insurrection he received a sentence of fourteen years.

In New South Wales, he was assigned to the Barrack Master along with Thomas MacFarlane, and was with him at least until 1825. In the November 1828 census he is recorded as being a miller, working for F Gerard of Sydney, to whom he may have gone after getting his Certificate of Freedom in December 1827. Thereafter there is no record of him, although he had collected his pardon in 1839.

William Smith (1779-1862)

Like Thomas MacCulloch he was Irish, but in 1820 was working as a weaver in Condorrat. It is unclear when he arrived in Scotland, and he was of age to have been 'out' in 1798, or at least aware of the circumstances of the Rising. Having become involved in reformist politics, he marched to Bonnymuir, where he was taken in arms and given a fourteen year sentence when his death sentence was commuted.

On his arrival he was appointed 'Overseer of the Female Factory' at Paramatta, for Rev Mr Marsden. In February 1822 he petitioned to have his wife, Lavinia, and children join him in the colony, as they were living in 'great distress' in Kilsyth. Admiral Fleming of Cumbernauld arranged to have his family join him, and Lavinia and two daughters arrived in early 1823. Two sons later joined them, William in late 1823. and James in 1830, and a third daughter, Elizabeth, was born at Paramatta in 1826.

He became 'Master Manufacturer of the Weaving Establishment' (salary £150) and proposed building a flax mill at Paramatta, but this did not materialise, in spite of Brisbane's support. Later Governor Darling granted him 320 acres in Northumberland, which his son used to set up a woollen manufactory.

William Smith died at Newtown in April 1862, and his descendants became prominent lawyers and educationists.

David Thompson (1798/8-1860)

Another radical Glasgow weaver, Thompson was given a fourteen year sentence for his part in the rising.

It seems he was unable to follow his trade in Australia, as he is recorded as being a shepherd. This was his occupation when listed in the return of convicts in 1821, and he was in service with Sir John Jamison at Penrith. The following year he was listed as being with G Collis at Windsor, and by 1825 at Cawdor with Dr Douglass, and was still there in December 1827 when he was granted a Certificate of Freedom.

The following year he was listed as being employed as a shepherd by Captain Barlow at Gundaroo and was still there in 1845, when he applied for a publican's licence to run a public house, the 'Traveller's Home.' His death certificate in June 1860 recorded his employment as 'shepherd', with no mention of him being a publican, although there is a note that he never married.

Andrew White (1804-1872)

White was only sixteen when he took part in the rising, and was living in Glasgow where he was apprenticed as a printer/book-binder. Sentenced to fourteen years, he was sent as a house servant to Dr Douglass, who had become unpopular with many of the settlers, who resented his aim of encouraging the welfare of the convicts that they used as cheap labour.

When in 1822, Dr Douglass was accused of acts of indecency against a young female convict, Ann Rumsby, by some of the leading citizens, White was a witness for the defence, corroborating, despite aggressive questioning, the girl's denial that anything had taken place. The magistrates, who also wanted rid of Douglass, preferring the account of their friends accused Ann of perjury and threatened to send her to the penal settlement at Port Macquarrie. Governor Brisbane wrote to Lord Bathurst defending the girl and Dr Douglass, explaining that the latter's service to the administration 'redounded to the honour of His Majesty's Government.' He then dismissed the five magistrates involved, set Ann free, and at the same time authorised her marriage to William Bragge.

In early 1824 Brisbane sent Dr Douglass to London to confer with the Colonial Office on the new court the Governor had set up, and to which he had appointed the Doctor as Commissioner. At the same time Brisbane granted an absolute pardon to Andrew White, twelve years before the other radicals, who was, it noted, to accompany Dr Douglass to London on his official business.

There is no record of White retuning to Australia with Douglass, and he may have remained behind when the doctor left. At some later date he returned to Glasgow where he resumed his trade as a printer and is recorded as living at 136 High St. In June 1849, he spoke at a reformist meeting in Birmingham's People's Hall about the 1820 Rising, as part of a campaign to secure the release of the Chartists sent to Australia after the Newport Rising in 1839.

He remained in Glasgow until his death in the Royal Infirmary on 20 November 1872. At his own request he was buried beside Baird and Hardie at Sighthill Cemetery. He and Thomas MacFarlane are the only two radical convicts who are known to have returned to Scotland.

James Wright (1798- ?)

This Glasgow radical has no recorded trade or occupation and, having been taken at Bonnymuir, was given a fourteen year sentence. According to his Certificate of Freedom, he had a number of tattoos on both arms; one showing a square and compass, which may indicate that he was a Freemason.

Employed by Dr Phillips and then Peter Cavanagh as 'a shopman', there is some evidence that he may have continued as a tailor afterwards, but details are scant. In 1827 he was granted a Certificate of Freedom, 'within the limits of this Government', but in 1834, he applied for a second Certificate of Freedom, which was unusual. It is possible that he had not at that time been granted his full pardon and wished to travel beyond 'the limits of this Government.' There may even be a chance that he returned to Scotland as there is no further record of him in Australia, but there is no evidence to prove this.

Conclusion

It is known that only two of the transported radicals returned to Scotland and that most of the others wanted to stay in the colony. The majority remained in Australia to make a new life and home there for themselves and their families. Some who were already married brought their family to join them, often assisted by friends at home, or sympathisers like Rear Admiral Fleming. Those who were unmarried frequently married convicts from the Female Factory and settled down in their new home. Most were successful and their descendants have made significant contributions to politics, the professions, and business life in Australia.

The reason for their success was a combination of factors. With one exception they were all trained craftsmen whose skills were required in the developing colony. They were educated at a time when few enjoyed the privilege, and so were in a position to contribute to the community; two of the Bonnymuir radicals became teachers. Most of the radical were active in their local church, won the respect of the authorities and established good relations with their neighbours, and some became senior members of their congregation.

They arrived at a propitious time, when the Governors had the foresight to recognise the possibilities of developing the prison settlement into a thriving colony. In the Scottish radical convicts, they found men with the skills to assist in doing just that, and with the tenacity to put these to use for the benefit of all. Among the free settlers, men like Dr Douglass were forward-thinking, and sought to look after the welfare of the convicts, not just to help them reform and improve their conditions, but to make of them useful citizens.

Finally, and perhaps most importantly, despite their convict status they were different from most of the other convicts as they were political prisoners rather than criminals. They were respected by other members of the community and by the authorities. And it is tempting to believe that as many of the senior officials in the colony at that time were Scots, they looked with favour on their fellow-countrymen.

11. 'BETRAYED BY INFAMOUS SPIES'

Ever since the publication of Peter Mackenzie's *Exposure of the Spy System* in 1832, controversy has raged over the involvement of government spies who informed on the radicals, and agents provocateur who, according to Mackenzie, actually set up the plot to entrap them.

> We are thoroughly convinced that Andrew Hardie and his unfortunate companions were the victims of *bloodthirsty scoundrels*, better known by the name of spies, who at that time infested this country, to the scandal - to the everlasting disgrace of its then government, by whom they were encouraged and protected.

Mackenzie believed that the strike and subsequent march to Carron were the work of people in government employ, whose role was to bring local radicals into the open so that they could be arrested and charged with treason. The actions of George Edwards, James Castles and J K Richards (aka William Oliver) in February 1820, in encouraging Arthur Thistlewood and his companions to attempt to assassinate the cabinet, had been quickly discovered to be a plot approved by the government. The main aim of the Cato Street Conspiracy was to portray the radicals as violent Jacobins, who would stop at nothing, including mass murder, to overthrow the constitution. Mackenzie saw a similar rationale behind the events later in 1820 in Scotland.

Almost at once, his views were denounced as anti-government propaganda and an attempt to portray as political martyrs, a group of desperate men who were prepared to take up arms to destroy the British constitution. This was not merely a Tory sentiment, but one shared by Whig reformists who, although advocating an extension of the franchise, had no intention of giving the vote to working men – the idea of women being given the vote probably never entered their minds. That the government had acted firmly and swiftly to suppress this French-style revolution would have allowed them to be seen as defenders of the constitution, saviours of the monarchy, and protectors of property: good publicity that was badly needed for Liverpool's unpopular government.

Informers

There is evidence that members of the public, like the residents of Cathkin House and the 'loyal citizens' of Strathaven, supplied information to the authorities. Such a one was the person calling himself 'A British Subject', who wrote to the Duke of Hamilton on 28 April providing details, albeit exaggerated, of events following the Greenock incident. He seems to have wanted a greater military presence to protect property, and hoped his information would achieve this.

Likewise, the factor at the Colzium Estate, who informed the authorities that Robert Gardner was a reformer and had him arrested, was acting partly out of revenge for having lost a legal case against Gardner, and partly out of a desire to be seen to want to suppress reform: he had earlier condemned a reformist meeting in Kilsyth.

Another informer, who doubtless saw himself as a good citizen, was the lawyer Robert Hodgart, who opened mail sent to the Paisley schoolmaster John Fraser to find the whereabouts of James Spiers, who had fled from Paisley soon after the general strike. That his illegal interference with the mail, which resulted in the arrest of both Spiers and Fraser on treason charges, was not regarded as a crime by the authorities clearly indicates that they were prepared to bend the law in pursuit of those they sought; or that they felt that the end justified the means.

Spies

But, relying on individuals to give information of events that they happened across as it was happening was not sufficient as the government was anxious to discover what was being planned at meetings of workers and reformers, and so sent agents to infiltrate and report on them.

As early as 1816, the Solicitor General, James Wedderburn, was receiving information about reform meetings in Glasgow from a number of unnamed sources. That same year, Captain James Brown, the Edinburgh police chief, travelled to Glasgow in disguise, where he attended reformist meetings, although he found nothing sinister happening. As the local police would have been recognised if they tried to get into meetings, the use of workers as informers was a viable alternative that was taken up by several officials. It was about that time George Biggar, a weaver, became a paid informed for Robert Hamilton, Sheriff of Lanarkshire.

Mackenzie gives an account of the recruitment of the former weaver Alexander Richmond by Kirkman Finlay to become his informer, and to report on the activities of radical groups in and around the city. Richmond, in turn, made use of John McLauchlane, a Calton weaver, and Macdowal Peat from Anderston, to report to him on the meetings they attended. Another member of this spy ring was the Calton weaver, George Biggar, who was already an informer for the Sheriff of Lanarkshire. Richmond had regular meetings with both Finlay, and the Town Clerk, James Reddie. But Mackenzie's accusations went further than that of spying, as he accused the authorities of using these spies, and others, to deliberately encourage the making of pikes and of hatching the plan for an armed rising throughout the central belt.

On 3 March 1817, another weaver, Alexander MacLaren, was tried on a charge of sedition for making a speech at a meeting in Kilmarnock in which he referred to 'the spirit of Bannockburn' and Scottish freedom, and a further charge of administering treasonable oaths. The shopkeeper Thomas Baird was similarly charged for publishing this speech. The jury found them guilty, but entered a plea for mercy on account of their previous good behaviour which Lord Gillies ignored and imposed sentences of six months imprisonment.

This case attracted political attention, with the opposition at Westminster claiming that government was using subterfuge to deliberately provoke unrest. Earl Grey, questioned the evidence in the case and told the House of Lords, on 16 June, that the basis for the trial lay with the authorities, as there was 'no longer any doubt that the alleged treasonable oaths were administered by hired spies and informers.'

In May, 67 year-old Rev Neil Douglas was reported as having used scripture to dishonour the Royal family, and was arrested. Wedderburn claiming it was 'improper' for ministers to use the pulpit to discuss political questions. In his defence speech, Francis Jeffrey pointed out that ministers were bound to refer to the civic as well as religious duties of their congregations, and were often expected to inform their congregations of government measures. When a jury found Douglas not guilty, Kirkman Finlay, was furious and condemned the perceived attack of the monarchy.

That spies were employed to infiltrate radical meetings is clear from several sources. The most important evidence comes from the correspondence, dated 29 October 1819, between Lord Advocate Sir William Rae and the Home Secretary Lord Sidmouth, that is held in the Devon Record Office. In these papers, the Lord Advocate explains that nothing material can be attempted by the Radicals without his prior knowledge, as he has 'two spies on the Secret Committee in Glasgow.' There are also two sheets justifying the use of spies. (Devon Record Office, Sidmouth Papers, 152M/C/1819/OH/39)

Alexander Richmond is perhaps the most obvious of these spies, and it was known at the time known that he who reported to the authorities in Glasgow at frequent intervals. James Anderson, writing in 1894, identified Richmond as the government spy who had stayed in the home of William Rodgers, secretary of the Airdrie Union Society in 1819. and he implied that he had encouraged the radicals meeting there to be more militant. In 1833, Richmond, having moved to England, sued the English distributors of *Tait's Magazine*, which had named him as a government, Lord Sidmouth.t spy, but lost his case, and was thereafter held in contempt by Scottish working class society.

While Richmond is the best known of the spies, far more effective was George Biggar, who was in the employ of the Sheriff of Lanarkshire, Robert Hamilton. He joined a number of radical societies and successfully worked his way onto the committee of several branches. He was instrumental in having the organising committee of the Thrushgrove meeting arrested. Another paid informer, but one with a lower profile, was James Logan, who passed information to the police chief at Ayr, although little has been recorded of his activities.

Agents Provocateur

Mackenzie was not alone in publicly accusing the government of having used spies to foment trouble with the aim of suppressing reform. In its edition of 1 January 1820, *Spirit of the Union* warned the public to be on their guard against being lured into trouble explaining,

> spies and incendiaries are abroad, and sent among you ... there is not a tap- room or pot-house in the metropolis, or scarcely in the country, without one or two of these worthies being in nightly attendance.

Gilbert McLeod, the editor of the *Spirit of the Union*, cited the example of an unnamed grocer in Hutchesontown who had been approached by two well-dressed men offering to sell him a pike head 'to defend his property', with the promise they could get more if he wanted. The grocer refused their kind offer, explaining he did not know how to use the weapon, and that his shop did not need defending. The men left, but the grocer got the impression that they were agents of the authorities trying to get him to buy weapons so that they could have him arrested. The newspaper ridiculed the blatant attempt to foment trouble, and suggested the public should not fall for this trick.

There were also claims that government deliberately used troops to provoke trouble. At a meeting of the Renfrewshire Political Union in October 1831, Mr Wallace of Kelly stated that troops had been brought into Paisley 'as formerly', to 'raise a commotion.' When this assertion was challenged by Sheriff John Dunlop, Wallace wrote, on 12 October, a highly critical letter about the earlier events.

I believe that persons in the confidence and employment of the Government were sent among the people to stir them up to mischief, and did stir them up to it in the years 1818 and 1819; and that troops were poured in at that time into all parts of the country at the request of the authorities – none of whom have ever contradicted the allegation, although a thousand times advanced, of hired spies and informers having betrayed the people into acts of insubordination.

He asked if Dunlop had knowledge of persons employed to spy on the people between 1818 and 1820, or of persons paid by Government for 'communication', or if he knew Alexander Richmond, or that he had been given a government pension.

In his reply, Dunlop denied all knowledge of a government spy system and answered 'no' to the first two questions, but admitted that he had heard of Richmond, but only through the press. He concluded by stressing that he and all the Sheriff Substitutes had acted properly and within the law, and that none had any knowledge of 'such a plot.'

Proof of the claim that agents were employed to incite trouble came from none other than Kirkman Finlay, who admitted to the *Glasgow Evening Post* in 1833 that he had paid 'three persons' to spy on meetings and 'stir up the people to revolt' in 1820. He particularly praised John King, by name, for his role in 'promoting action' at the meetings that he had infiltrated. While this can be interpreted as mere boasting after the event, the naming of King is of vital importance, for it is he who appears time and again in the events of 1820, from advocating violence during the general strike, to his role in the events leading to the Bonnymuir battle. The identity of Finlay's other two agents is not clear, but Craig and Turner figured prominently in distributing the Address with Lees, and in encouraging militant action among the Glasgow crowds assembled to read the notices and in other districts in the lead-up to the Rising.

Tom Devine has argued that the Address calling for the general strike was the work of 'three weavers from Parkhead in Glasgow rather than spies in the pay of the Crown', giving the lie to theories of a conspiracy to enable government to act against secret union societies. It has been suggested earlier that the references to English history are not sufficient proof that the author or authors were not Scots and could well have been local weavers, such as Turner, King and Lees. But the question then arises of what prompted the publication of a 'treasonable placard' at that particular time? If the perpetrators were members of the Organising Committee for a Provisional Government, then the authorities would have been expected to take drastic action against the members when they were apprehended, and their failure to do so has fuelled the fire of conspiracy theories.

Indeed, one of the enduring mysteries of this episode is the disappearance of the 28 members of the 'Organising Committee for a Provisional Government.' These men had been arrested by magistrates and police almost immediately after the spy John King left the meeting, but there is no record of any one of them having been apprehended. While James Mitchell informed Sidmouth of the arrests and his intention to keep it a secret to bring radicals into the open, there is no record of these leaders of a conspiracy to overthrow the government ever having faced trial, or being held in prison. Indeed, the police minute book for the period from March to August 1820 shows a normal series of meeting with only brief reference to 'disturbances.' The surprising absence of evidence in official records has led to the conclusion that there was a cover-up and that most, if not all, those arrested were agents working for the authorities, but unknown to each other. That the organisers of an armed rebellion would have been set free or even sent abroad without trial is unthinkable in view of the harsh sentences imposed later that year on the other participants who acted on their orders.

On the evening of the general strike John Craig was arrested by police as he was leading a group of armed men from Anderston towards Port Dundas, but when brought before the magistrate, Mr Houldsworth, only a fine was imposed, and this was paid by the magistrate himself, to allow Craig to be released. This raises the question of why the magistrate was so anxious to have Craig released when he was an obvious 'rebel' taken leading an armed group. The only logical answer is that Houldsworth knew who he was and what his plan had been– as is evidenced by there having been Hussars waiting at Port Dundas to capture radicals who they knew were coming that way – and had released him to allow him to continue with the scheme.

Clearly, agents were at work as the authorities were aware of what was about to happen, sometimes before the radicals themselves knew of the plan. This is most apparent in relation to the raid on Carron Ironworks, where Murray of Polmaise, commander of the Stirlingshire Yeomanry, sent troops on Tuesday 4 April to guard the factory from an attack that was expected the next day, when the Glasgow radicals were not told about the Carron plan until later that same evening. Likewise, Lieutenant Hodgson and the 10th Hussars having left Perth for Falkirk, were redirected from Stirling to Kilsyth to reinforce Lieutenant Davidson and the Kilsyth Troop of the Stirlingshire Yeomanry, who were waiting for the radicals on their way back from Carron.

Some days after the Address had been posted in Glasgow, a Sheriff Officer, Alexander Calder, tried to bribe one of William Lang's apprentices to swear that Lang had printed the Proclamation of the Provisional Government. His offer of £300 was turned down by the honest apprentice. Similarly, the smiths who had been asked to make pike-head by Sheriff Substitute Aiton of Hamilton, realised they were being led into a trap to have them charged with treason, and refused to make them.

Frequently the names of Turner, Lees and King figure large in the Radical War, thus making the case for a government conspiracy very strong. It was Duncan Turner who persuaded the Castle Street Union men that England was in arms and that they should set out for Carron, giving Andrew Hardie half of a card to match that held by the man at Condorrat who would lead the Radical 'army' there. Meanwhile, King/Andrews had made his way to Condorrat, where he gave John Baird the other half of the card and asked him to raise the local radicals and take command of the men from Glasgow. Baird's brother, Robert, had serious doubts about the man calling himself Andrews, and about the chances the small group that arrived had of success, but King persuaded John that others were on their way to join them, and a large radical group was waiting at Camelon that he was going ahead to meet.

Having left Condorrat, allegedly to bring reinforcements to join the radicals bound for Carron Ironworks, King's next appearance was near Radical Pend, and the Glasgow radical Keen, who had been sent with him, was not there. King explained that they became separated, but Keen was never seen again, leading to the suspicion that King had killed him at some point, and got rid of his body. Still convinced of his loyalty, Baird and the radicals followed King's instructions to wait on the hill out of sight of the road, while he brought the Camelon men to them, but shortly after his departure, the troops appeared and when Hodgson called on Baird, by name, to surrender, Hardie first suspected betrayal, as even he had not known his name until they met at Condorrat. During the Stirling trial, Hodgson testified that a 'gentleman' had directed him to the location of the radicals. That man could only have been King, as no other person had seen the men move up the hill or known where they were resting in a hollow out of sight of the road.

At Paisley, Lees convinced James Spiers to travel to Strathaven and get the local radicals to march on Glasgow, but had no success at Clydebank, where he faced lengthy questioning by local leaders that made him realise it was time to take his leave.

When the Strathaven radicals reached East Coldstream they were told that the rising had failed, and then at East Kilbride they discovered that troops had been waiting to ambush them, but had recently returned to Hamilton. This convinced James Wilson that the whole business was a plot to expose their numbers, and he returned home, although the remainder of his group travelled on to the Campsie Hills, before accepting that they had been set up.

John Anderson junior, son of the printer, who was arrested on charges of having printed the Address, claimed that his father had been persuaded to print it by Duncan Turner. He was held under special warrant until August, when he was escorted to a ship bound for the East Indies and given a government post there. It seems likely that rather than have Anderson testify and identify Turner as a government agent, Lord Sidmouth ensured his silence by bribery.

Conclusion

Over the intervening two centuries, there have been claims and coun-ter-claims about the government's use of spies to counter radical attempts to reform the franchise and the right of workers to form trade unions. The radicals have been portrayed by some as 'desperadoes who had no regard either to the laws of God or man', or, alternatively, as fools who were lured into armed conflict by persons who had no compunction about using them to advance their schemes for overthrowing the constitution. This last claim was made by some of the Kirk ministers when compiling the *New Statistical Account of Scotland* in the middle of the nineteenth century, although many others chose to ignore the rising completely.

Some have argued that the government would not have stooped to using agents provocateur to make radicals take up arms to reform the constitu-tion. Yet this is the same government that praised the Manchester and Salford Yeomanry for their actions at St Peters Field on 16 August 1819 when they killed eighteen men, women and children at a peaceful meeting, and wounded over 400 more. Government ministers greeted with approval the jury's deciding that four members of the Yeomanry tried in a civil case in April 1822 had acted justly 'to disperse an illegal gathering', and promptly arrested those responsible for organising the meeting and charged them with treason.

In early February 1820, Lords Liverpool and Sidmouth conspired with agents to encourage some radicals in an assassination attempt on the Cabinet at a dinner in Cato Street, despite there being no such meeting. The captured leaders of the conspirators were put on trial for treason in April, as the radical insurrection in Scotland was taking place, and they were executed on 1 May.

The government's actions to supress radicalism in England demonstrate that to some at least, and Sidmouth in particular, the use of spies to foment trouble that led to the identification, arrest and trial of radicals was not only justified, but a sensible means of identifying 'enemies of the state.' Similar action in Scotland would not have been unthinkable, particularly at the time of the Peterloo trial, and in view of the demand in the Address for a separate Scottish Parliament.

It has been pointed out that there is little in the way of documentary evidence to substantiate the claim that some government ministers deliberately instigated revolution with the aim of repressing the movement for reform. But the very absence of documents from the period has been seen as strengthening the case for the involvement of agents acting to incite trouble. That so many documents, particularly the record of the trials are lost, or were not held because they were not of 'sufficient importance', provides a strong, if circumstantial, case that the government did not want the public to have full knowledge of the methods it had employed to suppress popular opposition.

As a result, there remain several unanswered questions:

1.   What became of the Organising Committee arrested by police on 21 March? No records of their arrest or imprisonment, let alone their trial or punishment, have been discovered, despite exhaustive searches of record repositories over many years. Yet, of all those arrested in 1820, surely these, the planners behind the attack on the constitution were the most guilty, and deserving of severe punishment?

2.   Who were the authors of the Address calling for a general strike? Attempts by the government to place the blame on William Lang, to the extent of attempting to bribe two of his apprentices to give false evidence against him, when experts had earlier proved that the Address was printed by Duncan MacKenzie, would seem to confirm a plan to supress radicalism at any cost, by directing attention to the printer, and away from the author or authors, who may have been in the service of government, legal, or local authorities

3.   How did the military know to have troops waiting at Port Dundas for the Glasgow radicals on the evening of April 3? This could only have come from evidence by someone who knew the plan and betrayed

it to the authorities. That the magistrate, Mr Houldsworth, himself paid the fine he imposed on John Craig and immediately released this 'radical leader', would seem to confirm the theory that Craig was an agent whose role was to encourage radicals to take up arms and then lead them into a trap where they could be captured or killed, as a warning to others.

4. Where did Murray of Polamsie get the intelligence that there was to be a raid on Carron Ironworks on 5 April, before the radicals themselves had been informed, and that the radicals were to return to Glasgow via Kilsyth after the raid? The Major was able to send troops to defend the ironworks before the radicals in Glasgow knew that it was their target, and this information allowed him to direct Lt Hodgson to Kilsyth, where he knew the radicals intended to return from Falkirk. Again, this intelligence had to have come from someone with inside, and detailed, knowledge of the plan, i.e. a spy/agent who passed this intelligence on to the authorities.

5. Who was the 'gentleman' who met the troops at Bonnybridge and directed them to where the radicals were resting on the muir? That no attempt was made to find him and have him testify at the trials would indicate that the authorities were reluctant to have him identified, as this might provide proof of governmental manipulation of the radicals to have them arrested. Clearly, King was the only person known to have been there and who knew exactly where the men were resting, and the identity of their commander. His appearance at several critical points in the saga prove that he was deeply involved, as a spy or agent provocateur, or both, in enabling the authorities to crush the militant radicals in the west and centre of Scotland.

Finally, was the call for a general strike, and the encouragement given to the radicals to take up arms, a deliberate scheme by an unpopular, reactionary government to smash opposition and deter the lower classes from demanding rights which would threaten the power structure of the ruling elite? It is true the government and king had much to gain by deflecting public opinion away from the failings of the parliamentary system, and the sordid and embarrassing revelations about the royal family during the divorce proceedings, and action against 'rebels' threatening the country would ensure good publicity, especially with the assistance of a compliant press.

That Glasgow's police chief and the Home Secretary both chose to stress the creation of a Scots Parliament and the republican ideas of the reformers, would indicate an attempt to equate the Scottish Rising of 1820 with both the excesses of the French Revolution and the United Irishmen Rising of 1798, lending weight to the hypothesis that they were conducting a campaign to smear all reformists as violent revolutionaries. Public opinion had been shocked and horrified by the execution of the royal family and nobility in France, and propaganda warning that the same could happen in Britain stoked fear of change. At the same time, the influx of Irish immigrants at the end of the eighteenth century had prompted fear of a Catholic resurgence in Scotland, and the destruction of the Established Church. These were fears that government could play on. In this the support of the Church in Scotland could be relied upon and many ministers preached lengthy sermons against reform, condemning the radicals for disturbing the natural order, and warning congregations of eternal damnation and Hellfire for even contemplating change.

The truth is we will probably never know if agents were used. While the sacrifice of the radical martyrs in the cause of electoral freedom is commemorated, the events leading to their martyrdom is still shrouded in mystery. The evidence, if it ever existed, has disappeared and it remains to us only to recognise their contribution to our freedom. Within a century, the right to vote had been extended to all over the age of 21, women as well as men and women had been elected to Parliament at Westminster. Trade unions had become legal and were regarded as a normal and acceptable part of working life. It took longer for Scotland to have its own Parliament but before the bicentenary of the Rising, and the execution of those who sought such a body, the Scottish Parliament had been established and it has recognised the part played by Baird, Hardie, Wilson, and the men who were transported to Australia in helping bring this about.

12. POSTSCRIPT

The actions of the Scottish radicals had caused much alarm in Government circles, partly because there had been an armed rising that had challenged the military, and partly because they were seen as part of a more co-ordinated attempt at a rising that had involved cooperation with English radicals. The disturbances in Huddersfield, Sheffield, Halifax, Wigan, and elsewhere in April 1820 had been dealt with locally and, despite some of the marchers carrying weapons, had not led to armed confrontation with the military, whereas the insurrection in Scotland had necessitated the deployment of considerable numbers of troops.

Further, the English riots had been seen as confined to weavers and textile workers chiefly protesting at reduced wages at a time of economic distress. North of the border other trades, including smiths, tailors and bookbinders were represented, all of which had been involved in the general strike in the first few days of April. In addition, their demands were much more political and had gone much further, as in addition to demanding the right to vote and to form trade unions, they had demanded the creation of a separate Scottish Parliament. Even more disconcerting, to achieve these aims a number of men had been prepared to march in arms in an attempt to take over the armaments works at Falkirk. At the same time another band had set out for Glasgow from Strathaven to join radicals believed to be planning an attack on the city. All of which made the situation in Scotland seem much more dangerous.

The Scottish 'rebellion' that the government had anticipated for several months, was seen by Lord Sidmouth and the government as a more serious challenge to parliamentary authority than anything that had gone before. This accounts for the decision to use spies and agents provocateur to bring the radicals out into the open where they could be arrested, and for the draconian measures the government ordered to punish them. The trials were ordained to be conducted in accord with English Law, which was seen as more likely to secure convictions than Scots Law. They were to be show trials and followed by public executions for the purpose of instilling fear into the hearts of those who sought to change the political status quo. It is clear, however, from the repeated public protests in the days and weeks after Bonnymuir and from the reaction of the large crowds at the executions of the radical leaders that this plan had not proved particularly effective in suppressing opposition to the government, but rather had persuaded a more cautious approach in those still determined to achieve reform.

In late 1820, however, there was a recovery in trade that resulted in an increase in employment and better wages, which alleviated some of the worst grievances that had led to the original unrest. With the economic upturn bringing greater employment opportunities and leading to more secure incomes and better prospects, political reform became a less urgent issue for workers, and it was now the middle classes that sought to win the franchise. The new reformers were reluctant to turn directly to violence, preferring to work within the legal and constitutional system to win support for change. The economic boom lasted for almost five years and this, rather than the severe action of government, was the most important reason for a decline in radical activity in the years immediately following the Radical War.

The demand for a Scottish Parliament that had formed part of the 1820 Radical manifesto did, however, lead to Westminster politicians reconsidering their previous neglect of their northern neighbour and moves were made to recognise 'Scottishness.' In an attempt to distract the public from recent events and to offer a spectacle that would reflect well on the establishment, Lord Melville, Lord Liverpool's chief Scottish Minister, supported a plan proposed by Sir Walter Scott to have George IV visit Scotland: the first such state visit by a reigning monarch for over a century.

The arrival of the kilted king in his northern kingdom in 1822 led to the creation of 'Highland Societies' and began the Lowland love-affair with tartan. The kilt, which had previously been the symbol of Highland Clans and Jacobite sympathy, now became respectable and loyal Hanoverian-inclined nobles and lairds, who had previously shunned such garments, were quick to adopt the new 'national dress', thereby creating a new industry to provide tartan for a wealthy clientele. To commemorate the royal visit with a permanent memorial, Scott recruited unemployed weavers from the west of Scotland to pave a path round Salisbury Crags in Edinburgh: this became known as 'Radical Road.'

For a decade after the Radical War, there was little in the way of militant political agitation, other than a few 'old weaver orators' making occasional speeches that were generally ignored by the public. But one of the effects of the government's use of the spy system was to make people more suspicious of their neighbours, who might inform on them if they expressed criticism of the government or suggested constitutional change. The leadership of the radical movement had been shattered by the crackdown after Bonnymuir and critics of the system were viewed with suspicion, and the more extreme the language of the orator the greater the public suspicion of his intent.

One immediate effect of the failure of the insurrection was that working class energies were diverted into winning recognition for trade unions rather than into political action. This was seen as having a more immediate effect on their lives than changing the political system which would take longer to have an impact. There was also a move away from violence that carried over into the moral force wing of Chartism and even later agitation for the vote. Encouraged by the Kirk, people came to accept that 'respectability and restraint' were required and that improvement would come gradually and through the existing system, rather than through violence, militant action or drastic change. However, the lesson of working class solidarity was not completely lost, as the events of 1820 had demonstrated that different groups of workers could be brought together and put aside their occupational and religious differences to confront a corrupt political system.

By the second quarter of the nineteenth century, despite the crushing of the political aspirations of the lower classes, the workers had become more self-reliant. The Trustee Savings Bank movement, created in 1810 by Rev. Henry Duncan of Ruthwell in Dumfriesshire, to make banking available for working people to encourage saving to allow them to take responsibility for their future, gained momentum and branches opened in many towns for workers to save money on a regular basis. The movement spread rapidly and, together with the growth of friendly societies, gave greater financial security to many in the lower reaches of society. At the same time, those involved also became confident in their own abilities and more conscious that they had no role in making the laws that affected their lives, and consequently they looked for a means of getting the vote to solve their continuing social grievances.

Tory Reforms

The late 1820s saw a number of reforms by the Tory government designed, partly to alleviate some of the more oppressive legislation affecting the working class, and partly in response to Whig propaganda that successfully combined criticism of government sinecures and Catholic Emancipation with the extension of the franchise.

In 1824 the Combination Acts that had prevented public meetings and given magistrates the power to use the military to break up meetings that were deemed seditious, or of which they merely disapproved, were repealed. Scots, like the wealthy radical Joseph Hume and John McCulloch, editor of *The Scotsman*, had been prominent supporters of Francis Plaice, and they publicly welcomed what they regarded as progress towards greater democracy.

Further changes affecting Scots Law that had been advocated by the radical *Edinburgh Review*, were also enacted by parliament. These allowed jurors to be chosen by ballot, giving the accused the right to challenge the choice of juror, and reducing the penalty for sedition. In 1827, the Home Secretary, Sir Robert Peel, was persuaded to abolish capital punishment for many trivial offences

Perhaps the most significant reform was the passing of the Roman Catholic Relief Act of 1829. George IV had, albeit reluctantly, agreed to the repeal of the discriminatory Test and Corporation Acts the previous year which prepared the way for Peel and Wellington to grant Catholics the right to worship freely. In Scotland where there had previously been riots at the mere suggestion of any concessions to Catholics, repeal was greeted with large meetings of people across the religious divide showing support for the measure. With the influx of Irish, mainly but not exclusively, Catholic, Scots were prepared to tolerate the nationality and religion of the immigrants and, while religious tensions did not disappear, they became secondary to trade union and worker solidarity. In England opposition was stronger and the Relief Act led to the fall of Peel and the Wellington government.

As a corollary of greater religious freedom there was an expansion in education, particularly in denominational schools. This was not altogether altruistic but was as much a response to the needs of the new industries to recruit an educated, or at least literate workforce. Initially, however, the working class were unable to benefit as education was not free and for many families the priority was to have their children start work as soon as possible to supplement the family income. Over time, however, an educated working class emerged and it was more able to press the claim for greater political involvement.

The Tories reforming zeal did not, however, extend to changing the way that parliament was elected, as they agreed with Wellington's view that Britain had a 'matchless constitution' that did not need reforming The idea of parliamentary reform was not dead but took a new form and the leaders of this new movement were from the middle classes, who sought to gain a say in running the country that reflected their increasing economic and social power. These reformers were not men who were prepared to countenance the use of force when financial and social pressure could be brought to bear to achieve their ends.

The passing of the Catholic Relief Act was unpopular in England and led to the fall of the Tory government, and to the Whigs winning the election of 1830. By the late 1820s, there was a general feeling, especially among Whigs, that the electoral system was corrupt and in need of reform and even Tories were hard pressed to defend it. In his *History of the Working Classes in Scotland*, Tom Johnston quotes the Whig lawyer and politician Sir James Gibson Craig of Riccarton's depiction of the situation in Bute at election time in the early years of the nineteenth century.

> Mr Bannantyne, the Sheriff of Bute, got the writ for the
> election, named the day, and issued the precept for his own
> election; at the meeting he was the only freeholder present, so
> he voted himself to the chair, read himself the oaths against
> bribery, appointed himself clerk to the meeting, proposed
> himself as candidate, and declared himself elected. If he
> had any sense of humor, he must have capped the farce by
> proposing himself a vote of thanks, duly acknowledging the
> same to his own loud cheers.

During the reform campaign of 1830 to 1832 Whigs encouraged the working class to support their claim for an extension of the franchise, with the implication that they, the workers, would benefit. At meetings throughout the country the Whig speakers were cheered and supported by workers whose numbers swelled the crowds and impressed government by the surge in popular support for political change.

The Great Reform Act

The new Whig Prime Minister, Earl Grey, introduce a Bill in February 1831 to enfranchise the £10 burgh tenant and £10 county freeholder and rallies were organised to support the Bill, with thousands marching in Glasgow. When the House of Lords rejected the Bill there was outrage: at Hamilton, the Riot Act was read and cavalry charged the crowd; at Ayr the Tory MP had to be escorted from the town by troops; and Sir Walter Scott was barracked by weavers in Jedburgh. The Trades of Glasgow demanded the abolition of the House of Lords and the arming of the people to defend their rights, while violence erupted in Rothesay, Bo'ness and Montrose. There were strikes in Greenock and Falkirk and riots in several other towns, accompanied by a campaign of refusing to pay taxes. An attempt by the king to end the troubles by issuing a Proclamation ordering all Political Unions to disband was ignored and Whig organisers were believed to be prepared to instigate a workers' uprising.

Grey used the disturbances to persuade parliament to push through another Bill, basically the same as the earlier one, and this was passed by both Houses to become the 'Great' Reform Act of 1832. There was great rejoicing throughout the country that the right to vote had been extended, but this soon turned to disillusion and anger as it became clear that the change was limited to a few, rich people and excluded much of the middle class as well as the entire working class. The workers who had been encouraged by the new, moderate reformers to agitate for change and had been at the forefront of the more militant demonstrations gained nothing, as the Great Reform Act merely extended the right to vote to a few wealthy industrialists. Once in office, the middle classes espoused the belief that the vote should not be extended to the workers and adopted the earlier motto that those without property or an interest in the country had no right to have a say in how the country was governed.

Many of the disillusioned workers felt that they had been used by the middle classes for their own ends and that they should now concentrate on seeking change to allow them to strengthen trade unions in order to secure better wages and condition: matters that had a more immediate impact on their well-being. But the first step had been taken towards extending the franchise and with the growth of a wealthy and expanding middle class by mid-century, and a more educated and skilled working class later, it was inevitable that further reform would follow.

It is surprising that the Reform Bill was passed so soon after the Radical War, and, despite the disappointment of the workers that the 1832 Act did not grant them the right to vote it was a beginning and opened the road to further changes in the future. It could be argued that by taking up arms, the radicals of 1820, on both sides of the border had expedited change and their example was carried over into Chartism as the physical force element. That further political change was the result, meant the sacrifice of Baird, Hardie and Wilson was not altogether in vain, Andrew Hardie's mother did note in 1832 that her son had sacrificed his life for that cause.

However, the new Whig government was as uninclined to extend the franchise as the previous Tory one. The sense of betrayal, disillusion and anger felt by radicals is summed up in the poem 'A Radical Song', published in a collection of verses entitled *The Town's House on the Market Day*:

But Whigs grow Tories when "in Place",

And Tories, out, turn Whigs,

And I can tell them to their face

They're a' the same sow working class's pigs.

In spite of having won the support of the lower orders during the election campaign, the Whigs were prepared to introduce legislation that impacted heavily on the lower orders. In 1834, the Poor Law Amendment Act ended the traditional system of outdoor relief, replacing it with the workhouse system that forced those in need of help to enter institutions where conditions were designed to be harsh. The objective was to force people to stand on their own two feet and seek work by making 'charity' less attractive. The Act was implemented in response to the ideas of Thomas Malthus that population, unless checked, would increase faster than resources, and Henry Bentham's claim that people would rather live on poor relief than work. The new system quickly came to be hated and was seen as an attack on the poorest.

Another, often overlooked, piece of legislation but one that antagonised the poor, allowed the body of anyone who died in the poorhouse and whose body was not claimed by a relative to be given to the medical school for dissection. Designed to improve medical knowledge the Anatomy Act of 1832 (2&3 Will IV, c75) ruled that medical practitioners must study anatomy and to solve the problem of the severe shortage of cadavers and make the schools less reliant on the bodies of executed criminals, it decreed that any 'persons having lawful possession of a body' could donate it for 'anatomical examination', i.e. dissection. That any unclaimed bodies could be sent by the workhouse to a medical school, horrified workers, many of whom believed that their body had to remain whole for them to get to heaven. Those who had a miserable life on this earth were now, it seemed, to be denied an afterlife in heaven. This added to the stigma of the workhouse and was a source of worry for over a century: this Act was not repealed in England until 1983, and has never been repealed in Scotland, and was incorporated into the Human Tissues (Scotland) Act of 2006.

Disillusion, coupled with fear and hatred of the system spurred many workers to again support political action in an effort to improve their lot, and they threw their weight behind the new Chartist Movement.

Chartism

The Chartist Movement began in 1838 when the London Working Men's Association, led by William Lovett and Francis Place, drew up the 'People's Charter' to set out the aims of the reformers. It had six demands, many of which echoed the demands of the radicals of 1820: universal manhood suffrage, voting by secret ballot to prevent landowners taking action against tenants who rejected the landowner's candidate; annual elections to make parliament more accountable to the electorate, equal size constituencies, payment of MPs, and the abolition of the property qualification for MPs to allow workers to stand as candidates.

To achieve their aims Chartists set up committees in towns throughout the UK, and found a ready response in Scotland where the memory of 1820 was still strong. They even won support from some in the Church and ministers like Patrick Brewster of Paisley Abbey was a prominent supporter of reform, which led to him never being promoted to first charge of the Abbey, despite his popularity with the congregation.

As Gordon Pentland has demonstrated in his essay *Radical Returns in an Age of Revolutions* the Chartists were anxious to make the connection with earlier radical agitation. Thomas MacFarlane, 'the aged Bonnymuir martyr', was given a place of honour beside Fergus O'Connor, and presented with 'a handsome ebony staff, silver-mounted, and a sovereign to pay his expenses' when he attended the Chartist rally in Glasgow in 1841. Again, in 1847, he was present at the unveiling of the monument erected by the Chartists, to Baird, Hardie and Wilson at Thrushgrove, with his 'sabre wound' being mentioned in reports to show the connection of the Chartists with their radical 'pre-cursors.'

This identification with the militants of 1820 was not confined to Scotland. In 1849, the Bonnymuir Radical Andrew White, who appears to have become a Chartist to continue the cause for which he was transported in 1820, spoke at the rally in Birmingham on 9 June. There he demanded the release of the men sent to Australia as punishment for leading the Newport Rising of 1839. Having one of the transportees of the Radical Rising as a speaker emphasised the links between the two risings, and enabled the Chartists to claim that they were taking up the same cause. This desire to be associated with the 'Men of 1820' accounts for the erecting of monuments in places associated with the Radical Rising in the 1840s.

Although much was made of the important role that the men of 1820 had played in promoting the cause political and trade union freedom, change came about only gradually and with little in the way of serious violent action. The changing economic and social environment, coupled with the expansion of education over the succeeding century resulted in a gradual move towards democracy. Within a century of the Radical Rising the right to form trade unions was enshrine in law, and women as well as men had secure the right to vote, and before the centenary, women had been elected to parliament. The only demand of the radicals that had not been achieved was the creation of a Scottish parliament, and that was not attained for another half century.

What is more difficult to understand in light of the prominence given them by the Chartists, is why the sacrifice of the radicals of 1820 was not given any mention in the history of the growth of democracy in the United Kingdom. It is true that a few Independent Labour writers wrote about them at the start of the twentieth century but their works have long since gathered dust on library shelves, deemed too left-wing for educational purposes. In the 1960s, they were hailed as forerunners of those seeking Scottish independence and again were shunned by the establishment as too 'nationalistic' and not worthy of attention by 'serious' historians. The very idea of the events of 1820 being part of the history curriculum in Scottish universities and schools was anathema to those in authority and to head-teachers anxious not to upset the political establishment which regarded the events of 1820 as too radical to be studied, Even now, on the bicen-tenary of the Rising many have never heard of Baird, Hardie, Wilson and those transported for having sought rights that today is taken for granted – and, in the case of the vote, frequently not exercised.

In 2020, they will be remembered and honoured.

APPENDIX I: BRIEF BIOGRAPHIES OF THE MARTYRS

John Baird (Born 1 September 1790 - 8 September 1820)

The man who commanded the radical force in the Insurrection 1820, John Baird was born in Condorrat in the parish of Cumbernauld, and became a weaver and, lived in a house on the Airdrie Road.

During the French Revolutionary and Napoleonic Wars he enlisted in the British Army, joining the 2nd Battalion of the 95th Regiment of Foot (Rifle Brigade): a unit that was noted in official circles for its radical tendencies. He served for seven years and saw action overseas, first in Argentina and then in Portugal and latterly in Spain from 1808 to 1812 where he served under General Sir Thomas Moore during the Peninsular War. It was this military experience that was seen by the organisers of the insurrection as making him suited to be the commander of the radicals in their doomed march to take over the Carron Ironworks, and by the authorities as a dangerous threat that required drastic punishment to deter others similarly qualified.

When he was discharged he returned to Condorrat, living with his brother and his family and resumed his trade as a weaver. He became a member of the local Radical Society that was campaigning for better wages and conditions for workers, including the right to form trade unions, the extension of the right to vote and annual parliaments. This would have brought him to the attention of the authorities who were actively working to identify those they saw as possible troublemakers.

At the beginning of April he was persuaded by John King to lead the radical detachment that arrived in Condorrat from Glasgow to the Carron Ironworks. Despite his brother's reservations about the size of the force and uncertainty that there would be sufficient support forthcoming from Falkirk he agreed and led the men towards Falkirk.

At Bonnymuir when the cavalry approached he ordered the armed radicals to man the dyke and resist the attack, placing pikemen in the gap and those with firearms behind the wall. During his trial Lieutenant Hodgson of the 10th Hussars, who had confronted Baird after clearing the wall, commended his bravery during the brief, but 'fierce' resistance. Along with seventeen other radicals who were captured after the battle, he was taken to Stirling Castle but was separated from the others and held in chains. Taken to Edinburgh for interrogation he was lodged in the dungeons of the Castle for some weeks before returning to Stirling for trial.

After a trial at Stirling at which he was accused of being in arms and waging war against the king, he was sentenced to death and was hanged and beheaded in Broad Street on 8 September 1820 along with his second-in-command, Andrew Hardie. Together with James Clelland (who was later transported) they had seen military service and this would have made them more dangerous in the eyes of the authorities than the other radicals who had their sentences commuted to transportation.

His last words from the scaffold were,

> I do not mean to say much, only that what I have hitherto done, and which has brought me here, was for the cause of Truth and Justice.

Baird was 31 years of age and unmarried, but left two brothers and an aged father to lament his death. He is remembered in Condorrat where a plaque is mounted on the wall of his home in Airdrie Road and the local primary school is named after him: Baird Memorial School was opened in 1977. In 2011, a new memorial was erected beside Condorrat Library, with plaques in memory of Baird and the other Condorrat radicals of 1820, as well as those who lost their lives in the Auchengeich mining disaster of 1959, and in the two World wars.

Andrew Hardie (6 May 1793 – 8 September 1820)
Andrew Hardie was born in Auchinairn, but after his family moved to Glasgow he was educated there and became a weaver. When war broke

out with France he enlisted in the Berwick Militia and spent five years as a soldier, reaching the rank of sergeant. In the summer of 1815, he was discharged shortly after the battle of Waterloo and returned to the family home in High Street.

Like many weavers he was concerned about the deteriorating circumstances of his trade and the effect of industrialisation and became involved in politics. He became a member of the Castle Street Union Society, which was one of the many groups seeking reform of the franchise with the aim of improving the conditions of the working class, but he did not hold office in the organisation.

When the Proclamation was posted in Glasgow on 1 April he physically prevented its removal by a Justice of the Peace, James Hardie, and at his trial this was presented as evidence of his preparedness to use physical force in defence of his radical beliefs.

On 4 April he learned that there was to be a meeting that night at Germiston, and he went there, where he was told that the workers at Carron had taken over the ironworks and were waiting for a radical force to come for the weapons they had seized. But only 30 or 40 men were prepared to march to Carron as many others had doubts about the plan. After discussions with the Union Society leadership at Barony Church, and assured by Turner that reinforcements were on the way from Anderston and Camelon, he led his small group out of Glasgow, carrying half a card, the other half of which would be matched by a radical in Condorrat who would take command of the 'radical army.'

At Condorrat he met with John Baird and was appointed second-in-command of the force that was to Falkirk. Leaving at dawn they had breakfast at Castlecary before he went with a few men through Bonnybridge, while Baird took the main body along the towpath of the Forth and Clyde Canal. The two groups reformed at Radical Pend and moved to Bonnymuir, where, attacked by cavalry, they were taken prisoner after a skirmish with the troops.

At Stirling he was sentenced to death and was hanged and beheaded on Broad Street on September 8, along with John Baird. In his speech on the scaffold he declared,

Friends, I declare before God, I believe I die a martyr in the cause of Truth and Justice ... Please, after this is over, go quietly home and read the Bible, remembering the fate of Hardie and Baird,

He was 27 years of age and left an elderly, widowed mother and a sister. He was not married and wrote several letters to his girlfriend, Margaret McKeigh in the days before his execution. Thanks to Granny Duncan, the elderly lady who fed the prisoners and insane inmates at the castle, his written account of the rising was smuggled out in her porridge pot and later published.

When the Reform Act was passed in 1832, Mrs Hardie, Andrew's mother, placed a card in her window that read.

Britons, rejoice, Reform is won!

But 'twas the cause

lost me my son.

Originally buried in Stirling, in 1847 the remains of John Baird and Andrew Hardie were interred in a plot at Sighthill Cemetery in Springburn, Glasgow, which was then a private cemetery; it was not lawful to bury condemned criminals in public consecrated ground. In the same year Glasgow Chartists unveiled a memorial over their graves to commemorate their sacrifice, together with that of James Wilson who had been executed in Glasgow the same year.

James Wilson (3 September 1760 – 30 August 1820)
Born in Kirkyard Street, Strathaven in the parish of Avondale in Lanarkshire, he became a weaver and earned the nickname 'Purly' Wilson for having invented the machine for working the purl stitch. During the changes of the industrial revolution, he was employed in several other trades, and was for a time a tinsmith, a dentist, and repaired clocks and guns as well as training dogs.

He was sceptical of religion and particularly the control ministers had over the people and regarded himself as a free-thinker. With the House of Commons dominated by the landed class he disliked the government and favoured reform of the franchise to allow workers to have a say in the how the country was governed. He read Thomas Paine's *Rights of Man* and satirical publications like *The Black Dwarf* and *Cobbett's Register* and started campaigning for political reform.

Welcoming the French Revolution he hoped for change in Britain too and joined the Strathaven branch of the Society of the Friends of the People when it was it was set up by a group of Whigs. Although he and other workers were not at first very active, when the local landowner, the Duke of Hamilton, objected to the Society many members left and he became more active in maintaining the branch and was their delegate at the conventions. When the Friends of the People folded with outbreak of war with France Wilson preserved the local radical group to keep alive the idea of reform, and this expanded as soldiers returning from the French wars faced unemployment, and sought political change.

In 1816, he attended the great reformist meeting at Thrushgrove in Glasgow, where around 40,000 people assembled to demand an improvement to their social and political conditions. Like others who attended he became a target for government spies suspicious of the 'Jacobin' tendencies of anyone suggesting political reform.

On 1 April 1820 a notice from the alleged Provisional Government was posted in Glasgow and copes were taken to Strathaven where the local weavers and those from surrounding areas joined the strike. Four days later James Spiers arrived in the village with orders, allegedly from the Provisional Government, requesting the Strathaven radicals to take up arms. The next day, Wilson led a group, carrying a banner declaring, *Scotland Free or a Desart*, towards Glasgow.

Warned that troops had been waiting at East Kilbride he suspected a trap and decided to return home, although the others were keen to continue. He made his way back to Strathaven while the radical contingent carried on to Cathkin where they found there was no radical army and they too turned back

Shortly after returning home Wilson was arrested on a charge of high treason and taken to Hamilton before being transferred to Glasgow Jail to await trial. On 24 July 1820, he was found guilty of treason after proceedings before a Special Commission of Oyer and Terminer which he referred to as this 'mummery of a trial', and was sentenced to death. He made his political philosophy clear just before the judge pronounced sentence,

> I commit my sacred cause, which is that of Freedom, to the vindication of posterity ... I appeal to posterity for the justice which has in all ages and in all countries been accorded to those who have suffered martyrdom in the glorious cause of truth and liberty.

He was hanged and beheaded on 3 August 1820 and buried in the pauper's plot in Glasgow, but his family exhumed his body that night and had him buried in Strathaven with a funeral service which the authorities chose to turn a blind eye to. In 1846 a monument to Wilson was erected in the cemetery at Strathaven and his name is inscribed on the Martyrs' Monument in Sighthill Cemetery, close to where he had attended the 1816 Thrushgrove meeting.

The Radical Theme

In all three final speeches there are echoes of the last words of the radical lawyer Thomas Muir as he faced the court at the end of his trial for sedition in 1793,

> I have engaged in a good, a just, and a glorious cause – a cause which sooner or later must and will prevail: and by a timely reform save this nation from destruction.

Clearly the theme of the need for a change in the constitution to allow a wider representation of the people had not diminished in a generation, and the will to continue the struggle remained strong, in the face of government opposition.

APPENDIX II: Grand Juries

Prior to the prisoners being put on trial English Law required the prosecution to confirm that there was a case to answer, and for this the Crown evidence had to be presented to a Grand Jury of twenty-three men, who would decide if it was worthwhile taking the case to trial. This meant that there had to be a hearing in each of the areas where a trial was to be heard and a decision had to be made by the jurors in each location.

Stirling: 23 June

Foreman: Hon. George Abercromby

Sir Thomas Livingstone, Bart.	Sir James Riddell, Bart
Peter Spiers, Esq.	William Morehead, Esq.
Ninian Lewis, Esq	Samuel Cooper, Esq.
James Bruce, Esq.	George Callander, Esq
Francis Simpson, Esq.	Alexander Gartshore Stirling, Esq.
John Henderson, Doctor of Physic.	John Baird, Esq.
John Kincaid, Esq.	William Archibald Cadell, Esq.
Alexander Littlejohn, Esq.	Patrick Muschet, Doctor of Physic.
John Murray, Esq.	James Russell, Esq.
Duncan Robertson, Esq.	Joseph Stainton, Esq.
Thomas Campbell Haggart, Esq.	Alexander Ramsay, Esq.

Glasgow: 27 June

Foreman: Hugh Bogle Esq.

John Lang, Esq.

Norman Lockhart, Esq.

Patrick McAdam, Esq.

James Stewart, Esq.

David Sim, Esq.

William Pollock the Younger, Esq.

James Coutts Crawford, Esq.

James Bruce, Esq.

Archibald Lothan Cuthill, Esq.

Archibald Lamont, Esq.

John Rowat, Esq.

Humphrey Ewing McLae, Esq.

James Fyfe, Esq.

George Miller, Esq.

George More Nisbet, Esq.

Nathaniel Stevenson, Esq.

Archibald Kier, Esq.

Thomas Falconer, Esq.

Alexander Campbell the Younger, Esq.

James Gourlay, Esq.

David McHaffie, Esq.

James Hutton, Esq.

Dumbarton: 29 June

Foreman: Rear Admiral the Hon. Charles Elphinstone Fleming

John Buchanan, Gentleman

Robert McGown, Gentleman

John Mc Allister, Gentleman

Walter Duncan, Gentleman

John Grey of Sauchiehall, Esq

James Smith, Gentleman

George Shaw, Gentleman

John Goodwin, Merchant

John Grey of Bedcow, Gentleman

Charles Stewart, Gentleman

James McKean, Gentleman

James Dennistoun, Gentleman

David Arthur, Gentleman

Patrick Mitchell, Gentleman

John Freeland, Gentleman

Walter Aitken, Gentleman

John McKean, Gentleman

Alexander Corbet, Gentleman

John Paterson, Gentleman

Robert Stewart, Gentleman

John Gardner, Gentleman

William Calder, Gentleman

Paisley: 1 July

Foreman: Sir William Milliken Napier Bart.

William Mure, Esq.

James Stuart, Esq.

William Wilson the Younger, Esq.

Matthew Brown,, Esq.

Robert Wallace, Esq.

Charles Cunninghame, Esq.

Andrew Moody Esq.

John Hamilton ,Esq.

Adam Keir, Esq,

John Craig, Esq.

William Maxwell, Esq.

Henry Dunlop, Esq.

William Stewart, Esq.

William Carlile, Esq.

Quinton Leitch, Esq.

Robert Stewart, Esq.

James Watt, Esq.

Archibald Falconer, Esq.

Robert Barclay, Esq.

William King, Esq.

John Lowder, Esq.

Robert Cochrane, Esq.

Ayr: 4 July

Foreman: Sir James Montgomery Cunningham, Baronet

John Boyle, Esq

Robert Crawford, Esq

John Ferrier Hamilton, Esq

John Cunningham of Thornton, Esq

John Smith, Esq

John Cunningham of Carmelbank, Esq

Hugh Brown, Esq

William Neill, Esq

James Miller, Esq

William Heron, Esq

William Hay-Boyd, Esq

Captain James Shaw, Esq

Hugh Brown Younger, Esq

John McKindlay, Esq

James Cuthbert, Esq

John Andrew, Esq

James Porteus, Esq

William Wallace, Esq

William Rankine, Esq

James McCubbin, Esq

Robert Montgomerie, Esq

Robert Beaumont, Esq

APPENDIX III: Parliament and the Legal Establishment

In the nineteenth century it was common practice for members of the legal profession to become Members of Parliament. Under the old system, with its very restricted franchise, the government as well as certain landowners had the right to nominate the local MP, making it simple to install as MP for any vacant seat a member of the legal profession, especially those who had been elevated to the justiciary. It was not required that the MP should actually reside in or near the constituency that he supposedly represented with the result that several Scots found themselves MP for English and Irish boroughs.

By 1820, it was normal practice to appoint newly promoted Scottish judges to seats in Parliament and several members of the High Court of Justiciary had served as MPs. The members of the legal establishment involved in the trials were no exception and their parliamentary appointments are listed below.

Which raises the question of just how open they were to political change or to understanding the need for such change, and if their views were not so opposed to the cause for which the radicals had taken up arms that they were not capable of being objective when hearing the cases.

Lord Justice General James Graham, 3rd Duke of Montrose (1755-1836) represented the borough of Richmond from 1780 and then that of Great Bedwyn, in Wiltshire, from 1784, until he inherited the dukedom in 1790. In addition, he was appointed Lord Lieutenant of Stirlingshire in 1795, and of Dunbartonshire in 1813, holding both positions until his death in 1836.

Lord President of the Court of Session Charles Hope (1763-1851) had served as MP for Dumfries Burghs from July to December 1802, and as MP for Edinburgh, a seat in the gift of the Dundas family, from 1803 to 1805.

Lord Justice Clerk David Boyle (1772-1853) had been MP for Ayrshire from 1807 to 1811.

Lord Adam, William Adam of Blair Adam (1751-1839) was MP for Gatton, the most notorious of the English 'rotten boroughs' from 1774 to 1780, then represented Wigtown Burghs from 1780 to 1784, Elgin Burghs from 1884 to 1790, Ross-shire from 1790 to 1794 and Kincardineshire 1806 to 1812.

There is no detail of George Ferguson of Hermand (1743-1827), Adam Gillies of Gillies (1760-1842), David Moneypenny of Pitmilly (1769-1850), or Archibald Campbell of Succoth (1769-1846) having been appointed to Parliament, although the father, son and grandson of the last were MPs.

The Solicitor General Alexander Maconochie (1777-1861), who had prosecuted the organisers of the Thrushgrove meeting in 1817, was raised to the bench in 1818 as Lord Meadowbank. He had been the member for Yarmouth from 1811 to 1818, and then for Anstruther Burghs from 1818 to 1819.

Sir William Rae (1769-1842), the Lord Advocate who was responsible for bringing the charges against the radicals was, at the time of the trials, MP for Anstruther Burghs (1819-1826), and went on to be the member for Harwich from 1827 to 1830, Buteshire from 1830 to 1831, and again from 1833 to 1842, and from 1831 to 1833 was MP for Port Arlington in Ireland.

Sir Samuel Shepherd (1760-1840), former Solicitor General and Attorney General for England and Wales, who was appointed as Lord Chief Baron of the Scottish Exchequer in 1819, and as adviser to the Scottish Judiciary on English Law during the radical trials, had served as MP for Dorchester from 1814 to 1819.

Henry Monteith, Lord Provost of Glasgow at the time of the Rising, was later elected to parliament as the member for Linlithgow and served from 1820 to 1826 and again from 1830 to 1832.

Even the great defender of the radicals Francis Jeffrey (1773-1850), in spite of his Whig leanings, was to follow the footsteps of others who became judges and was the representative for Perth Burghs from January to March 1831, Malton from April to July the same year and then Perth Burgh from late 1831 to its abolition in 1832, when he became the MP for Edinburgh serving until 1834.

From the above, it is clear that many in the legal profession saw politics as a natural part of the system and would have had no reason to seek change. What is also demonstrated is that members frequently had no connection with the constituencies which they allegedly represented. It is obvious from the short periods which some served, and from the fact that their appointments were for places in England and Ireland, with which they had no connection, that their political function was not primarily that of representing the people of whom they were 'representatives', but rather to support the government.

APPENDIX IV: HARDIE'S ACCOUNT OF THE RISING

Andrew Hardie wrote an account of the events of the Glasgow Rising as he was awaiting execution. The papers were smuggled out of Stirling Castle by 'Granny' Duncan who, with her daughter, was responsible for feeding the prisoners. The condemned men were permitted to write to their relatives and friends, but some of the correspondence, this one especially, would not have been permitted. She attended Baird and Hardie in the days before their execution, and carried letters to and from the prisoners past the guards by hiding them in the bottom of the dish in which she brought their porridge.

This brief history was among the papers she brought from the castle in her pot, and it was given to John Fallon of Raploch, Stirling, who then forwarded it to Robert Goodwin in Glasgow, who had it published by P Walsh, 24, Greenbank Street, Rutherglen, at the end of 1820. Thanks to 'Granny' Duncan's ingenuity, and bravery, history has an account of the rising, from one of the leading radical participants.

Stirling Castle 1st August, 1820

My dear friends,

The following is an account of the whole of our proceedings to, and at the Battle of Bonnymuir & etc. I hope you will look over any repetition of sentiment, and the ungrammatical manner and style in which it is written, when you consider that while I was writing it, I was always in fear of being discovered, as it is against orders. I would very willingly write another copy, as I could make some improvements in it, both the subject and the writing, but I am afraid that they will suspect me by getting so much paper, and for these reasons, I hope you will not look upon it with the eye of a critic. Let it suffice to say, that it contains nothing but the truth. I could have dwelt much longer upon it, but for the above reasons, I made it as short and comprehensive as my weak ideas would permit. You will see by the ending of this, that I intend a continuation of it, as soon as I get paper and an opportunity.

I am, my dear friends, yours & etc,

A. Hardie

To Mr Robert Goodwin, Glasgow,

Care of Mr John Fallon, Raploch, Stirling.

On the 4th of April 1820 (the night I left Glasgow with two men, whose names I forbear to mention), we arrived at Germiston, where we found, as expected, a number of men in arms, whom I immediately joined, and after some delay, expecting some more, as we were told, from Anderston and other places (but which did not come forward), we got notice where we were to go, and received a very fine address from a man I did not know. I was made to understand the nature of our affair by the two men, and, likewise, that the whole city would be in arms in the course of an hour afterwards, and he who addressed us told us likewise; and that the coach would not be in the following morning; and that England was all in arms, from London downwards, and everything was going on beyond our most sanguine expectations; and declared that there were no soldiers to oppose us betwixt that and Edinburgh; and further that the whole was ready to receive us, and well armed, and that those that wanted would get arms by the road, refreshments and every thing necessary. I heard likewise through the course of the day, or early in the evening that there was going to be a turn-out, but I did not get information of the nature of it before our departure. I asked if there was no person going along with us who had instructions how to proceed, or take the charge of us. There was one Kean told me that there was a person with us who would give us every satisfaction, and had every necessary instruction for our proceedings, but that I might take command until we came to Condorrat, where we would be joined by a party of fifty or sixty men, and get one there to take command of the whole; but this I did not assume until we came within a mile of Condorrat, when we halted, and proposed to form ourselves in regular order, and I was appointed by the men themselves to do this, which I did by forming the front and rear rank, and sized them accordingly, and likewise numbered them the same as a guard; my reason for doing was because we were strangers to one and other, and did not know our names, that if anything was wanted, we might answer by our numbers. After this was done, I led the party and went before them (with Kean) to find out Mr Baird, and when we found him, there was one King had been waiting with him, upon us coming forward. This King belongs to Glasgow, but what he is I do not know, but this I know, that he acted a very unbecoming part with us. King had told Baird that there was a party of two hundred well armed men coming out, and that they were all old soldiers. When I arrived at Condorrat with Kean, I did not stop with him and Mr Baird, but joined the party, and went in to a public house to get refreshments, which consisted of one glass of whisky, and a bit of bread. Now during the time we (the party) were in the public house, one of them told Mr Baird a quite different story than which we were made to believe, and apologised for the smallness of our party, by saying that the Anderston party & etc. had mistaken the road, and had gone by Airdrie; he likewise said that there was a party gone to Hamilton to stop the coach there. But to proceed, after some time was spent in fixing pike heads & etc. we proceeded on, but in place of being joined by fifty or sixty men, I think we got only six, but had a sufficient force come from Glasgow, it would have been far otherwise; yet it was quite reasonable for people to decline from coming out, when such a small force could only be brought from Glasgow. Yet, in consequence of this great disappointment, we were not at all discouraged, but proceeded on in the most orderly manner. After we left Condorrat, our first halt was at Castlecary Bridge, where we received half a bottle of porter, and a penny worth of bread each man, which was paid for, and a receipt obtained for the same. We again proceeded, but I should have observed before this that King left us at Condorrat, and went before on the pretext of getting the Camelon and Falkirk people ready by the time we should be forward, and in case we should miss them, or the party that was to meet us, I, with other four or five stout men, went by the road and the main party went by the canal bank. The first we met, after leaving the main party, was a gentleman on horseback, whom we, in a very civil manner, asked if he was going to Glasgow – he answered in the affirmative; we then told him (as we were made to believe ourselves) that there was sad work going on there, and advised him to turn, but he did not turn at that time; however, in a short time he came past us, and told us he would take our advice. We went into a house, a little way off the road, and got a fowling piece, for which we offered a receipt, but it was not accepted; the gentleman to whom it belonged was very civil, and did not say much against us taking it away, and asked when he should get it back. Soon after we came upon the road again we saw a Hussar at a little distance; upon this we drew ourselves upon the road, and called to him to halt, which he did immediately; we then agreed that we should do him no *harm, and desired him to come forward which he did, and stopped when he came up to us, and told a very good story that he was a friend of our cause, that he was a weaver, and had a wife and five children & etc. I told him it was no matter what he was, we should do him no harm; he answered every question we put to him very correctly; he said he was going to Kilsyth, and that he had fallen behind his detachment. Henderson then gave him one of the addresses, and some conversation passed, which I do not remember, and we let him pass. We proceeded along the road about a mile and a half past Bonnybridge, where we got a signal from the party on the bank to join them, for King had come to them and said, that we should have to go up on the moor and wait there until we got reinforcements from Camelon; the whole of us turned and went through an aqueduct bridge, and went up about a mile into the moor, and sat down on the top of a hill, and rested (I think) about an hour, when the cavalry made their appearance; upon this we started upon our feet, and at once resolved to meet them. I proposed forming a square where we were, but Mr Baird said it would be much better to go under cover of a dyke, which was not far distant; we then immediately ran down the hill, cheering, and took up our positions. There was a slap in the dyke, which we filled with pikemen. The cavalry took a circular course through the moor, and came under cover of a wood at our right flank. As soon a they made their appearance past the end of the wood, firing commenced immediately – I cannot say who commenced firing. I think the cavalry had fired a shot or two before they came to the wood, with intention, probably, to frighten us, for they afterwards told us they did not expect we would face them. However, this is a matter of no importance. They came right up to the dyke – the Hussars in front led by their officer, who called out to us to lay down our arms, but this was not agreed to. After firing some shots at us, they made an attack on the slap, and got through, but were repulsed and driven back. They, in general, stood a little distance from the dyke, so that our pikes were rendered unserviceable. One of the Hussars came close up to the dyke, a little to the right of where I stood, and one of our party made a stab at him. The Hussar fired at him in return, and he fell forward on his face. They made a second attack on the slap, and got through, but were kept at bay in the inside and the officer again called on us to surrender, and he would do us no harm, which most of the men took for granted, and threw down their arms and ran. (It will be here necessary to observe, that some of our men never came into action at all, but made their way into a wood at some distance.) But those that tried to make their escape after our surrender, (viz. after the officer had called out the second time, and by this time was on the inside, our side of the dyke) were instantly pursued,* but were not all taken, and some of them wounded in a most shocking manner; and it was truly unbecoming the character of a British soldier to wound, or try to kill any man, when he had it in his power to take him prisoner, and when they had no arms to make any defence. One of the Yeomanry was so inhuman, after he had sabred one of the men sufficient, as he thought, to deprive him of life, as to trample him under his horse's feet; but here, my friends, the horse had more humanity than his master, and would not do as he wished, but jumped over him, in place of trampling upon the wounded and mangled body; and after he had returned from doing so, he called out (speaking very broad) that he had left him lying wi' his head cloven like a pot. There were several others wounded, but I will not say any more about them, as I suppose you have heard all particulars long before this. Mr Baird defended himself in a most gallant manner; after discharging his piece, he presented it at the officer empty, and told him he would do for him if he did not stand off. The officer presented his pistol at him, but it flashed and did not go off. Mr B. then took the butt end of his piece and struck a private on the left thigh, whereupon the sergeant of the Hussars fired at him; Mr B. then threw his musket from him, and seized a pike, and, while the sergeant was in the act of drawing his sword, wounded him in the right arm and side. Before this the officer was wounded in the right hand, and his horse was also wounded; yet notwithstanding, he would not allow one of his men to do us any harm, and actually kept off, with his own sword some of the strokes that were aimed against us. One of the Hussars recognised one of our party who, he said, had wounded this officer, and would have instantly sabred him, had not the officer speedily interfered, and told him there was too much done already. Although my enemy, I do him nothing but justice by saying that he is a brave and generous man; he came up in front of his men, and I am truly happy (but surprised) that he was not killed, as I know that there were several shots fired at him. After the wounded men, and those who had tried to make their escape, were all brought together, we were taken off the moor. Mr Baird and I assisted one of the wounded men, until we got a cart and were put into it; one of them was dreadfully wounded in the head, I think in four places, and shot through the arm. Another old man, with a frightful looking wound in has face, so much so that his jaw bone was seen perfectly distinct; and the third with a sabre wound on his head; and two or more left on the field for dead; but I was truly happy to hear afterwards that it was not so, but that they had recovered and got safe off. The officer of the Hussars asked who was our captain and if his name was Baird, which made it evident, that some person who knew him, had given them information. We were all very fatigued by being up all night, and having got no victuals but what is before mentioned, viz. a penny loaf and a drink of porter, we made application to the officer of the Yeomanry to halt and let us get a drink of water, but Alas! that small favour could not be granted, - you must observe that the officer of the Hussars was at that time absent, getting another horse, as his was so wounded that it could carry him no farther; when he came up to us he granted our request immediately. After we arrived at Stirling, we were all put into one room, and being uncommon tired, it was not long before the most of us buried all our cares in a sound sleep, having previously obtained some bread and water. Mr Baird and I went to bed together, but he was taken away from us shortly after, and put in a dungeon, and had about four or five stones of irons put upon him. After being at Stirling Castle a day or two, we were all examined, and on being asked the reason why I was in arms, I told them I went out with the intention to recover my rights; they then asked me what rights I wanted? I said annual parliaments and elections by ballot. Question – what reason had you to expect those rights? Answer – because I think Government ought to grant whatever the majority of the nation requested, and if they had paid attention to the people's lawful petitions, the nation would not have been in the state that it at present was, or words to this purpose; but this last part of my answer they did not think proper to put down; when I told them so, they looked at one another, but said nothing. A number of other questions were put to me, which are not worth notice. Concerning our proceedings on the road & etc. I was examined time after time; after we were taken to Edinburgh, and everything that took place on the road was put to me precisely as they had happened, which at once led me to understand that **** had told all that was transacted; he had made no less that fourteen pages of declaration before we left Stirling, beside what he gave in Edinburgh, which I suppose was much more. I knew well that he told all he could concerning me, by the questions asked at my examinations, and I was told by a soldier on sentry in the new jail that one of us had turned King's evidence, and well I knew who it was; but after they had made him their tool, and got all they wanted out of him, they have, to all appearances turned him over with the rest, which was not what he expected for he told since he came to this Castle, a few days before our trial, that Captain Sibbald was to get him work in Edinburgh. I allow that we were very justly examined, as they told us not to answer any questions but as we choosed ourselves; but, on the other hand, I was plied with unwearied importunity by Captain Sibbald, which was not his duty to do, but he might as well have saved himself the trouble, for I would not tell him a word, although he foretold me my fate; neither did I in my declaration about what passed on the road, because I knew it was all told before they asked me. I will not trouble you with an account of my imprisonment, but shall close this long letter with a few observations on my trial and witnesses. The first in order is Mr Hardie; it is not at all necessary that I should give you the sum of his evidence, and I do not deny preventing him from taking down the bill and asking him his authority for doing so; neither shall I mention the abusive language he gave to me, nor what I said to him. But as I have a good and just God to answer, and to whom I must give an account of my actions, in a very short time, I hope you will form a more favourable opinion of me than to think I would tell you any lies. He said that I had seized him by the collar and driven him off the pavement twice, but it is very strange that I mind all that passed and cannot charge my memory with doing so, and yet two other witnesses corroborated his evidence. I remember perfectly well of telling Mr Stirling that I knew his principles, and that he was taking up arms against those from whom he had his bread, or words to that effect. And likewise of Mr Anderson, that he had said in a certain house that the Radicals were going to plunder and divide property and etc. and that he was supported by the Government, or perhaps his opinions would be the same as mine. But driving Mr Hardie off the pavement is entirely out of the question; but according to his own statement, there were about thirty persons there, and I trust that some of them will have in their remembrance all that passed. The next I shall mention is Hugh Nicol Baird, of the Kilsyth Yeomanry Cavalry, who actually swore that he met ten or twelve of us on the road, and that we demanded his arms, and he, in return, presented his pistol at us, and said he would give us the contents of it before he would do so. In the name of common sense, what could tempt this coxcomb to swear a notorious lie as this to face and frighten ten or twelve well armed men; he is worthy of being classed with Sir William Wallace. I am astonished that after such a feat, he did not petition the officer of Hussars to fight the whole of us on the moor himself; but he had done enough for one day. But the truth of the matter is this, we never saw him on the road at all. He had got notice of our approach and putting more confidence in the swiftness of his horse than his own valour, had either turned or hid himself until we passed; and I understand there are about twenty people who could testify that he did not pass until we were off the road altogether. How different was the evidence of the Hussar from this Don Quixote, who told the truth and stated our number to be five or six, yet he had more policy than to offer to attack us, and very prudently capitulated with us, and told us, after we were taken prisoner, that he thought we were a set of damned dangerous looking fellows; and yet this imaginary hero, i.e. the Yeoman, identified me, the prisoner at the bar, as one of the party! I was more than astonished when I saw him come forward and assert such falsehoods, and went immediately and told one of my counsel that it was altogether lies. I saw the newspapers (when I was in the steamboat going to Edinburgh) an exaggerated account of the battle, stating our numbers to have been about 100; but if there had been that number, I am of the opinion that I should not be sitting here, this day, a solitary prisoner, under sentence of death. But the truth is, there were only 24 or 26 of us, and there were three or four who never came forward at all, so by that means our number was reduced to about 20; and although those men had come forward, they would have been of little service, as I believe they had no arms, for I remember there were two or three without arms, and in all probability it was these that did not come forward. The numbers of the Hussars and Yeomanry cavalry were, I think, according to the officer's own statement, 32; yet they found some difficulty in subduing us. The paper gave an account of us meeting a yeoman on the road, and likewise the Hussar, which made me think that the gentleman whom we first met had been him, as he had a tartan cover on, and saddle bags, and I thought he might have been armed and in regimentals, although unseen to us, as his tartan cloak was sufficient to cover them; yet I am certain it was not so, for that gentleman was a lusty, stout man – but the Kilsyth hero was quite the contrary; so I shall now leave this son of Mars. You will observe that I promised to give you some observations on my Trial, but this I think unnecessary, as no doubt, it will be handled by an abler pen than mine; and as the short time allowed me is drawing to a close, and as I have matter of much greater importance to take up my attention, I shall now confine myself to a few observations. You will be curious no doubt, to know what views I now entertain of those principles which induced me to take up arms.

My suffering countrymen! As I am within view of being hurried into the presence of my Almighty Judge, I remain under the firm conviction that I die a Martyr in the Cause of Truth and Justice, and in the hope that you will soon succeed in the cause which I took up arms to defend; and I protest, as a dying man, that although we were outwitted and betrayed, it was done with a good intention on my part, and I may safely speak for the whole of those who are here in the Castle, that they are in the same mind; I have had several interviews with them, and I was happy to find them all firm to the cause. I intended to speak at some length on the scaffold, but I have changed my opinion on that point, as I am a little quick of temper, and more particularly when I enter upon that subject; I have found by experience, when I entered upon politics with some of the clergymen who visited me, particularly one who introduced the subject of the French Revolution, and tried to point out the fatal effects arising from it, I was completely nettled at this, and *was much the worse for his visit; as it took me some pains to get it erased from my mind; neither do I think it proper for a person so near to eternity to enter upon these matters. However, I may speak a few words – farewell, my suffering countrymen; may God send you a speedy deliverance from your oppression, is the earnest prayer of yours,*

Andrew Hardie

APPENDIX V: LETTERS FROM RADICALS

John Barr to his brother and sister

Stirling Castle 17 July 1820

To Andrew Barr

Bells hill

by Holy town

Dear Brother and Sister,

I write you an answer to yours of date 4th and have received no letter from you since. No doubt you will have heard of the proceedings which I have gone through since I wrote you last; but to let you know a little of that proceedings; on the thirteenth we were placed at earthly Tribunal at 9 o'clock a.m. and a carle of the name of Andrew Hardie was first to the barr and he pleaded not guilty and after a large trial which lasted until 2 o'clock next morning was found guilty and on the 14th we were again put to the barr when John Baird also pleaded not guilty and after a long trial was found guilty and on the 19th we were again put to the barr and by the advice of our council the rest of us pleaded guilty and then we were dismissed from the court and now wait our Sentences; I am very happy that you delayed to come here as you would not have got in to see me; but I have received information this day that our friends will be admitted to visit us twice a week namely on Wednesdays and Thursdays at 10 o'clock and you may take your own means of coming here. Not I am very much obliged for the trouble that you have taken in my behalf and I would also write you to act a little more by agents dong every thing in our favour and if you could use any influence with General Bailie to get him to use some influence with any of his aquaintances of the higher circles will be very much respected in this case of our and any thing that you may get either to forward them to the agents that is acting for us and the directions you will put upon them ie – Mr David Blackie writer to the signet of 13 Albion Street Edinburgh – and if you would be so good as to write me and (damaged) me know how you are and also your wife; this leaving me in good health and hoping they will find you in the same and you will be so good as forward the formerly issued articles as soon as possible as there is no time to loose; I am also still of the same mind putting my trust in God knowing that he is able to save even until the very uttermost and able to support and redeem all aflictions and trials. I add no more.

Your

Affectionate but concerned

Brother

John Barr

P.S. give very best respects to all enquiring friends and aquaintances

Postmarked Glasgow 20 July 1820

Alexander Hart to his brother

The Convict Ship Speke,

London

11 December 1820

Dear brother,

I now write to you from the convict ship which I entered yesterday and I can form but a faint idea of what this place will be, yet I may state there are 9 men and 10 boys in the apartment and we will only remain here about a fortnight or so in order that we may send word to our friends and get word from them. I have been in a miserable condition this some time back. I do not know whether I will be any better or not but I am happy at leaving the hulk for I assure you that they are no better than they are called … we had a good character from the Bellerophon. the minister invited us to take part in the sacrament at Christmas a thing quite unusual in the ship but as he says himself would leap the hedge to the Scotch Reformers seven of us gave in our names all except Clarkson and Thomson but now that the Bay ship having come he said in his address to us the last night we was before him he stated that him his wife and Captain Owen some pain that we would not sit in communion with them but would pray for us and hoped we would do likewise … Dear Brother I do not know if you will can read this letter or not there is 10 boys here in this small place and I assure you you can form no idea of such wretches as they are it is of no … to speak to them I scarcely know what I am writing however if I can get any better convenience I will write another before I leave this I hope you will write me before I leave this and give some news about my friends as it will be a long time before I hear from you again.

Andrew Hart

John Baird to his brother;

Edinburgh Castle

5 June 1820

Dear Brother,

I received your kind and welcome letter dated 9th of May and I wrote you shortly after, but I understand by Thomas Cowie's letter that it has not come to your hand; so I have wrote you again. You wished to know if I was in possession of a Bible; I got one as soon as I was admitted to the Castle, and I spend a good deal of my time in scanning its pages. I hope you will all study as much as possible against grieving on my account, for you can do no good by sorrow for me, but ill for yourself. I am well looked after; I am visited eight times a day, and sometimes oftener; I am in a cell by myself; the precognitions are not yet closed; I will let you know as soon as you can to see me. I am very sorry that you did not get the last letter that I sent off on purposes for you; there was something in it that that I wished an answer to; but it has gone out of the way. I imagine, on that account., it can do little good to them that kept it, and it can do little ill to me that lost it; but it is keeping you out of an answer to your letter; however, we must put up with disappointments; there is no certainty in the things of this world. I wrote, my brother, Robert, but I have never got an answer from him. You may let my father and friends know that I am wel. No more at present from,

Your affectionate friend

John Baird

N.B. I took it very kind in your franking your letter – when I came here I could not have paid for one; my money was all taken from me in Stirling and kept up. The high powers do as they please, and I dare not say what doest thou.

Yours

John Baird

John Baird to Daniel Taylor of Kilsyth:

Stirling Castle

September 4 1820

Dear Friend,

I take this opportunity of sending you my long and last farewell. On Friday I am to be made immortal. Although man may mangle my body, yet blessed be God, he has kept the most noble part in his own hand. I do not mean to say anything about them who have been so sore against me, for I have made it my study to forget and forgive all men any wrong that they have done to me. I received your kind and welcome letter. It cheered my very heart to think that you will go so far as to see my grave; and it gave me some consolation to hear you say you will write my dirge. All this, you have said, I hope you will do. It gives me no small concern to think that any person blames you concerning me; that I never could do; I look on you still as my trusted friend; but you know men oft are blamed, when they are not worthy of it. I hope that you will let all animosity cease, and let love and harmony abound, is the sincere wish of your dying friend.

Let troubles rise and tyrants rage,

And days of darkness fall;

But those who wait upon the Lord,

Shall more than conquer all.

"If God be for us, who can stand against us?" "It is God that justifieth, who is he that can condemn?" No more from your dying friend, a martyr to the cause of liberty. May the grace of God protect you and yours. Give my kind love to all friends of liberty.

John Baird

On the same letter, is written:

Dear Sir,

This comes from a hand you never saw, to the best of my knowledge -from a hand that in a few days must mingle with its native dust. Hard is our fate, my dear unknown friend; yet, I resign my life without the least reluctance, knowing that it is for the cause of truth and justice; and to the which I remain under conviction. I die a martyr –

" I die firm in the cause, like a magnet to its pole,

With undaunted spirit and unshaken soul."

My dear friend, I must bid you farewell; and I hope you will keep in your remembrance the cause for which Baird, Hardie and Cleland died on the scaffold. No more, farewell.

I am, sir, your most obedient servant,

Andrew Hardie.

P.S. Since writing this, I am happy to announce that Cleland has got a respite.

Andrew Hardie to his fiancée, Margaret MacKeigh

Stirling Castle

September 7ᵗʰ 1820

My dear and loving Margaret,

Before this arrives at your hand I will be made immortal, and will be, I trust, singing praises to God and the Lamb, amongst the spirits of just men made perfect, through the blood of our Lord and Saviour, Jesus Christ, whose all-sufficient merits are infinitely unbounded, then even all the sins of a sinful world -and he is able and willing to save to the uttermost all those who are enabled to come to him by faith in his blood. What consolation does this render to me, who, while writing this, and within a few short hours of launching into eternity, where I am not afraid to enter, although a poor, unworthy, miserable sinner, and not worthy of the least of this notice. Yet I trust he will put on his unspotted robe of righteousness, and present my poor and unworthy soul to his Father, redeemed with his most precious blood. Think, my dear Margaret, on the goodness of Almighty God to me in the last and closing period of my life. O think on it, and draw consolation from that source from whence I obtained it, and from whence consolation and real fortitude can alone be obtained. Could you have thought that I was sufficient to withstand such a shock, which at once burst upon me like an earthquake, and buried all my vain earthly hopes beneath its ruins, and at once left me a poor shipwrecked mariner on this bleak shore, separated from thee, in whom all my hopes were centred? But, alas, how vain are the earthly hopes of us weak sighted mortals. How soon are they all buried in oblivion. Mt dear Margaret, put yourself to no concern about me – O may that good and gracious God who has supported me so peculiarly support you in every gracious dispensation of his Providence that he is pleased to visit you with. O that he may send his ministering angels and sooth you with the balm of his comfort. O may they approach the beauteous mourner and tell you that your lover lives = triumphs – lives – though condemned, lives in a nobler life. My dear Margaret, I hope you will not take it as a dishonour that your unfortunate lover died for his stressed, wronged, suffering and insulted country; no, my dear Margaret, I know you are possessed of nobler ideas than that, and well do I know that no person of feeling or humanity will insult you with it – I have every reason to believe that it will be the contrary. I shall die firm in the cause in which I embarked, and although we were outwitted and betrayed, yet I protest as a dying man, it was done with good intentions on my part. But well did you know my sentiments on that subject long before I was taken prisoner. No person could have induced me to take up arms to rob or plunder; no, my dear Margaret, I took them for the restoration of those rights for which our forefathers bled, and which we have allowed shamefully to be wrested from us; but I trust the innocent blood which will be shed tomorrow, in place of being a terror, wil waken my countrymen – my poor, suffering countrymen. From that lethargy which has so overwhelmed them! But, my dear Margaret, this is not a pleasing subject to you, so I will leave it, and direct your attention to matters of more importance – to the one thing needful. Recollect, my dear Margaret, that we are, one and all of us, lost and miserable sinners, and that you have, as well as me, to stand before a great and just God, who is infinite and pure, and who cannot look upon sin but with the utmost abhorrence, and that it is only through the blood of a crucified Saviour that we can expect mercy at this awful tribunal, my dear Margaret, I will be under the necessity of laying down my pen, as this will have to go out immediately.

"O may God's grace your life direct,

 From evil guard your way;

And in temptation's fatal paths

Permit you not to stray."

You will give my dying love to your Father and Mother, James and Agnes, Mrs Connell and Jean Buchanan, and I exhort you all to a close walk with God, through our Lord and Saviour, Jesus Christ; and when you have fulfilled a course of life agreeable to his word, that we may be united together in the mansions of peace, where there is no sorrow – Farewell – a long farewell to you and all worldly cares, for I have done with them. I hope you will call frequently on my distressed and afflicted mother. At the expense of some tears I destroyed your letters. Again, farewell my dear Margaret, may God attend you still, and all your soul with consolation fill, is the sincere prayer of your most affectionate and constant lover while on earth.

Andrew Hardie

Thomas McCulloch to his wife;

Sydney

New South Wales

October 12 1821

Dear Wife,

I send you these few lines, hoping they will find you and the children in good health, as they leave me at present thank God for it. We arrived here on the 18th of May, all in god health (after being at sea five months); I was taken off the stores by a Mr Panton1 a native of Scotland, and employed by him as a labourer; but not agreeing with me, he was so kind as to transfer me to a Captain Irvin, and am to be with him as a house-servant, and am going to remove about 40 miles up the country.

If you think of coming here, there shall be nothing wanting on my part to bring you, as I have every encouragement from several Gentlemen that can enable me to do so, as your presence here will free me from bondage; as any man's wife that comes out here as a free settler, can take her husband from Government employment or being a servant to any man. Captain Irvin has

---

1   George Panton was the Postmaster of the New South Wales colony.

promised to do every thing for us to make us comfortable. By our friends applying to the Secretary of State at London, you could obtain for us 300 or 400 aces of land. It is Andrew Dawson's wish that his wife would come here also, and we will endeavour to get you out both together; but if you do not think of coming, I hope that you and the rest of my friends will do all they can to obtain a mitigation of my sentence, as my mind never be at rest till I be with you and the rest of the family.

Sir Thomas Brisbane arrived here two days ago, he is to be our new Governor and the Governor can pardon any man he thinks proper; a great many have obtained their liberty since we arrived here; Captain Irvin, Mr Wyeems, Commissary-General, and other Gentlemen, have promised to befriend us; and the whole of our party is much respected here by the respectable people in this country, and if you will only come out, a steady man and woman can do very well, as they are very rare articles to be found here.

Andrew Dawson, James Cleland, John McMillan, and Allan Murchie, are kept in Government employment, on account of their being blacksmiths, who are very valuable in this part of the world; W Clarkson and John Anderson is with Mr Lord, a respectable Gentleman, who much esteems them. Alex Johnson a principal servant to the Commissary-General; Thomas McFarlane and Thomas Pink are with the Barrack Master; James Wright is shopman to a Dr Phillips; Benjamin Moir, John Barr and David Thomson is with Sir John Jamieson; Andrew White, Bookbinder and Alex Hart, cabinet-maker, are in Paramatta with Dr Douglass; Wm Smith is also at Paramatta with Mr Marsden; Robt Gray and Alex. Lattimer, is in Van Dieinan's Land with Mr Mulgrave.

This is a fine country, and will grow anything that will grow in Any other country, and in general have three crops a year. Loaf bread is 3d a lb., butter 2s per lb. beef and mutton 10d, eggs 2s a dozen, tea 2s. 6d. per lb., sugar 6d, potatoes 10s. per cwt. A free labourer gets from 25s. to 30s. a-week, and a tradesman who has a trade to suit this country the country can make it a great deal better. I see Gilbert McLeod2 often, he is very well and is acting as a schoolmaster.

Yrs etc.

Thomas McCulloch

---

2   Editor of *The Spirit of the Union* who was sentenced to five years in New South Wales in 1820 for sedition.

Alleged Dying Declaration of James Wilson

This document was sent to Peter MacKenzie who used it to prove that James Wilson had been reluctant to take part in the Strathaven Rising, but had been pressurised into taking up arms. The Strathaven Radical and historian, John Stevenson believed that the so-called Declaration was a forgery, as he had been a participant in the rising, and the contents did not agree with what he saw of Wilson and his actions. He thinks the forger convinced MacKenzie that it was genuine and he hoped that publishing it would prove Wilson's innocence.

Stevenson's opinion is corroborated by Wilson's family, who stated that when they talked with him in Glasgow Jail, it was through a grilled door, and that a jailor was present at all times, making the passing of a document impossible.

The original document (ref. GD. 185/12/11) is among the papers of Peter Mackenzie held in the William Patrick Library, Kirkintilloch

Being desirous of a correct account of my conduct in the matter for which I am to suffer should go to the public, I have to submit the following short narrative, which neither conceals nor misrepresents the truth - I am just entering the sixtieth year of my age; was born in the village of Strathaven, of respectable parents; was bred a hosier; was married about thirty years ago, and never once left the house in which I was born till I was lately confined to prison; I will readily be believed, therefore, when I mention that my life was peaciable, and harmlessly passed away; and indeed I know no one in my neighbourhood that can say that I even injured of offended them. In was not till Thursday the sixth of April last that this inoffensive life was interrupted by an occurrence which, in the little I had to do in it, I will now detail.

In the morning of that day, almost twenty men, mostly belonging to Strathaven, came to my house, and said that a person of the name of Shields had brought some news from Glasgow, which had inclined them to set off immediately for that place: and they added, they were determined I should go along with them. I never heard of this person Shields before. I refused to go; but they threatened to blow my brains out if I did not accompany them. I said I had no arms; when the persons noticed the blade of a sword, which had no hilt, and was broken at the point, and which I used for a bow for my stocking frame, and they observed, I might take it. At length, carrying this useless blade with me, we left my house for Glasgow; but when near to Kilbride, which is half way, we heard that we were deceived by the Glasgow committee having turned all traitors. I then left these persons, and, after stopping a short time at a friend's house by the way, I returned home, where I had scarce arrived when I was secured by the officers of the law, and conveyed to Hamilton Barracks, where I lay till Sunday, when I was taken to Glasgow prison. I was now charged with taking up arms, and levying war against the king, and am doomed to suffer the extremist punishment of the law, as one who has committed High Treason. My trial is before the world; the facts of my case are already public, and I refrain, in present situation, from making any observations on those singular proceedings. I meet my fate in the calmness and tranquillity of a man who is decidedly conscious of suffering innocently. I most solemnly deny that I took up arms to levy war against the king. I indignantly reject the imputation that I comitted or intended to comit High Treason. Of that crime, or of any offence done or meditated against the lives or properties of my fellow creatures, my heart does not accuse me; and the humane and discerning will, I am sure, with difficulty persuade themselves that the facts above detailed merited the name and the punishment of treason. I acknowledge that I die a true patriot for the cause of freedom for my poor country, and I hope that my countrymen will still continue to see the necessity of a Reform in the way of the country being represented (and am I Convinced that nothing short of unifersal suffrage and anual parlements will be of any service to put a stop to the present Corrupted State of the house of Commons; therefore, I hope my dear Countrymen will unite and stand firm for their whole rights.

In order to confute a most scandalous falsehood that has been circulated by two men of but very indifferent characters (viz) of my having burnt a Bible, as a dying man I solemnly deny that I ever did anything of the kind, and I do solemnly declare it to be false. I therefore do declare and firmly believe the Bible to be the word of God; and I do believe that Jesus Christ is the son of God and the Saviour of the words, and I do place all my hopes and confidence in the mercy of God the Father, and in the merits and meditation of Jesus Christ, my Lord and Saviour. Amen.

James Wilson

Glasgow Jail, Iron-room.

20th August, 1820

(William Patrick Library, Kirkintilloch: GH 185/12/11)

APPENDIX VI: POEMS BY THE RADICALS

While in prison in the dungeons of Stirling Castle awaiting execution, Allan Barbour Murchie, the Glasgow blacksmith, and Andrew Hardie turned their minds to composing poetry. Both wrote about their plight, under the title *Bonnymuir*, with Hardie versifying the events that took place on the muir on 5 April.

Your wish is granted, I did say,

Then steered our course along the way,

But when we came near Camelon town.

We saw no men of great renown,

Him we saw who had us sent

And on the cause he still was bent,

In one short hour I will you meet –

With twenty men, equipped, complete.

You'll speed your way up on the moor:

You and your men may rest secure,

For all is going on so well –

Yes, more than mortal tongue can tell.

Then to the moor we went with speed

And on the heather laid our head:

But there we did not long remain

Until we saw a dreadful train.

Men and horses in armour bright,

Advancing speedy in our sight.

Up we sprang, to arms we flew

And this we then designed to do,

Close to the dyke to run with speed,

And then to face the prancing steed,

To keep them back as long's we could

Or in the cause to shed our blood.

With anxious eye we looked in vain

To see this hero and his train

To help us in the time of need

Against the rider and his steed.

Firing commenced on every side,

Swords and pikes did next succeed,

Thro' the dyke a few advanced,

But back we drove them with the lance.

'Him who sent us' refers to John King, the government agent.

The poem appears to be unfinished, perhaps Hardie did not want to finish it.

Murchi's poem, on the other hand, concerned itself with plight of the men, under sentence of death, and waiting for information about appeal for mercy. His song was sung by his fellow prisoners to the tune, *Hey! Johnnie Cope*. When Thomas MacFarlane attended the meeting of the Working Man's Association of Airdrie. On 15 January 1840, this song was sung during the entertainment afterwards.

BONNYMUIR

Although our lives were ventured fair

to free our friends from toil and care,

The English troops we dint to dare,

And wish'd them a' god mornin'.

It's with three cheers we welcom'd them

Upon the Muir of Bonny Plain,

It was our rights from them to gain

Caused us to fight that mornin'.

With pikes and guns we did engage;

With lion's courage did we rage –

For liberty or slavery's badge

Caused us to fight that mornin'.

But some of us did not stand true,

Whish caus'd the troops them to pursue,

And still it makes us here to rue

That e're we fought that mornin'.

We're a' condemned for to dee,
And weel ye ken that's no a lee,
Or banish'd far across the sea
For fightin' on that mornin'.

But happy we a' hae been
Since ever that we left the Green,
Although strong prisons we ha'e seen,
Since we fought that mornin'.

If mercy to us all shall be shown
From Royal George's kingly crown,
We will receive't without a frown,
And sail the seas some mornin'.

Mercy to us has now been shown
From Royal George's noble crown,
And we're prepared, without a frown,
To South Wales some mornin'.

ILLUSTRATIONS

Unless otherwise attributed, photographs are by the author.

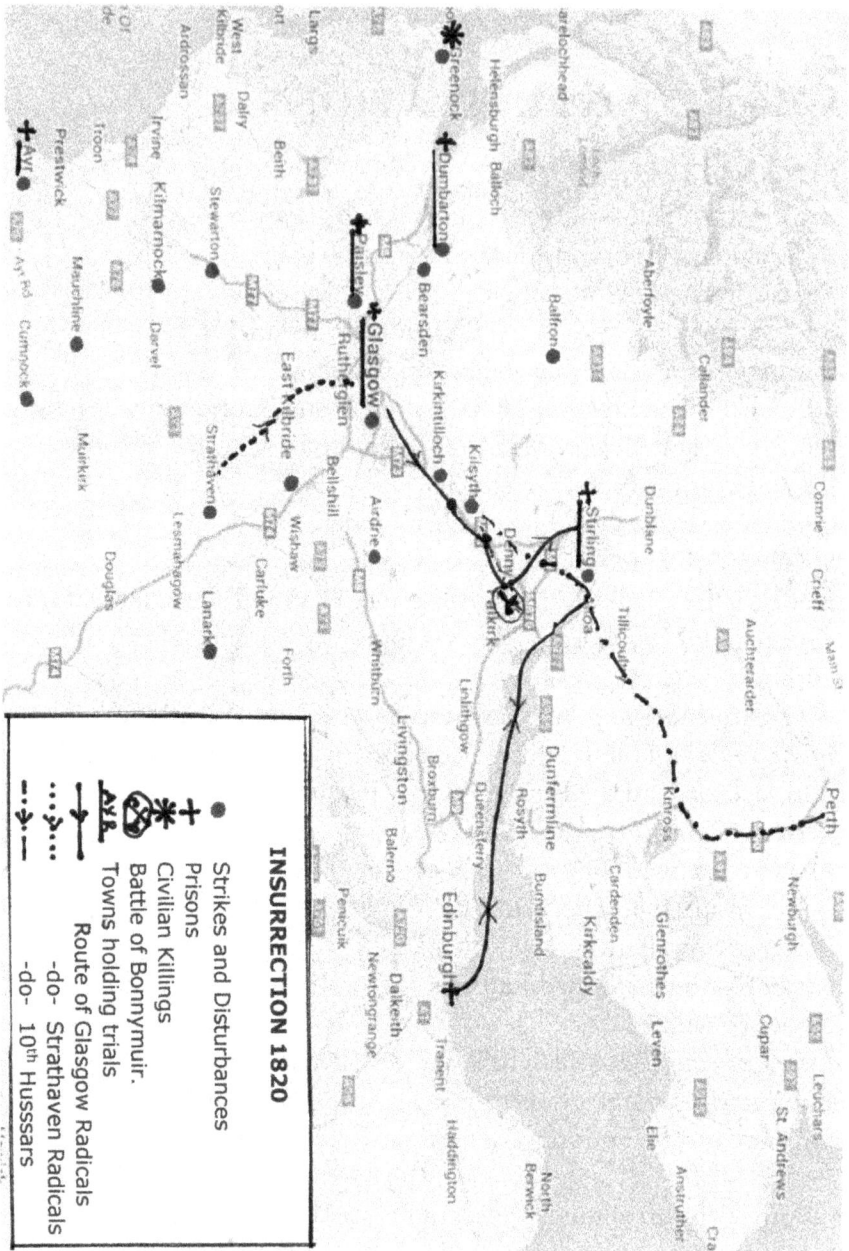

INSURRECTION 1820

- Strikes and Disturbances
- Prisons
- Civilian Killings
- Battle of Bonnymuir.
- Towns holding trials
- Route of Glasgow Radicals
- -do- Strathaven Radicals
- -do- 10th Hussars

Plan of the
CITY of GLASGOW
1821

Barony Kirk, Glasgow (Theglasgowstory: ImageTGSAO4807)

Gallowgate Barracks, Glasgow (Wikipedia Common Creative Licence)

Radical Pike Head (National Museum of Scotland)

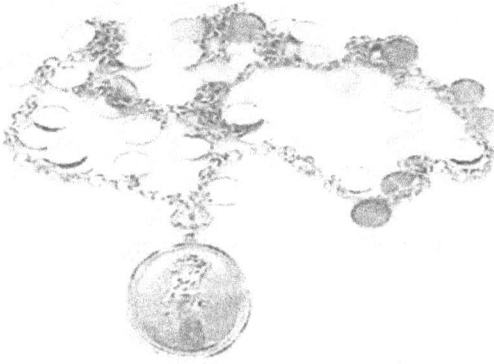

Airdrie Provost's Chain, with Close-up of the Volunteer Badge added in 1828 (Courtesy Councillor David Stocks)

Duntreath Arms Hotel, Kilsyth
(Kilsyth Library, Culture NL: Bill Mowat Local Photograph collection)

The Cross, Kilsyth 1905 (Antique Postcards of Scotland)

Radical Pend on the Forth and Clyde Canal, where the Radical groups met.
Radical Pend (© Lairich Rig - geograph.org.uk/p/1903153)

Site of the Battle of Bonnymuir

Aerial view of Stirling Castle (Wikipedia Creative Commons Licence)

Bridewell Prison Glasgow (Scott Harp, TheRestorationMovement.com)

Glasgow Police Uniform 1820 The Baird Home, Condorrat
(Courtesy Glasgow Police Museum) (Courtesy A & M Macfarlane)

Edinburgh Dungeons   **Hardie's Account**

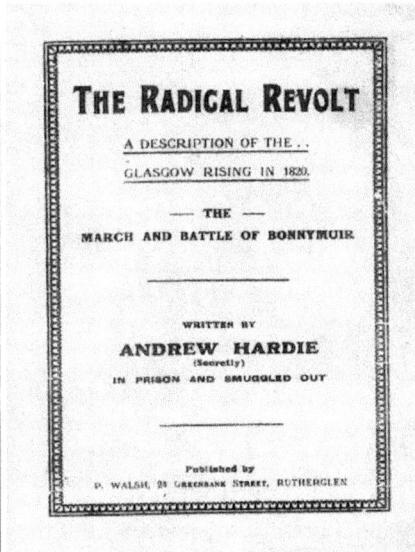

Dumbarton Castle from an old print by Roger Griffith

Riverside Church Dumbarton, where the trial was held

St George's Church, Paisley, where the trial was held (Wikipedia CCL)

Paisley Barracks, opened in 1821 as a result of the Rising

Alexander Hart   **Alexander Johnston**
(Courtesy their descendants and M and A Macfarlane, Australia)

Kirkman Finlay MP   **Serjeant Mr John Hullock**
(Wikipedia Creative Common Licence)

Broad Street Stirling

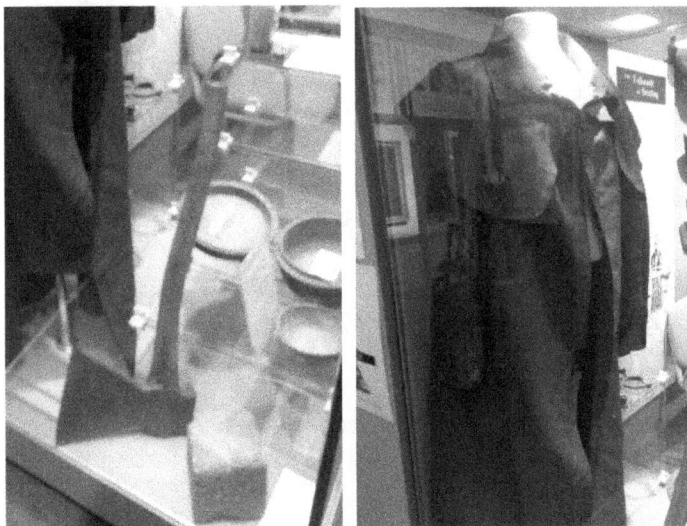

Axe & Baird's Grave Marker Executioner's Gown
(Courtesy Smith Art Gallery and Museum, Stirling

HMS *Bellerophon, 1815, with Napoleon on board*
(John Chalons, Royal Museums, Greenwich)

Convict ship, wrecked off Victoria (collections,slsa.sa.gov.au)

Port Jackson 1821, showing Sydney and Harbour (portraitdetective.co,.au)

(Illustrated Sydney News, 3 October 1889)

Unto the ... honour
the Lord Justice Clerk and
Lords Commissioners of Justiciary

The Petition of Sir William Rae
Bart His Majesty's Advocate
for His Majesty's Interest

Humbly Sheweth

That John Cameron Currier, Edward
McGoun Labourer, Alexander Foster Shoemaker,
Dugald McCaulay Smith, Darby Canning
Labourer, John Linnot Hatter, Robert
Bole Joiner, and John Calder Smith all in Greenock
were lately committed to the Tolbooth
of Greenock on a charge of High
Treason, and it is desireable for
the safe custody of said persons
that they should be removed from
said Tolbooth to the Castle of
Dumbarton, and whereas the same
cannot take place without the
authority of this High Court.
        May it therefore please
Your Lordships to Grant
        warrant.

persons of the said
John Cameron, Edward McGoun, Alex
Porter Dugald McAulay, Darby Canning,
Wm Sims, Robt Bole, & John Calder
from the Tolbooth of
Greenock to the Castle at
Dumbarton thence to
remain until liberated
in due course of law
according to Justice &c

W.M. Rae

Garscube 15th April 1820
The Lord Justice having considered this
Petition Grants warrant for removing
the persons therein named described from the
Tolbooth of Greenock to the Castle at
Dumbarton thence to remain until
liberated in due course of law —

Archd Campbell

Letter of Lord Advocate to Lord Justice Clerk re Greenock Prisoners, with his
reply (Right) Courtesy Arts and Heritage West Dumbarton Council (1018/1, D21,
Letters to Major General Ferrier)

To His Excellency Gen May ...
Lt Governor of Dumbarton Castle

Sir

In consequence of the manyfold favours
we have received from you we consider
it our duty previous to our Examination
to return you our most humble thanks
not knowing whither we may return
to your charge again or not, We trust
Sir you will be pleased to accept of
although returned in a vulgar style,
We assure you Sir our minds are free
and this is done from the sincerity of
our hearts, for few would have granted
the indulgences in your situation of
life, as you have done, considering the
crime which we are alledged with,

Dumbarton Castle
28 June 1820

George Munroe
William M'Phee
William Smith
Robert Munroe
Patrick M'Devitt
Matthew Bennie
Wm Blair
Richard Thompson
Jas Hamilton

Letter thanking Gen Ferrier Dumbarton Castle from the Duntocher Radicals
Courtesy Arts and Heritage West Dumbarton Council (1018/1, D23, Letters to Major General Ferrier)

Letter of John Barr, from Stirling Castle to his Brother
(Courtesy of Allison Symon, a descendant of John Barr's family)

No 2   GD 185/1/4

Colonial Secretary's Office
Sydney, 2nd February 1836

His Excellency the Governor directs it
to be notified, that the Right Honorable
the Secretary of State for the Colonies, had
signified in his Despatch dated 10th August
1835 No 37 His Majesty's gracious permission
that Absolute Pardons be issued to the
eighteen individuals undermentioned viz

    Burr John ------ Spike
Clarkson or Clarkin William Do
        Hart Alexander ----- Do
        Johnson Alexander   Do
        Latimer Alexander   Do
        Weir Benjamin   Do
        McCulloch Thomas   Do
        Poke or Polk Thomas Do
        Glacht William   Do
        Thompson David   Do
        White Andrew   Do
        Wright James   Do
        Clelland James   Do
        Ferguson Andrew   Do
        King Robert   Do
        Strickland Thomas   Do
        McMillan John   Do

By O?

Letter to Peter MacKenzie naming the pardoned Bonnymuir Radicals
(Courtesy EDLC Archives, Kirkintilloch, GD185/1/4

Courtesy of EDLC Archives, Kirkintilloch   GD185/1/9

Letter from James McMillan to Peter MacKenzie about Royal Pardons
(Courtesy EDLC Archives, Kirkintilloch, GD185/1/9)

RADICAL MONUMENTS

Bonnymuir Sighthill (The 1820 Society)

Strathaven Woodside Paisley
(Gordon Brown, Creative Common Licence) (The 1820 Society)

Greenock Jail and Memorial to those killed by troops, 8 April 1820
(Courtesy WordPress.com and Lairich Rig, under Creative Commons Licence)

Condorrat Memorial to the 1820 Radicals, Auchingeich Disaster and the dead of two World Wars, unveiled 2011

BIBLIOGRAPHY

Primary Sources

National Records of Scotland
RH1/2/930, Letters of Andrew Hardie
RH4/187, Murray of Polmaise Papers
JC21/ 1, Commission of Oyer and Terminer, 1820
JC21/2, Stirlingshire
JC21/3, Lanarkshire
JC21/4, Dunbartonshire
JC21/5, Renfrewshire
JC21/6, Ayrshire
JC21/7, Writs of certiorari
JC21/8, Writs of Capias against prisoners not brought to trial
CD 224/31/17, Miscellaneous Correspondence.

National Library of Scotland
LC1/73, An Account of the Executions at Stirling 1820
Ry.111.a.2(12), Broadsheet Concerning the Execution of the Radicals, Andrew Hardie and John Baird, 1820
Acc. 13901. 12 Letters of John Barr
CC.BT40, A R Richmond, *Narrative of the Condition of the Manufacturing Population (London, 1825)*

Mitchell Library, Glasgow
E1/1/10, Police Minute Book No 11; Report by Commissioner of Police James Mitchell

Dumbarton District Library: Heritage Centre

10/8/1 Letters of Mjr General Ferrier, Lt Governor Dumbarton Castle, 1790-1824

D21, Letter to Lord Justice Clerk and Lords Commissioners of Justiciary, 14 April 1820, with Postscript from Lord Succoth, 15 April 1820.

D22 & 23, Letters of thanks from Prisoners.

Outline of the Life of Ilay Ferrier of Belsyde, 1744-1824

15/1/3 Prison Record Book, 1812-1224

1/1/9 Council Records, 1808-22

Falkirk Archives, Callendar House

CH/2/79/12, Cumbernauld Parish Church, Burials, 1817-1846

CH/2/79/13, Cumbernauld Parish Church, Burials, 1847-1854

Stirling Archives Library

GD 189 Murray of Polmaise

1/81, Letters from Rev Robert Rennie, Kilsyth

Condorrat Library.

Letters of John Barr: CD and manuscript.

William Patrick Library, Kirkintilloch

GD 185/1, Peter Mackenzie Papers: Correspondence re James McMillan.

GD 185/12/11, Copy of Narrative of the Case of James Wilson by Himself, written in Glasgow Jail, accused of High Treason, 29 August 1820

The Scottish Police Memorial Trust

Roll of Honour

State Library of New South Wales
A.1193; Applications for Convict Families to join them
D.574-5, Discharge Letters
DOC.1940b, Letters of Andrew Hart
QO.41/C, Letters of Thomas McCulloch

State Library of Queensland
Convict ship records
Lists and details if individual convicts

Public Record Office, Kew
HO 11/3, Prisoners transported on the *Speke* 1820
HO 17/6 & 23, Criminal Petitions, 1820
HO 44/9, Domestic Correspondence 1773 to 1861, J G Knapp, 1820
HO 102/22, Home Office Correspondence (Scotland), 1812
HO 102/32, Letters to Home Office from Glasgow, 1820
HO 102/33, Calendar of Prisoners Charged with High Treason at Stirling, 1820

Devon Record Office, Essex
152M/C/1819/OH and 1820, Sidmouth Papers

Published
Andrew Hardie, *The Radical Revolt* (Rutherglen, 1820)
John Stevenson, *A True Account of the Radical Rising in Strathaven* (Glasgow, 1833)
Trial for Libel: Alexander B Richmond v. Simkin & Marshall & Others (1834)

Contemporary Newspapers/Periodicals

Ayr Advertiser
Blackwood's Magazine
Caledonian Mercury
Cobbett's Political Register
Dundee Advertiser
Edinburgh Evening Courant
Edinburgh Gazetteer
Edinburgh Review
Edinburgh Weekly Journal
Glasgow Chronicle
Glasgow Courier
Glasgow Herald
Glasgow Saturday Evening Post
Greenock Advertiser
Inverness Courier
Manchester Times
Northern Star
Scots Magazine
Stirling Journal
Sydney Gazette and New South Wales Advertiser
Sydney Morning Herald
The Black Dwarf
The Scotsman

Secondary Sources

Anderson J W, *Reminiscences of Sixty Years Ago* (London, 1894)

'A Ten-Pounder' (P MacKenzie). *Exposure of the Spy System Pursued in Glasgow During the Years 1816-17-18-19 and 20* (Glasgow 1832)

Bamberg C, *A People's History of Scotland*, (London, 2014)

Bayne I, The 1820 Radical Rising, in *Scottish Local History,* Issue 35, (October 1993), 16-21

Brown R, *The History of Paisley: from the Roman Period down to 1884* (Paisley, 1886)

Clark S, *Paisley: A History* (London, 1988)

Clark S, The Crime of Rebellion, in *Scottish Local History,* Issue 29, (October 1993), 5-10

Cowan E J & Finlay RJ, *Scotland Since 1688: Struggle for a Nation* (2000)

Crainey T, *The Hidden Story of the Kilsyth Weavers,* (Glendaruel, 2013)

Crainey T, Radical Kilsyth 1820, *Scottish Local History,* Issue 105 (Spring 2020)

Davies M T, Prosecution and radical discourse during the 1790's: The case of the Scottish sedition trials, *International Journal of the of the Sociology of Law,* Vol. 33, Issue 3, (September 2005), 148-158

Devine T M, *The Scottish Nation 1700-2000,* (London, 1999)

Devine T M, *Conflict and Stability in Scottish Society 1700-1850* (Edinburgh, 1990)

Devine T M, et al., *People and Society in Scotland* Vol, 1 (Edinburgh, 1998)

Devine T M & Jackson G, *Glasgow, Vol 1: The Beginnings to 1830,* (Manchester 1995)

Dickson T & Clark T, Social Concern and Social Control in Nineteenth Century Scotland: Paisley, *Scottish Historical Review* Vol. 65, Nos 179-180 (1986)

Dictionary of National Biography (Oxford, 1981)

Donnelly F, The Yorkshire Rising of 1820, *Albion Magazine Online,* Vol.4, Issue 2 (Summer 2007)

Donnelly M, *Thomas Muir of Huntershill* (Bishopbriggs, 2016)

Donnelly T K, The Scottish Rising of 1820: A Re-interpretation, in *International Review of Scottish History,* Vol. VI, (1976), 27-37

Donnelly T K, *General Rising of 1820* (Sheffield, 1975)

Dowds T J, The Condorrat Radicals of 1820, *Scottish Local History,* Issue 85, (Spring, 2013), 11-16

Dowds T J, 'We're a' Radicals Here': The Paisley Radical Trial of 1820, *Scottish Local History*, Issue 90, (Winter 2014/15), 11-16

Dowds T J, Muir's 'Good Cause'1820, *Thomas Muir of Huntershill: Essays for the Twenty First Century,* (Edinburgh, 2016), 249-274

Dowds T J, Dumbarton and the 1820 Rising, *Scottish Local History*, Issue 105, (Spring 2020)

Dowds T J, James Wilson and the Strathaven Rising, *Scottish Local History*, Issue 106 (2020)

Duffy S, The Scottish Radical Rising of 1820 in Glasgow and the West of Scotland, in *Scottish Family History Society Newsletter* (March 2008), 5-6

Ellis P B & Mac a' Ghobhainn S, *The Scottish Insurrection of 1820* (London, 1989)

Fraser W H, *Conflict and Class: Scottish Workers 1700-1838* (Edinburgh, 1988)

Galbraith A F, *Dumbartonshire Military Forces, 1798-1816* (1840 Reprint from the *Lennox Herald*)

Glen J, *History of the Town and Castle of Dumbarton* (Glasgow, 1847)

Green C J, *Trials for High Treason, in Scotland, Under a Special Commission, Held at Stirling, Glasgow, Dumbarton, Paisley, and Ayr, in the Year 1820,* in 3 Volumes (Edinburgh, 1823 reprinted 2012)

Grigor I F, *Highland Resistance: The Radical Tradition in the Scottish North* (Edinburgh, 2000)

Halliday J, *The 1820 Rising: The Radical War* (Glasgow, 1993)

Howie J, *An Historical Account of the town of Ayr for the last fifty years* (Kilmarnock, 1861)

Hutchison J, *Weavers, Miners and the Open Book: A History of Kilsyth*, (Cumbernauld, 1986)

Johnston T, *The History of the Working Classes in Scotland* (Wakefield, 1974)

Knox J A, *Airdrie: A Historical Sketch* (Hamilton, 1921)

MacFarlane M & A, *The Scottish Radicals, Tried and Transported to Australia for Treason in 1820* (Stevenage, 1981)

Mackenzie P, *Reminiscences of Glasgow and the West of Scotland* (Glasgow, 1865)

McPhail I M M, *A Short History of Dunbartonshire* (Dumbarton, 1962)

Meikle W H, *Scotland and the French Revolution* (Glasgow, 1912)

Mileham P J R, The Stirlingshire Yeoman Cavalry and the Scottish Radical Disturbances of April 1820, *Journal of the Society for Army Historical Research,* (1985), Vol. 63 No. 253, 20-30 & No. 254. 104-112

Miller H B, *Historical Cumbernauld* (Cumbernauld, 1968)

Murphy J & Moffat R, *Patrick Brewster: The Paisley Prophet* (Glasgow, 1997)

Pentland G, *Radicalism, Reform and National Identity in Scotland 1820-1833 sw* (Suffolk, 2008)

Pentland G, 'Betrayed by Infamous Spies'? The Commemoration of Scotland's 'Radical War' of 1820, *Past and Present* Vol 201, Issue 1 (November 2008), 141-173

Pentland G, Radical Returns in an Age of Revolutions, *Études Écossaises,* 20 (2018), 91-102

Roach W M, Alexander Richmond and the Radical Reform Movements in Glasgow in 1816-17, *Scottish Historical Review* Vol 11 (1972), 212-228

Sherry F A, *The Rising of 1820* (Glasgow, 1968)

Smout T C, *A History of the Scottish People 1560-1830* (Edinburgh, 1985)

Steele T, *Scotland's Story* (1984)

Strang J, The Waterloo Club, in *Glasgow and its Clubs* (Glasgow, 1856)

Stevenson J, *A True Narrative of the Radical Rising,* (1835)

The New Statistical Account of Scotland (Edinburgh, 1845)

Volume 6, Lanarkshire;

Volume 7, Renfrewshire;

Volume 8, Dunbartonshire, Stirlingshire and Clackmannanshire.

The Third Statistical Account of Scotland (Edinburgh):

Glasgow (1958)

Dunbartonshire (1959)

Lanarkshire (1960)

Renfrewshire and Bute (1962)

Stirlingshire and Clackmannanshire (1966)

Weir D, *History of the Town of Greenock* (Greenock, 1829)

Whatley C, *Scottish Society 1707-1830* (Manchester, 2000)

Young J D, *The Rousing of the Scottish Working Class* (London, 1979)

Young J D, *The Very Bastards of Creation; Scottish International Radicalism 1707-1995* (Glasgow, 1996)

Website

www.ConvictRecords.com.au:*Convicts transported to Australia*

Historical Fiction

Lannon T, *The Boys from Bonnymuir* (Edinburgh, 1985)

INDEX

140, 172, 192.
Fallon, John of Raploch, 191.
Fallow, James, 68, 109.
Faulds, James, 124.
Faulds, Robert, 124.
Ferguson, Sir David, 145.
Ferguson, George, Lord Hermand, 188.
Ferguson, Peter, 97.
Ferrier, Lt. Gen. Ilay, 72, 81, 230-1.
Finlay, Kirkman MP, 16, 24, 27, 32, 38, 58, 85, 88, 156, 157, 159, 224.
Firth, Joseph, 53.
Flanagan, William, 56.
Fleming, Admiral, 84, 150, 152, 185.
Forran, John, 84-5.
Forth and Clyde Canal, 60, 76, 217.
Foster, Alexander, 81, 229.
Foxbar, 49.
France, 18, 30.
Fraser, John, 89, 98, 118, 155.
Fraser, Malcolm, 122.
Fraser, Marjory, 118.
Freeland, John, 185.
French Revolution, 9, 22, 29-39, 33, 53, 92, 197.
Friends of the People, Society, 17, 68, 182.
Fulton, Robert, 44, 90.
Fyfe, James, 185.

Gallowgate, 38, 46, 216.
Galston, 87, 98.
Gardner, Robert, 75, 155.
Gardner, John, 185.

Gardner, William, 75.
Gatton, 180.
George III, 34, 84, 95.
George IV, 28, 35, 78, 90, 168, 170.
Germiston, 56-7, 191.
Gerrald, Joseph, 17.
Gettie, Joseph, 87.
Gibson, John, 116.
Gilchrist, James of Gilfoot, 107.
Gilfillan, Moses, 97
Gilfillan, Mr (Glasgow Volunteer), 87.
Gillies, Adam Lord, 100, 231, 188.
Gillies, George, 97.
Gilmour, David, 88.
Gipps, Sir George, 147.
Girvan, 38.
Glasgow, 10, 14-16, 19, 24-7, 37-9, 59, 66-7, 84-5, 94, 97, 99, 115, 144, 145-9, 150-2, 164-5 , 189, 191-2, 200, 207-8, 215, 216, 230..
Glasgow Sharpshooters, 47, 59, 66, 84.
Glasgow Trial, 105-111.
Glass, William, 100.
Glassford, 69.
Glenmavis, 147.
Goldie, John, 98.
Goodwin, John, 185.
Goodwin, Robert, 192.
Gourlay, James, 185.
Graham, Alexander, 97, 110
Graham, Capt. 69.
Graham, David, 76.
Graham, William, 76.
Grainger, John, 19.

76, 90-1, 99.
Hussars, 25, 46, 48, 58, 61-3, 70-1, 74, 83,92, 115, 161, 193-6, 198.
Hutchison, John, 44.
Hutton, Andrew, 100.
Hutton, James, 185.

Immigrants, 9, 18, 87, 145, 149-50,166.
Ireland, 21, 47, 71, 188.
Irwin, Capt., 146, 205-6.

Jamieson, Sir John, 141, 148, 150, 206.
Jamieson, Oliver, 49, 78-9, 81, 115.
Jeffrey, Francis, 100-2, 104-5, 116, 136, 157, 188-189.
Johnston, Alexander, 65, 97, 100, 137, 144-5, 207, 224, 232..
Johnston, Allan, 100.
Johnston, Mary, 142.
Johnstone, 99, 120, 121, 118.
Johnston, John, 97, 105.

Keen (Kean), John, 60, 62, 162.
Keir, Adam, 186.
Keith, John, 27.
Kellett, Col., 19.
Kendall, Rev Thomas, 139.
Ker, Allan,116.
Kerr, James, 80.
Kerr, Robert, 98.
Kier, Archibald, 185.
Kilbarchan, 47, 49.
Kilbride, 69, 209.

Kilmarnock, 88.
Kilsyth, 22-3, 30-1, 33, 46, 48, 58-9, 61, 73, 86, 102, 132, 146, 155, 161, 165, 193, 197, 202, 218.
Kincaid, John 184.
Kincardinshire, 188.
King, John, 37-8, 57-8, 60, 62, 63-4, 67, 159- 62, 192-3.
King, William, 186.
Kinloch of Kinloch, 33, 67.
Kirkintilloch, 57, 74, 76.
Kirkland, Andrew, 97.
Knapp, Thomas, 93-5, 100, 125-6.

Lady Lindley, 53.
Laird, David of Balornock, 107
Lamont, Archibald, 185.
Lanark, 50.
Lanarkshire, 144.
Lang, Andrew, 37.
Lang, James, 112.
Lang, John, 89, 98, 116, 123.
Lang, John (juror), 185.
Lang, Rev. John Dunsmore, 144.
Lang, William, 84, 89-90, 160, 164.
Lapslie, Rev. James, 73-4, 128.
Larbert, 65.
Latimer, Alexander, 65, 97, 100, 137, 143, 145, 206, 232.
Latta, John, 112.
Leeds, 31.
Lees, Robert, 44-5, 51, 90, 159-62.
Leggatt, William, 25.
Leiper, Alexander, 116.
Leitch, Quinton, 186.
Lennox, George, 97.

McKindlay, John, 186.
MacKinlay,Andrew, 27.
MacKinlay, Robert, 72, 97, 112.
McKinnon, Archibald, 80.
McLachlan, Archibald, 112.
McLae, Humphrey, Ewing, 185.
MacLaren, Alexander, 156
McLaughlane, John, 156.
MacLean, Archibald, 97, 112.
MacLeod, Gilbert, 34, 158, 206.
MacMillan, Jane, 147-7.
MacMillan, John, 97, 105, 137, 143, 144, 147 -8, 206, 232, 234.
MacNab, Daniel, 72, 97, 112.
McNaught, John, 116.
Maconochie, Alexander, 26-7, 100, 106, 188.
McPherson, Capt. Peter, 139
MacPhie, William, 72 97, 228.
McPhunn, Hugh, 46, 102.
Macquarie, Lachlan, 137-8, 140.
McWhinnie, John, 80.
Malmesbury, 16.
Malthus, Thomas, 19-20, 174.
Maltman, William, 56.
Malton, 188.
Manchester, 23, 28, 52, 163.
Maori, 139.
Margarot, Maurice, 17.
Marsden, Rev., 150, 206.
Mauchline, 98, 115.
Maxwell, William, 186.
May, John, 97, 110
Mercer, Agnes, 143.
Millar, (Airdrie), 31.
Miller, George, 185.

Miller, James, 186.
Mirfield, 52.
Mitchell, Capt. James, 34, 37, 44, 58, 84, 160.
Mitchell, James (juror), 106.
Mitchell, Patrick, 185.
Moir, Benjamin, 65, 97, 100, 137, 187-8, 208, 232.
Moneypenny, David, Lord Pitmilly, 34, 106, 123, 125, 187.
Monteith, Henry, 16, 24, 32, 34, 36-7, 46, 52-2, 58, 77, 84, 87, 89, 188.
Montgomerie, Robert, 186.
Montgomery, William, 124.
Montrose, Duke of, 93, 188.
Moody, Andrew, 186.
Moore, Thomas, 128-9, 134-5.
Morehead, William, 184.
Morrison, Archibald, 82.
Morrison, John, 67, 69, 97.
Motherwell, William, 120.
Muir. Thomas, 9-10, 17-8, 73.
Muir Thomas of Muirpark, 107
Mulgrave, Mr & Mrs, 139, 143, 145, 206.
Munro, Alexander (juror), 104.
Munro, Dr. Alexander, 82.
Munro, Hugh of Novar, 54.
Munroe, George, 72, 97, 167.
Munroe, Robert, 72, 97, 114, 167.
Murchie, Alan, 65, 97, 100, 137, 149, 206, 211, 233.
Mure, William, 186.
Murray, James, 65, 102.
Murray, John, 184.

Port Glasgow, 79, 80.
Port Glasgow Armed Association, 49, 78-9.
Port Jackson, 137, 227.
Portland Head, 141.
Provan, Walter, 97.
Provisional Government, 34, 35, 41, 49, 57, 60, 61, 84, 89, 104 160.

Quarrellstone, 121.

Rae, Sir William, 15. 51, 54, 82, 83, 100, 106, 110, 112, 114-5, 116-8, 123, 126, 157, 188.
Rait, James, 97.
Ramsay, Alexander, 184.
Rankin, John, 72.
Rankine, William, 186.
Rayburn, James, 98.
reading clubs, 22-3.
Reddie, James, 24, 32, 152.
Reid, Andrew, 97.
Reid, James, 100.
Reid, William, 87, 89.
Renfrew, 15, 115.
Rennie, Rev. Robert, 73, 86.
Reynall, Mjr. Gen., 51, 87, 129-30.
Rice, William, 53, 143.
Richmond (borough), 187.
Richmond, Alexander, 23-5, 32, 156-7.
Riddell, Sir James, 184.
Rifle Brigade, 47, 58, 76, 81, 83, 129-30.
Ritchie, Mrs, 131.
Robertson, Alexander, 65.

Robertson, Duncan, 184.
Robertson, Ross, 49.
Robinson, William, 97.
Rodger, Matthew, 116.
Rodger, William, 31, 32, 186.
Rogers, Benjamin, 53
Roney, William, 72.
Rony, Matthew, 68, 112.
Ross-shire, 188.
Rothesay, 172.
Rowan, George of Holmfauldhead, 109.
Rowat, John, 185.
Roxburgh, Alexander, 98.
Roxburgh, James, 98.
Royal Veterans Battalion, 49.
Rumsby, Ann, 151.
Russell, James, 67.
Russell, James (juror), 184
Rutherglen, 15, 28, 70, 190.

St Aubins, 145.
St.Ninian, 97.
St Peter's Field, 11, 28, 52, 163.

Salmond, George (Fiscal), 83-4.
Sandford, Erskine Douglas, 106, 113, 116, 120, 124.
Saxelby, Sgt., 63.
Scone (NSW), 145.
Scots Greys, 89.
Scott, Sir Walter, 153-4, 155-6, 168, 172.
Scottish Parliament, 11-2, 34, 37, 167-8, 176.
Selkirk, 36-7.

Wemyss, William, 144, 206.
Westminster, 11, 14-6, 55, 125, 138, 166, 168.
White, Andrew, 65, 97, 100, 137, 143, 151-2, 176, 206, 232.
Wigan, 52, 169.
Wigton Burghs, 188.
Williams, Lt. Col., 83.
Wilkes, John, 29.

Wilson, Alexander (juror), 100.
Wilson, Alexander (Paisley poet), 16.
Wilson, Alexander (Radical), 98
Wilson, Hugh, 113.
Wilson, James, 4, 10, 18, 68-70, 74, 97, 106- 11, 128-31, 162, 166, 173, 181-3, 207-8.
Wilson, James (juror), 116.
Wilson, John, 100.
Wilson, William the younger, 186.

Windsor (NSW), 148.
Woddrop, John of Dalmarnock, 107.
Wooller's Gazette, 22.
Wright, James, 65, 97, 100, 137, 207, 144, 152, 232.
Wright, John, 100.
Wright, Thomas, 116.
Wyllie, Andrew, 98, 123.
Wyllie, James, 98.

Yarmouth, 188.
Yeomanry, 58-9, 61-5, 66, 71-2, 75-6, 87-8, 144, 175-6, 196-7.
York, 100
Yorkshire Revolt, 52-3
Young, John, 79, 98.

ZENO, see McGrugor.

Tom Dowds was among the first graduates from Strathclyde University and taught history in secondary schools in Paisley and Cumbernauld before becoming a tutor in the Centre for Lifelong Learning at Strathclyde. He is the author of a number pf books, including *The French Invasion of Ireland 1798, The Forth and Clyde Canal: A History,* and *The Origins of Scotland's National Identity,* and contributed to *The Compendium of Scottish* Ethnology, and *Thomas Muir of Huntershill: Essays for the Twenty First Century,* and is the author of a number of articles.

He is currently Honorary Vice President of the 1820 Society.

THE 1820 SOCIETY

Founded in 1969 as a non-party political group to preserve the memory of the Insurrection of 1820, the Society holds annual commemorative meetings at Strathaven, Greenock, Paisley and Glasgow in memory of those who were killed and transported for seeking the right to vote and form trade unions, and for a Scottish Parliament. For further information about the Society see:

www.the1820society.com

www.ingramcontent.com/pod-product-compliance
Lightning Source LLC
Chambersburg PA
CBHW060014100426
42740CB00010B/1481